LAUGH YOURSELF SILLY AT THESE

FRASIER™

SHOW-STOPPERS!

FRASIER *(on Maris's 112 unpaid parking tickets):* "What do you expect from a woman who thinks a chocolate allergy entitles her to use a handicapped space?"

◆

NILES *(excusing himself from the table):* "Oh dear, look at the time. I have a session with my multiple personality. Well, not to worry. If I'm late, he can just talk amongst himself."

◆

FRASIER *(to caller):* ". . . And while I agree that washing his hands twenty to thirty times a day would be considered obsessive-compulsive behavior, bear in mind that your husband is a coroner. Thanks for your call, Jeanine. Whom do we have next, Roz?"

FRASIER™

JEFFERSON GRAHAM

POCKET BOOKS

New York   London   Toronto   Sydney   Tokyo   Singapore

An *Original* Publication of POCKET BOOKS

POCKET BOOKS, a division of Simon & Schuster Inc.
1230 Avenue of the Americas, New York, NY 10020

Copyright © 1996 by Paramount Pictures. All Rights Reserved.

All script excerpts and photographs (except photos on pages 36, 39,
and 40) ™ & © 1996 Paramount Pictures. All Rights Reserved.

FRASIER THEME on page 287 a/k/a TOSSED SALAD AND SCRAMBLED
EGGS Copyright © 1993 by Bruin Music Company. Written by Darryl
Phinnessee and Bruce Miller.

All rights reserved, including the right to reproduce this book or portions
thereof in any form whatsoever. For information address Pocket Books,
1230 Avenue of the Americas, New York, NY 10020

ISBN: 0-671-00368-2

First Pocket Books trade paperback printing October 1996

10   9   8   7   6   5   4   3   2   1

POCKET and colophon are registered trademarks of
Simon & Schuster Inc.

Text design by Stanley S. Drate/Folio Graphics Co. Inc.

Printed in the U.S.A.

FRASIER™

A radio interlude . . .

ROZ: We have Nina on line two, with a question about fantasies.

FRASIER: Yes, Nina, I'm listening.

NINA: Dr. Crane, I've been very happily married for twenty years. I wouldn't dream of cheating but lately, when we're making love, I find myself fantasizing about . . . people other than my husband.

FRASIER: That's perfectly normal. There's no harm in enhancing your lovemaking by secretly imagining yourself having a tryst with a sports figure, say, or a movie star . . .

NINA: Or a radio psychiatrist?

FRASIER: I beg your pardon?

NINA: It's your voice, Dr. Crane. You must have the most sensuous voice on earth.

FRASIER (*sensuously*): I don't know, Nina. The earth is a big place.

NINA: I've never seen your picture. Would you mind describing yourself?

FRASIER: I really don't think that's appropriate.

ROZ: Then I'll do it.

FRASIER: Roz, I don't think . . .

ROZ: He's about six one, with a granite jaw, the broad shoulders of a marine . . .

FRASIER (*giving in*): Oh, all right.

ROZ: . . . he's been wearing his hair short lately. But that only accentuates his cobalt blue eyes, chiseled cheekbones, and full, provocative lips.

NINA: God. I'd better go. My husband's home in fifteen minutes and I've got to fire up the Jacuzzi.

FRASIER: Well, this is Dr. Frasier Crane, feeling a little red in his chiseled cheeks. Thanks for listening. Join us again tomorrow on KACL 780-AM.

ONE

THE FRASIER STORY

"Six months ago I was living in Boston. My wife had left me, which was very painful, then she came back to me, which was excruciating. On top of that, my practice had grown stagnant and my social life consisted of hanging around a bar night after night. I was clinging to a life that wasn't working anymore and I knew I had to do something, anything. So I ended the marriage once and for all, packed up my things, and moved back here to my hometown of Seattle. Go Seahawks!"

And with those words, Dr. Frasier Crane explained to his radio listeners, as well as the millions of TV viewers who knew him from eight years of sitting at the bar on *Cheers*, just how he ended up on the other side of the country.

Over the next few weeks, we would learn that Frasier had lied considerably to Sam, Norm, Cliff, and the rest of the Cheers gang about his background. He wasn't an only child, as he had said, and not only was his father not dead, he was alive and kicking in Seattle.

Viewers willingly accepted Frasier and his new family: brother Niles, who outpompoused Frasier in the stuffy department; retired cop Martin Crane, the blue-collar polar opposite of Frasier; Martin's physical therapist, the daffy Brit Daphne Moon; and Frasier's man-hungry and wisecracking radio producer, Roz Doyle.

Frasier debuted on September 16, 1993, and broke the spin-off curse that has fallen on so many shows, such as *After M*A*S*H*, *The Colbys*, *The Tortellis*, and *Models, Inc.* The usual problem is that the second edition pales in comparison to the original. But like the successful *Lou Grant*, which showed a popular sit-com sidekick moving to a new town and starting a new life, Frasier Crane migrated to Seattle and America met his new gang of zanies.

But unlike most sit-coms, whose lead character is usually a straight man reacting to the loonies around him, on *Frasier* our hero was saner than he was on *Cheers*, but still rather crazy after all these years.

Frasier, NBC's highest-rated rookie of the year in 1993, has been a top 20 staple ever since, and the show has won every award imaginable, including back-to-back Emmys for best show and actor, and Peabody, Golden Globe, Directors Guild of America, Writers Guild of America, American Comedy Award, and Television Critics Association nods.

- ◆ Witty.
- ◆ Urbane.

* Sophisticated.
* Literate.
* Great sophisticated and physical comedy.
* People-pleasing dog tricks.

Just some of the words used to describe all that is *Frasier*.

In these 276 pages, you will discover the makings of a hit Emmy-winning show, from start to finish, learn that one member of the *Frasier* troupe was actually once an actor from an even higher-rated NBC sit-com before being fired three days into production, find out how they teach Eddie (whose real name is Moose) to do all those great dog tricks, and laugh yourself silly with great moments from *Frasier*.

The doctor is listening . . .

"We have a shocker for you," announced the *Frasier* creators when they went to NBC to formally present their concept. "We're presenting a family show to you." The producers, David Angell, Peter Casey, and David Lee, had been adamant in the past about their expertise in doing gang comedies, and had said openly many times that they weren't in the business of creating family shows.

Consider NBC surprised.

They mentioned actors' names as possibilities to help the NBC executives visualize their characters. When they brought up Frasier's father, they said, "Think John Mahoney," to which NBC said, "If you can get John, he's approved." (Networks have to approve the casting, and usually make actors read for the part first.) They brought up David Hyde Pierce's name for Niles, and NBC said the same thing. They knew his work from *The Powers That Be* and said they'd love to have him on the show. When they talked about Daphne, they said they were thinking of making her either Latin or British. NBC Entertainment President Warren Littlefield said if they decided to go British, "We love Jane Leeves," and the producers decided to go in that direction.

NBC ordered thirteen episodes, sight unseen, of *Frasier* for the 1993–94 TV season, but that didn't mean much to John Mahoney, the veteran actor, who has appeared in over thirty-five films (including *In the Line of Duty* and *Moonstruck*). Angell, Casey, and Lee flew to Chicago, where John Mahoney lives, to try and talk him into joining their show. They took the actor to dinner to Shaw's Crab House, but Mahoney had one concern: "Where's the script?" he asked. The producers had the story in their head. They said they'd get back to him.

The good news was that Mahoney had worked at Paramount before, on a later episode of *Cheers* as a seedy jingle writer hired to come up with a commercial tune for the bar. Casting director Jeff Greenberg approached him during his *Cheers* stint to ask if he would ever consider doing a sit-com. "If it's as good as *Cheers*, sure," Mahoney told him.

After their dinner, the producers left early the next morning to return to Los Angeles to finish the script. When it was done, they sent it off to Mahoney and got a positive response the next day.

Two down, three to go.

David Hyde Pierce was also discovered before the writing began. Sheila Guthrie, who works on casting for Grub Street shows with her boss Jeff Greenberg, came across Pierce's photo and suggested the producers take a look at him as a possible brother, if for no other reason than his uncanny resemblance to the young Frasier.

But after doing *Wings*, a show about two brothers, the last thing Casey, Angell, and Lee wanted was to give Frasier a brother. The show was going to be the awkward prodigal-son relationship between the highbrow shrink and his blue-collar ex-cop dad, the antithesis of everything that Frasier is.

"They said, 'Yeah, he looks like him. So what?'" Pierce recalls. The producers had their agenda and didn't plan on altering it. But Guthrie urged them to at least get acquainted with Pierce's work by scanning tapes of him from the short-lived NBC series *The Powers That Be*, in which he played the part of Theodore, a congressman and the suicidal son-in-law of Senator William Powers (series star John Forsythe).

The producers were impressed, and quickly agreed to change direction. Pierce was offered the job without even having to audition. "I went and met with them, and I called my agent after the meeting and said, 'Well, I think it went really well,'" says Pierce, "and she said, 'Well, it must have, because they just offered you the part.' And I was all excited, and then about an hour later I realized I had agreed to do a part that I knew nothing about."

Adds Casey: "When we met with him, we didn't have a script to show him, so we just said that Niles was a psychiatrist like Frasier, only stuffier." They added that Niles was Frasier—if he hadn't gone to Boston and met all those people at Cheers and become an actual human being. To get snobbish, intellectual, neurotic Niles down, Pierce watched Frasier's earliest appearances on *Cheers* and tried playing Niles as Frasier then, as "a Crane who hasn't been exposed to life, like Frasier was in Boston."

In an interesting piece of what-if-trivia, casting director Greenberg's two top candidates for Niles and Martin, in case things didn't work out with Pierce and Mahoney, were Peter MacNichol (who was also on *The Powers That Be* before getting the part of lawyer Alan Birch on *Chicago Hope*) and Robert Prosky (who took over for Michael Conrad as the new head sergeant on *Hill Street Blues*).

"The beauty of finding David," says Grammer, "is that we got to keep Frasier. Because David is the old Frasier. My Frasier is somebody else now. It was such a wonderful device and such a great character, and it provided so much room for all that silly stuff. David carries that mantle now, which is wonderful."

Like Pierce, prior NBC experience also paid off for Jane Leeves, cast as Daphne, Martin's physical therapist. She had appeared on several episodes of *Seinfeld*, including the most talked about one of the 1992–93 season, "The Contest," in which the gang bet each other that they couldn't go a few days without sexually pleasing themselves solo. Leeves played the woman Seinfeld called "The Virgin," who ended up in bed with (a fictional) John Kennedy Jr. by the end of the episode.

NBC was delighted with her work on *Seinfeld*, and wanted to find something else for her. The producers weren't sure about how to play Daphne. In fact, the pilot script was written to say simply "Health care professional enters." Daphne could have been a Rosie Perez type, a Latina with a loud voice, but instead they settled on a British working-class ally for Martin to prick the pomposity of Frasier and Niles.

Grammer, however, was opposed to the concept. "I thought, oh, my God, it's *Nanny and the Professor*," Grammer recalls. "I'm not going to do it. I said, 'You've got to convince me it's not a stereotype and it's not going to be just a silly little device in the show.'"

The producers disagreed, and to settle it they asked him to just read a scene with Leeves and four other British actresses. Grammer came around after working with Leeves. "Hire her," he said. "She's fabulous." Leeves had two other firm offers on the table at the time, and Grub Street had to move fast.

The character of Roz is named after the late Roz Doyle, who worked with Angell, Casey, and Lee on *Wings* as a producer. "She took care of the technical things, oversaw the building of the set," says Casey. "She was one of the finest people I've ever worked with in this business."

Doyle succumbed to breast cancer in 1991 at the age of forty-nine, and "we were crushed," says Casey. "It was absolutely gut-wrenching for all of us." So they decided to name Frasier's producer after her, as "our little tip of the cap, a way of showing our affection."

Peri Gilpin wasn't the first actress cast as Roz. But more on that in a minute. Gilpin, who hails from Texas, originally met Angell, Casey, and Lee in 1990 when *Wings* was being formed. She auditioned for the role of Helen, who was originally written as a sultry Greek, and in fact, she was the producer's first choice for the role. But NBC had other ideas, and the role eventually went to Crystal Bernard, as Helen changed from Greek to southern. Gilpin went on to series guest roles on such shows as *21 Jump Street* and *Max Monroe*, nabbed a tiny part in the short-lived NBC series *Flesh 'N Blood* as Irene, the best friend of costar Lisa Darr, and also a part in the sequel, *Local Heroes*, a series NBC canceled in the midst of production and never aired.

Cut to 1993, and after auditioning nearly five hundred actresses "of every ethnicity, size, and shape," according to Greenberg, the part of Roz was winnowed down to two actresses: Gilpin and Lisa Kudrow. "We took them both to NBC, and at that point, it was anyone's guess for how it would go," says Greenberg. The decision was to go with Kudrow, who, of course, went on to magazine cover, Emmy nomination, and Nielsen fame as the ditsy Phoebe on NBC's smash hit *Friends*. But after a few days at *Frasier*, says Lee, they realized she wasn't right for the part. "It wasn't a proper wedding of actress to character."

"Roz was supposed to be a tough-talking, whiskey-drinking broad," says Casey. "With Frasier being in the unfamiliar area of radio, she would be his superior in that she knew her way around. With Lisa as Roz, it added a different kind of spin to the role, and we really liked it. We brought the two actresses to NBC, and NBC sparked to Lisa instantly. She got the laughs, so we hired her and went into rehearsals."

The writers found themselves adjusting the material to Kudrow's strengths and came to realize that the kind of character they wanted and who Lisa was playing were two different things, and decided that they needed to make a change.

"Think of Lisa and Kelsey at the radio station," says Lee. "Kelsey's presence was just overwhelming. The energy was just eating her alive. He needed somebody who could stand toe to toe with him."

It was director James Burrows, in fact, who said to Greenberg after the first run-through, "Who's your second choice?" When informed it was Gilpin, whom he had directed on one of the last episodes of *Cheers* as well as *Flesh 'N Blood* and *Local Heroes*, Burrows concurred that she would be the better Roz.

"Lisa was wonderful," says Burrows. "I had worked with her on an episode of *Cheers* and since on *Friends*. But what was needed for Roz was somebody with chops, and

that's not what Lisa does. Nobody can do Phoebe (the ditsy masseuse and struggling songwriter from *Friends*) better than Lisa. The spin she put on Roz was not the spin we needed. We had to have somebody who could go up against Frasier, and Peri does that beautifully." Three days into the rehearsals for *Frasier*, the producers made the switch. Greenberg tracked down Gilpin at LA's Orso restaurant to tell her the news, where she was dining with her agent, who wanted to make sure the actress wasn't taking the rejection too hard. A waiter informed her that she had a call and brought over the phone. "I understand that there was a scream that came from the phone that was heard throughout the restaurant," says Greenberg. In fact, Gilpin says she was so stunned she left the restaurant and forgot to pay her bill.

Of course, after the good-news call, he then had to deliver the bad news to Kudrow. "Lisa's very smart and a very cool lady and she understood why we were making the change," says Greenberg. "But it was really a dark day for us."

Adds Burrows: "I felt bad for Lisa, but when I directed

the pilot of *Friends* I went up to her and said, 'You have arrived. This is your part.' She understands that now."

The last member of the cast to join was Moose, as Martin's dog Eddie. The idea for the dog was that with so many things going wrong in Frasier's new life, adding a dog who did nothing but stare at him would be a funny comedic element. Angell, Casey, and Lee had an animal-training service meet them at Balboa Park in the San Fernando Valley, where ten dogs in a van pulled up, and one dog after the other was brought out. "I wish I could tell you it was a long, drawn-out process," says Lee. "But we just looked at ten dogs and picked the one we liked the best. We had no idea how funny that face was. We got much more out of him than I ever imagined."

When they were at *Cheers*, producers Angell, Casey, and Lee didn't spend a lot of time socializing with the actors. They didn't have the time. They were usually locked in the writers' room, working on scripts. They were as friendly with Kelsey Grammer as they were with any of the other *Cheers* troupe. But they certainly never talked about one day going off to do another show together. "I always liked Kelsey and considered him a wildly talented actor," says Casey. "And a lot of people thought that if anybody would be spun off *Cheers*, it would be Frasier and Lilith, but I certainly never expected we'd be the ones doing it."

Angell, Casey, and Lee did, however, talk about striking out on their own. In 1990 the three producers left *Cheers* and formed Grub Street Productions. (Grub Street is an in-joke, British slang for hack work.)

They went to the Beverly Garland hotel in North Hollywood, shared a booth in the restaurant, and came up with the idea of *Wings*, about two brothers who run a small commuter

David Angell, Peter Casey, and David Lee, the three creators of *Frasier*

airline in Nantucket, and (initially) lust after the same woman, Helen, the owner of the airport diner. Tim Daly and Steven Webber starred as the two brothers, and Crystal Bernard played Helen.

Critics called it *Cheers at the Airport*, or *Cheers II*, and the producers don't deny that they were inspired by their previous home.

"We hadn't done a show on our own before," says Lee. "It was a daunting task, so we did the natural thing and did a variation on what we knew. We had done a gang comedy, so that's what we did again, and I think it was the wise decision. We really had to prove ourselves the first time out, so we were less inclined to take chances with something different."

Wings premiered on April 19, 1990, and was an instant top 10 hit, helped, no doubt, by the fact that it aired directly after *Cheers* on Thursdays at 9:30 P.M. in a season when *Cheers* was the number one show on television. For that reason, many in the TV industry thought of *Wings* as a "time-slot hit," which suggested that people were just too lazy to get up and change the channel.

Right or wrong, *Wings* took a nosedive from the top 10 to the bottom of the charts the following fall when NBC forced *Wings* to make a layover on Fridays at 9:30 P.M., in a time slot that lasted just a few months. By January, *Wings* was flying again on Thursdays at 9:30, staying there until February 1993, when it moved to 8:30 P.M., and then to Tuesdays in September 1994. The show finally came into its own and beat down the "time-slot hit" rap by winning the ratings race and ending the domination ABC's *Full House* had had over the time slot for years.

Before the Tuesday move, before *Wings* really started to dominate the competition, NBC was always looking for ways to promote the show, and the natural requests seemed to center on the Grub Street guys finding ways to have the *Cheers* gang—since they lived in Boston, a few hundred miles from Nantucket—come through town.

Norm and Cliff stopped in, as did Rebecca, and eventually, Frasier and Lilith. Not only did the Frasier/Lilith episode do well in the ratings, but Grammer was nominated for an Emmy for his guest spot on the show, a story about Frasier and Lilith visiting Nantucket to peddle the "Crane Train" self-help seminar scheme. A few months after it aired, Grammer stopped by the Grub Street office and made an offer. "I'd be interested if you were interested in working together again," he said, adding that whether *Cheers* came back or not, "this is my last season. I'm tired of doing this character. I've done him long enough."

A few weeks later, Ted Danson made his announcement that he wanted to leave *Cheers* too, and that spelled the end. After eleven years on NBC, the network's then top-rated program would go out with a bang in May 1993 with a ninety-minute finale in which Diane Chambers (Shelley Long) would return to *Cheers* for the first time since exiting in 1987.

Grammer had a deal with Paramount for a new show, in place since the eighth season of *Cheers*, and it was accelerated in the wake of the *Cheers* announcement, as NBC wanted to whisk the new show onto the airwaves the following fall to ride the crest of "Goodbye, *Cheers*" publicity.

But first, they needed a concept all could agree on. Grub Street's first idea was that Grammer would play a magnate modeled after the late Malcolm Forbes, an eccentric billionaire running his empire from his bedroom after a motorcycle accident. The producers ran it by Grammer, who liked it, but found great resistance from John Pike, the then head of Paramount's Network Television division. "When we pitched it, he looked at us like we were nuts," recalls Casey. "We haggled around and kept trying to find a way to make it work, and he kept saying one word. Frasier. Frasier. It's Frasier. We have to keep the franchise alive."

They mentioned to Pike that Grammer didn't want to do Frasier anymore, but Pike wasn't fazed. "Leave that to me," he said.

Frasier Crane was invented three years into *Cheers* as a device to break up Sam and Diane and bring jealousy into the bar. At the beginning of the show's third season, in the fall of 1984, we learned that Diane had checked herself into the Golden Brook sanitarium and met staff psychiatrist Dr. Crane. They fell in love and he followed her to Boston. They eventually became engaged to be married and went to Europe to exchange their vows, but, unable to get Sam out of her mind, Diane jilted Frasier at the altar and returned to Cheers.

Frasier followed Diane back, refusing to give up on her. He eventually stuck around, and his love life improved when he met the ice princess Lilith, a fellow psychiatrist. They married in early 1988, and she later gave birth to young Frederick.

Frasier (and Lilith, for that matter) was supposed to be on *Cheers* for only a few episodes, but the producers enjoyed the interplay between the seemingly two stuffiest people on the planet, Frasier and Diane. And, as Grammer himself revealed in his autobiography *So Far* (Dutton, 1995), Long campaigned so strongly to get rid of Frasier (he says she didn't like the character and wanted Sam and Diane to be back together) that the producers were equally determined to keep him. And so, Grammer remained with the show through the end, to the close of its eleventh season. And Paramount saw great potential in Grammer, who was nominated for an Emmy twice for his "Frasier" portrayal, offering him the deal for his own show during *Cheers*'s eighth season.

Cheers had been NBC's highest-rated series for eleven seasons, and NBC clearly wanted to keep the income from that cash cow flowing, in some form or other. And Paramount knew that it would be much easier to launch the series with a known character, à la Frasier. Just ask George Wendt, whose CBS *George Wendt Show*, debuting a year and a half after the premiere of *Frasier*, lasted less than a month.

"I was hesitant," says Grammer, "but John Pike said, 'Kelsey, we have a built-in audience. I think we're going to hit a home run if we keep Frasier. You want to hit a home run, don't you?' Well, yeah, I did."

NBC Entertainment president Warren Littlefield, who began his career as the program executive assigned to *Cheers*, says that when it became clear the show would be ending, "John and I began talking on a daily basis to plot how we were going to get Kelsey to continue as Frasier. What we didn't want to do was start from scratch. We had an unbelievably strong asset in the character of Frasier and felt that was the only way to go."

NBC had attempted only one *Cheers* spin-off before, *The Tortellis*, in which Carla's ex-husband Nick (Dan Hedaya) moved to Las Vegas with his new wife Loretta, a spacey blonde who was trying to launch a show-biz career. The show lasted five months and NBC never tried again, since the response from creators Glen and Les Charles and James Burrows was always, "We won't discuss it until *Cheers* is over," says Littlefield. NBC threw around some possibilities, like giving Norm and Cliff their own show, or putting Norm on his own, as well as the idea of Frasier and Lilith. "We always felt," says Littlefield, "that Frasier was a character who could grow and expand and that as an actor, Kelsey had such range that he could be moved from a character who was not at the center of the show to have the shoulders and strength to be at the center."

That especially became clear, he adds, in the later years of *Cheers*, once the writers started devoting more time to Frasier and Lilith and their new son Frederick.

A few days later, after their meeting with Pike, the Paramount exec ran into the producers at the Paramount commissary. "Kelsey will do Frasier. What about you guys?"

Now that they agreed the show would be about Frasier, they had to figure out what he would be doing. They knew that it wouldn't be the Frasier and Lilith show, because Bebe Neuwirth at that point was concentrating on stage work and Grammer wanted the chance to fail or succeed on his own. "This is my shot," he told the producers. "I've worked for it for a long time."

They thought about Frasier opening a practice in a new city, but decided against that one when they realized it would be too similar to the old *Bob Newhart Show*. While at *Cheers*, they had toyed with a story about Frasier filling in for a week as radio shrink. And that story came back to life. "It was not only a different way to see Frasier, but it would be something new for him too," says Casey.

The show was set in Seattle because the producers wanted to get as far away from Boston and *Cheers* as possible. "We wanted to avoid that constant breathing down our neck from the network every three weeks to get a *Cheers* person to stop by," says Angell. "If we were in Seattle, it wouldn't be as easy for them to get there."

At first, the entire show was going to be set at the radio station, with a full range of characters that included a station manager, head of advertising sales, and a bombastic Rush Limbaugh–type commentator. But now the producers felt like they had another "gang comedy" like *Cheers* and it was too similar to *WKRP in Cincinnati*. In fact, it felt like *WKRP in Seattle with Frasier.*

David Lee had a brainstorm. His father had had a stroke recently, and so the problem of aging parents was hitting home for him. He suggested making Frasier both a workplace and a home-based comedy, and said it would be interesting to see Frasier taking care of a disabled father. "The problem of parents who are aging is something that a lot of us are going through, and by having Frasier in that position, it seemed like a nice balance between work and home," he says.

So they scrapped most of the workplace characters (except for radio producer Roz and the occasional appearance of Bob "Bulldog" Briscoe, the sports talk guy) and focused the show on Frasier's home life, specifically, on Frasier reacquainting himself with his father in middle age.

By putting Frasier into the home setting, he became a different sort of person than people were accustomed to seeing. "That cartoony, pompous Frasier Crane would not carry a series," says Angell. "We needed to find ways to pop that pomposity and deal with some real emotion."

Frasier was forced to confront the father he hadn't seen in years, and comment and erupt at his situation at home—

with a cranky father, daffy physical therapist, and a psychiatrist brother who was even stuffier and more elitist than
Frasier. Add to that mix the daily dose of wackies and zanies
who called up Frasier's radio show for advice.

Frasier's estranged wife Lilith and their son Frederick
stayed behind in Boston. And instead of having Norm and
Carla deflate and irritate Frasier with their one-liners and
practical jokes, Dad and Daphne were at home to do that for
him.

The producers wrote the pilot script in two weeks. "Everything just fell together," says Casey. "We spent three
weeks on the initial *Wings* pilot script, but NBC didn't like the
story and we had to go back and do it again. On this one,
there were no notes. Everything just fell into place, and it was
a pretty painless process."

"The Good Son" had a simple story. Frasier now had the
perfect life. He was a free man, single again, with a great
apartment and new job. But he was forced to alter his plans
greatly by having his dad, dog, and health care worker move
in with him.

Speaking of family connections, one thing Angell, Casey,
and Lee didn't think about before they wrote "The Good Son"
was Frasier's family tree. On *Cheers* he said that his parents
(both scientists) were dead and that he was an only child. (It
was when Frasier and Lilith were making their wedding
plans, and Frasier said he wouldn't be inviting his parents because they were dead.) "We missed that particular episode of
Cheers," says Casey, "and when we told Kels about our idea,
he reminded us that Frasier's father was no longer alive."

Casey's reply: "That's okay. It was one line in one of 275
episodes. We'll take the consequences and answer the letters
from fans. As far as I know, to this date, we have received no
letters of complaint."

But speaking of *Cheers*, "The first thing NBC said to us
when we pitched the show was, 'How often will Norm, Cliff,

and Woody stop by," says Lee. "We said never. We could have had Frasier say 'I'm giving up psychiatry and open a little tavern.' But I think it would have been deadly for us to copy *Cheers*."

They were adamant that *Frasier* not be *Cheers II*, but instead an all-new show that happened to feature a character from a popular series. They strived to make *Frasier* as different as possible from its predecessor.

Yes, there's a hangout, but no hard drinks are served, and the Café Nervosa coffee bar really just serves as a place for Frasier and brother Niles to meet during the workday and discuss things that are on their minds. Seattle is known for its coffeehouses, so the producers decided that a coffeehouse would be a good nonwork/nonhome setting.

(*Nervosa*, by the way, is a psychological term meaning "the debilitating psychological addiction to an object, belief, or behavior pattern.")

Frasier and Niles share some coffee at Café Nervosa.

Speaking of *Cheers*, the final episode was filmed on March 31, 1993, on Stage 25 at Paramount Studios. The Charles brothers returned to oversee the last few episodes, which were nostalgic affairs penned by *Cheers* writers who had contributed so much over the years, including Ken Levine and David Issacs, who wrote more *Cheers* episodes than anyone else, and Angell, Casey, and Lee (the next-to-last *Cheers*, where Sam enrolls in a program to deal with his sex compulsion). The Charles brothers wrote the ninety-minute finale, featuring Sam's short-lived reunion with Diane, and the tying up of loose ends for the other characters.

NBC's then most popular show ended as the third longest-running sit-com ever—after *The Jack Benny Show*, with fifteen seasons, and, tied for second place with twelve seasons each, *My Three Sons*, *The Lucy Show/Here's Lucy*, and *The Danny Thomas Show*.

One month and a few days after the final scene with Ted Danson locking up Cheers was filmed, director Burrows, his *Cheers* crew, Grammer, and the new *Frasier* cast came to Stage 25 on April 21 to begin rehearsals for the pilot of *Frasier*.

The bar was taken down and stored in a North Hollywood warehouse. There was talk of it going to the Smithsonian, but the bar is too big, and for now it still sits in the warehouse, awaiting a more permanent home. Meanwhile, workers at the Paramount shop spent the weeks between *Cheers* and *Frasier* building the swanky new Seattle digs for Dr. Crane, as well as KACL studios and the Café Nervosa.

"When I left there was a big bar on Stage 25," says Burrows. "And when I came back, a brand-new upscale apartment was in its place."

The $200,000 set was designed by Roy Christopher, a veteran art director who also handles those chores for *Wings*, *Murphy Brown*, and *NewsRadio*. Angell, Casey, and Lee's notes were simply that it would be the *Frasier* show, and they wanted something contemporary that would leave the traditional Boston behind. They wanted a look that symbolized Frasier's new life. "The producers let me go out as far as I wanted," says Christopher. "It was great to give Frasier a fresh start in a sleek, contemporary setting."

Christopher sat at his desk and began drawing possibilities. He came up with the high-rise apartment, feeling that a man of Frasier's stature would surely want to live there. His assistant Wendall Johnson made models of Christopher's ideas, and the producers approved them. At the last minute, David Lee called Christopher and said, "Oh, by the way, there has to be a grand piano in the living room." Christopher felt that this was a big "by the way" but that the addition made the set what it is today. It not only adds a little more class to the apartment, but it also has given the producers several opportunities for comedy, since pianists Grammer and Pierce are able to noodle on the keyboard.

Frasier's snazzy apartment at the Elliott Bay Towers

Two decorators—Sharon Viljoen and Ron Olsen—were hired by Christopher to find Frasier's upscale furniture, the Chanel-style sofa, Eames chairs, and African objets d'art.

"We were lucky," says Christopher. "We knew who his character was from *Cheers*. We knew he was a pompous intellectual, and we knew that in the script they talked about an Eames chair and a Corbusier lamp. Frasier was somebody who knew about classic contemporary design. We didn't have to imagine that he was a man who was aware of his surroundings and a connoisseur. We knew that already."

(Not everything was authentic. Those killer views of Seattle from apartment 1901 are really forty-by-twenty-foot photos.)

Christopher, who creates at least one new set per week at *Frasier*, says he has received more attention for his *Frasier* set than for any other show he's worked on—and his career goes back to the 1960s, with the *Dean Martin Show*.

"It's really amazing," he says. "The set has gotten fan letters. It's been featured in *Metropolitan Home*, *Redbook*, *TV Guide*, and *Entertainment Weekly*. Sets work when they reflect the character of the show that lives there. I've done a lot of shows with stunning sets that don't click with the public as much because they didn't like the show. In this case, people love Frasier and people feel like this is a place where Frasier would live—and a place they'd like to visit."

Angell, Casey, and Lee wanted Burrows, considered the premiere TV sit-com director in Hollywood, to help launch *Frasier*, and he was keen on it too, saying he had a "proprietary interest" in making sure the show got off to a good start, since he was a cocreator of *Cheers*.

The pilot production process began the same way virtually every other sit-com does: with the actors sitting around a table, reading their lines aloud. The director then works with the actors on where to stand and how to interpret the lines.

Director Burrows helped contribute to who Niles is in his very first moment with Frasier at Café Nervosa. "I went to sit down in the chair to talk to Frasier, and Jim said, 'Hey, why don't you take a handkerchief out of your pocket and wipe off the chair?'" recalls Pierce. "That whole element of the character, which is his fastidiousness and his anal-retentiveness, was not something that was necessarily written in, but it's become a big part of the character."

Burrows also suggested the concept of Daphne's purse being filled with all sorts of odds and ends. "When she comes for her interview, Jimmy's idea was that all these bizarre things would come out of her purse, which was a funny note," says Casey. "That's just one of the many indications of what a great director Jimmy is. He always see little things like that and adds them, and makes us look good."

But Burrows's main goal was simply to change the image of Frasier for the new show. "The most important thing that happened was that Kelsey became a leading man," he says. "We wanted to turn Frasier the boob into Frasier the leading man and make Niles the boob. The show took off because Kelsey was capable of playing the new Frasier. Kelsey had to show much more emotion and vulnerability than on *Cheers* and say a lot of straight lines. When I was directing the pilot, I kept saying he's got to be more emotional, he's got to be more like Sam, and we were all in agreement."

Frasier was filmed before a live studio audience on May 4, 1993, handed in to the network two weeks later, and given a prominent position on NBC's fall 1993–94 schedule at 9:30, after *Seinfeld*. Advertisers predicted that the radio shrink and

Grace Under Fire, starring the new southern comedienne Brett Butler, would be the two big hits of the fall.

There were no growing pains.

Frasier premiered on September 16, 1993, and Peter Casey remembers going out the morning the show premiered, driving to a newsstand, and buying every newspaper he could find—the *Los Angeles Times*, *USA Today*, the *New York Times*, the *Los Angeles Daily News*, *Daily Variety*, and the *Hollywood Reporter*, to read the reviews. "They were all good," he says. "Many of them were raves and there wasn't a bad one in the bunch."

- *Variety:* "Smartly written, witty and absurdly human, Frasier looks to have an extended, successful practice. The doctor's in—and will be for a long, happy time."
- *New York Daily News:* "May go down as the most creatively impressive sit-com spin-off sequel in TV history."
- *Miami Herald:* "In a season of too many three-child sit-coms, Frasier reminds viewers how good an adult sit-com can be."
- *New York Times:* "[Grammer and Pierce] and the rest of the cast are putting on a splendid act."

The first season was an unqualified success, with *Frasier* hitting an instant chord with viewers and critics. By the end of the 1993–94 season, it was tied for number seven, season to date, NBC's best-performing rookie. (At the time, NBC was clearly the number three network and had few new hits. In fact, the gap was wide between *Frasier* at number seven and its runner-up, *Someone Like Me*, at number forty-two, a short-lived vehicle for young performer Gaby Hoffman.)

"We all agreed to play up to the audience," was how Grammer explained the instant success of the show. "People want to be entertained on a sophisticated level. If you do that, you'll get a great response. The results have borne out that theory."

Says Casey, "We kept the story very simple, which gave us the room to do a lot of character humor. We painted very vivid characters, we had a lot of laughs, but also dramatic moments, and the very first episode showed what kind of range the show could have. Frasier's problem was real. Everyone could relate to it. I don't know if Frasier and Niles are people everyone would want to be friends with, but they're endearing, because you can laugh at their ridiculousness and the way they look at the world."

And based on the success of *Wings*, the producers felt they now had the clout to alter the form a bit and take some chances. "We consciously fought against what was happening at the time," says Lee. "The world of the sound bite was being translated to TV scenes, and they were becoming shorter and shorter. So with *Frasier* we decided to try longer scenes, and we also tried to not show the scenes you would expect to see. For instance, in the pilot, we didn't have Frasier go to his father to talk him into moving in with him. We just skipped it and gave the audience credit for knowing what we did."

They also skipped over the obligatory exterior shots of the building (think about how many times you saw Mary Richards's Minneapolis apartment to show that you were about to visit her home) or music cues (little bursts of music to signal that a tender scene was about to come up).

Stuck in third place in the ratings, NBC felt strongly enough about *Frasier*'s potential at the end of its first season that they decided to go for broke for year two. The plan: to move *Frasier* from its comfortable Thursday night berth and head over to Tuesdays, to help build a new comedy night and take on *Roseanne*, which had been a top five show for much of its life.

NBC even went as far as to charge $230,000 to advertisers for thirty-second ads, NBC's third-highest fee, even though the peacock network had been an also-ran on Tuesdays for many seasons.

"This was the boldest scheduling move we ever made," says Littlefield. "Most of the world thought we were insane, that we were taking a hit and destroying it."

When NBC came up with this plan, they asked Kelsey Grammer to fly to New York and make the announcement to the advertisers. He refused. He later said it wasn't because he was upset but instead had previously scheduled time with his daughter. Either way, NBC later responded to his obvious concerns by handing Grammer the keys to a shiny new $55,000 red Chrysler Viper. It was a gesture, Grammer notes, "to take the sting out of moving."

Not that the stars and producers of the show weren't shy about making their feelings known about being sent packing to Tuesdays.

"We were not happy at all," Casey told the *Los Angeles Times*. "We felt we earned that spot and performed incredibly well. We wanted to remain there."

"I was really shocked," says John Mahoney. "I just thought, 'Well, you don't get very long to rest on your laurels, do you?' "

The actor has worked several times with *Roseanne*'s Laurie Metcalf and Estelle Parsons, and spoke with them about NBC's decision. Their reaction: "Extremely, extremely confident, and [they] sort of patted me on the back. You know, 'Sorry about this,' as if our career [was] going straight down the tubes."

Littlefield says that if NBC was ever going to catch up with ABC (then the dominant network) "we had to be more than a one-night network. The only choice we had was to go at ABC with a group of comedies. We felt *Roseanne* was vulnerable and maybe we wouldn't beat her from day one, but shortly thereafter, we knew we could take her.''

ABC took the *Frasier* threat quite seriously. They knew that *Roseanne* was declining, and they weren't ready to give up their Tuesday dominance lightly. So they countered NBC's move by switching *Roseanne* to Wednesdays, so that their number one show, *Home Improvement*, could go head-to-head against *Frasier*.

Observers expected NBC to make a countermove, as at the time *Home Improvement* was TV's most popular show, a program ABC would sometimes run two or three times a week to solid top five ratings.

On paper, it looked like *Home Improvement* might do real damage to *Frasier*, a case of a literate, thinking man's comedy up against the most mass market of sit-coms. After all, just two years earlier, when *Home Improvement* and *Seinfeld* went head-to-head, Jerry and company were decimated.

''There's no way we'll beat *Home Improvement*,'' Lee told *USA Today* in September 1994, the week before the big showdown. ''But we might take a few viewers away.''

NBC's Littlefield was publicly optimistic, saying there was no way *Frasier* could be hurt by *Home Improvement*. ''It's too popular a show. It's a rocket ship right now. Nothing can stop it.''

Luckily for all of them, once again, the angel was on *Frasier*'s side. *Frasier* was the Queen of the Emmy ball that year, winning five statues for best comedy, best actor (Kelsey Grammer), best script (Casey, Angell, and Lee's ''The Good Son''), best direction (Burrows for ''The Good Son''), and best editing.

The story became really juicy. Show popular with critics and viewers gets moved to a new night and takes on the most popular show on TV, a program so hot that ABC often ran it twice a night. A week before the big move, *Frasier* shocks some prognosticators by dominating the Emmys.

The hubbub surrounding the move dominated the media pages all summer long, and Grammer told reporters that it "certainly hasn't hurt the show. People became more interested in us because of all the nonsense. It's flattering to be such a spoiler. But you've got to laugh about it. It's all so silly."

Maybe to some elements of the TV community. But not certainly to NBC, which had millions of dollars riding on the decision. When the two shows went head-to-head, *Home Improvement*, as expected, easily won the time slot, but not by as big a margin as had been expected. *Home Improvement* tallied a 22.7 rating and 34 share, to *Frasier*'s 14.5/22. It was *Improvement*'s highest-rated premiere in four seasons, but NBC was still delighted, as *Frasier*'s numbers were 67 percent higher than the network had been doing a year earlier with *The John Larroquette Show*, at 9:00 P.M.

"We're walking on air," Littlefield told *USA Today*. "Most of the [share] estimates from the advertising agencies were high teens for *Frasier*. We always felt we could do better, so we're thrilled."

Bottom line: both shows could successfully exist. By the end of the season, *Home Improvement* was no longer the number one show on TV, falling to number 3, as *Seinfeld* took over top spot and NBC's new *ER* came in second. *Frasier* was number fifteen, down from the year before, but a major player now on a night where NBC had been treading water a year earlier.

The following season, NBC would overtake ABC as the top network, and Littlefield would credit the move of *Frasier* for putting the wheels into motion, for giving the network much-needed exposure on another night besides Thursday. ("The most important move for NBC's turnaround back to number one was *Frasier*," he says. "Without it, we're not number one.")

And even though Casey had been against the move, he re-

alized later that it was the best thing that ever happened to the show, because it showed local stations, who were buying *Frasier* for reruns beginning in the fall of 1997, that *Frasier* was strong enough to exist on its own, without the benefit of a strong lead-in. According to *Daily Variety*, stations have forked over an estimated $300 million for the right to air *Frasier* reruns, one of the biggest investments among stations ever.

With *Wings*, Angell, Casey, and Lee launched a respectable, quiet hit. But with the *Frasier* ratings, critical acclaim, back-to-back Emmys, the Golden Globes, Peabody, American Comedy Award, and Directors Guild of America nods, the producers have been thrust into the other side of the Hollywood spotlight.

"*Wings* was a totally different experience," says Angell. "It was like pushing a rock up the hill to get any notice. We used to beg the cast to have affairs, just to get any kind of publicity. *Frasier* has been the opposite side of the coin. We've had to turn down things because there's been so much. And the show came together so easily. We did the first one, and it felt like it was our hundredth. And that's very rare.''

Frasier and Niles on . . . Brotherly Love

N I L E S (*to Frasier*): You unprincipled charlatan, you unconscionable fraud! If this were another era, I'd horsewhip you!

F R A S I E R : Niles, what are you talking about?

N I L E S : You spoke to a patient of mine today, Marlene, and thanks to your fast-food approach to psychiatry, she left me. Two years of my hard work wiped out in one of your two-minute Mc-sessions.

F R A S I E R : I merely suggested she consider a change.

N I L E S : Based on what?

FRASIER: My assessment of your work with her. Only I didn't know it was you at the time.

NILES: Yes, well, the day I start telling you how to be a deejay is the day you may tell me how to be a psychiatrist.

FRASIER: I am still a psychiatrist.

NILES: The side-show version. "Speak quickly ma'am. You only have two minutes, then my next patient steps into the tent."

(After a fight, the brothers both demand an apology.)

NILES: It's your turn. I apologized first the last time.

FRASIER: No you didn't.

NILES: I did so. I remember clearly. It was after the shouting match at the Monet exhibit. I had my secretary leave a heartfelt apology with your service.

(Niles and Frasier go to a couples therapist to deal with their sibling rivalry. His prognosis:)

DR. SCACHTER: In thirty years as a couples therapist I have never said what I'm about to say. Give up. It's hopeless. You're pathologically mistrustful, competitive to the point of sickness. . . . Just see each other at weddings and funerals, and the rest of the time, stay as far the hell away from each other as you possibly can.

(At the Café Nervosa)

NILES: I just spotted someone. My least favorite patient.

FRASIER: Not the couch-wetter?

NILES: Worse. The man's a compulsive womanizer. He goes through so many women, he calls them all by the same odious nickname, "Sunshine," to avoid slipups. Frasier, what do you do when you don't like a patient?

FRASIER: Well, it's a tricky issue. How long have you been treating him?

NILES: Six months and we've made no progress whatsoever. Sometimes I feel he comes to me not so much to be helped, as to brag. He claims to have been with, at last count, one hundred and fifty women.

FRASIER: A hundred and fifty.

NILES: As though anything over say . . . seven isn't absurd.

FRASIER: I would say eleven, but I get your point.

TWO

GUEST VOICES

Like lending your voice to *The Simpsons*, being an unbilled caller to the *Frasier Crane Show* on KACL is considered one of the fun perks of celebritydom in Hollywood.

It all began when casting director Jeff Greenberg mentioned to the producers that it might be fun to have celebrities do the guest voices of the callers to KACL. The producers liked the idea, and Greenberg called on favors from friends to see how it would work. He got Linda Hamilton (*Terminator 2: Judgment Day*) and executive producer Christopher Lloyd got Griffin Dunne (*After Hours*) to sign on. All found that it worked.

"It gave the show a little cachet," says Greenberg. "And since they're wonderful actors, it made the scenes a little more special." Plus, viewers enjoyed scanning the end credits to see what famous names were hidden in tiny letters.

Since the stars don't have to come into the studio (they can actually record their lines over the phone!) Greenberg has received great response. "Christopher Reeve (before his accident) called in from Calgary, Patti LuPone from London, Tom Hulce from Seattle, of all places," says Greenberg. "James

Spader was on the phone, trying to keep his infant quiet while he recorded his bit."

As far as salary, *Frasier* contracts have a "favored nation" clause that says each of the guests providing voices gets the same fee. You won't get rich doing it, but it's worth more than a talk show appearance and less than showing your face on camera.

Finally, these aren't voices, but appearing in your body on *Frasier* can do wonders for your career. Eric Lutes had never appeared on television before. From the New York theater scene, he had auditioned for Greenberg a few times but never passed. Greenberg gave him another shot as Frasier's gay radio station manager boss in the classic episode "The Matchmaker," and within a few months, Lutes was an overnight sensation and costarring on NBC's *Caroline in the City.*

Same thing happened for Harriet Harris after she did the first of her guest spots as Bebe, Frasier's agent. "The response the next day was like nothing I can recall," says Greenberg. "We got call after call saying 'Who is that woman?'" Glaser went on to costar in CBS's short-lived *The Five Mrs. Buchannans,* and has been back to *Frasier* three additional times. Says Greenberg: "She's our favorite guest star."

The Guest Voice List

- Linda Hamilton: Broke up with her boyfriend and couldn't get over it.
- Griffin Dunne: Depressed because he felt that his life was going nowhere.
- Christopher Reeve: An agoraphobic who was afraid of large open spaces.
- Patti Lupone: Had a problem with her in-laws. They dropped over without calling.

- Mel Brooks: Traumatized by the Christmas he found a dead puppy from Santa.
- Rosemary Clooney: Fell down so many times they couldn't fit any more pins in her hip.
- Henry Mancini: Hated his voice.
- Joe Mantegna: A local columnist who hated Frasier and challenged him to a fistfight.
- JoBeth Williams: Before making her bow as Madeline, the sportswear entrepreneur who goes to Bora Bora with Frasier, the actress lent her voice as a French-woman who was having a problem with her ''meu-theot.''
- Jay Leno: Complained that he couldn't lose weight, call-ing from the drive-in window at a fast-food restau-rant.
- Carl Reiner: Couldn't decide what to name his new cabin cruiser.

Jay Leno
(Photo credit: Eric Vanderwerff, Director of Photography at NBC)

- ◆ **Eddie Van Halen:** Had a problem with his neighbor. Never talked about it because he kept trying to hear himself over the radio.
- ◆ **Jeff Daniels:** Concerned that his mother doesn't do anything and hangs around the house all day.
- ◆ **Robert Klein:** Sought marital advice. She wanted to go to Italy and he wanted to buy a sump pump.
- ◆ **Ben Stiller:** On Christmas, he couldn't stop crying to discuss his problem.
- ◆ **Dominick Dunne:** Watching *The Sound of Music* was his cure for the holiday blues.
- ◆ **Elijah Wood:** School bullies beat him up because he was smart.
- ◆ **Christine Lahti:** Lost all her hair from a bad perm.
- ◆ **Reba McEntire:** Her husband insisted on keeping an urn of his late wife's ashes on their bedroom dresser.
- ◆ **Sandra Dee:** Found Seattle a depressing place.
- ◆ **Garry Trudeau:** The KACL restaurant critic Gil Chesterton got his reservations at Maximillians after he forgot it was his anniversary.
- ◆ **Steve Lawrence and Eydie Gorme:** They couldn't say "I love you" to each other.
- ◆ **Mary Tyler Moore:** Couldn't confront her boss.
- ◆ **Lily Tomlin:** Felt overwhelmed raising four kids alone.
- ◆ **James Spader:** Wanted to know if it was okay to let young children climb into bed with their parents.
- ◆ **Patricia Hearst:** Couldn't break through a barrier with her in-laws.
- ◆ **Amy Madigan:** She went out with a guy twice and he sent her roses everyday. She listened to Roz and dumped him.
- ◆ **Sydney Pollack:** A politician running for office who called in to say that America would be a much better place the day more people like Frasier were off the air and more pols like the caller were elected.

- **Alfre Woodard:** A depressed receptionist at a pest-control company.
- **Art Garfunkel:** His wife felt that he was just wasting his life doing nothing. He was willing to hold until Frasier started his show the next day.
- **Kevin Bacon:** Had problems with women.
- **Mary Elizabeth Mastrantonio:** Nina, the woman who fantasized about Frasier while making love with her husband.
- **Tom Hulce:** A cop on his love for doughnuts.
- **Matthew Broderick:** Liked to watch himself on the video camera at the mini-mart.
- **Carrie Fisher:** A late-night caller in the episode where Kate banishes Frasier and Roz to the late-night shift. She complained of insomnia at a time when Frasier had fallen asleep on the radio console. "If I don't get some sleep soon, I'll go crazy," she said. Frasier misses that thought, and wakes up suddenly. His counsel: "Things look better in the light of day. My advice is to sleep on it."
- **Teri Garr:** Told Frasier she was wearing nothing.
- **Blair Brown:** A girl on the other side of a glass had an urgent message for her, but she was unable to receive it.
- **Billy Crystal:** Bulldog fan who enjoyed the way the sports jock makes fun of Frasier.
- **Ed Harris:** Another Bulldog freak, he suggested naming Seattle's newest team the Bulldogs.
- **Brooke Adams:** Lived in Wisconsin near Roz's cousin Billy Rayburn.
- **Laura Dern:** Likes to listen in on stranger's conversations in restaurants.
- **Cyd Charisse:** Called in to the radio show when Frasier was filling in for the Happy Chef, saying she was out of cinnamon.

Kevin Bacon (Photo credit: Mark Hom)

- **Paul Mazursky:** Lost a pinkie ring at a lady's house and called in to the show, hoping one of his conquests might be listening.
- **Ray Liotta:** Called from the airport at Christmastime. Wasn't sure whether to go home and see his parents or to go to Maui instead.
- **Armistead Maupin:** After Frasier appealed to listeners to befriend him, Gerard called and offered to comb Frasier's hair.
- **Jodie Foster:** Said that if she and her husband didn't have sex within the next two days, she would go to a department store and pick up a stranger.
- **Faith Prince:** In the episode "A Word to the Wiseguy," in which a shady figure asks Frasier to repay a debt by telling his girlfriend on the radio to marry him, Brandy called and said her would-be hubby wasn't there for her, wouldn't let her work, and was too quick in bed.

Said Brandy, in recalling their most recent postsex conversation: "I said to him last night 'What the hell was that? I been vaccinated slower.'"

- ◆ Randy Travis: Said three words. "Yeah. Thanks, Doc."
- ◆ Joan Allen: Complained of receiving obscene phone calls.
- ◆ Katarina Witt: Called and asked Frasier to hold as she got her other line.
- ◆ Jerry Orbach: Had trouble with his neighbor and his leaf blower.
- ◆ Billy Barty: Snuck into neighbor's backyard and shoved shrimp into the air conditioner.
- ◆ Eric Idle: Put a hundred scorpions into a Federal Express package.
- ◆ Jane Pauley: Tried to settle an argument with her landlord by sticking a garden hose into the window of his Cadillac and turning it on full blast.

Jane Pauley
(Photo credit:
Eric Vanderwerff,
Director of
Photography
at NBC)

+ **Mrs. (Debi) Fields:** Convinced her husband was having an affair with his secretary.
+ **David Duchovny:** Has sex with his girlfriend every morning and night and three times a day on weekends, but not sure they have anything in common.
+ **Sherry Lansing:** Frasier's first caller in the flashback "You Can Go Home Again" episode. Her husband has died and she's quite upset.

Another radio interlude . . .

FRASIER: We have Ethan on line three. He's having a little trouble in school. Hello, Ethan. I'm listening.

ETHAN: Hi, Dr. Crane.

FRASIER: How old are you?

ETHAN: I'm thirteen.

FRASIER: How can I help you?

ETHAN: Well, I'm having a lot of problems with the other kids at school. They're always beating up on me because I'm smart. I have a one sixty IQ. I'm in the astronomy club and I hate sports.

FRASIER: Well, Ethan, don't worry. These kids are acting out of jealousy and immaturity. But in a few years, you'll have the last laugh.

ETHAN: That's it?

FRASIER: Yes.

ETHAN: Frankly, Dr. Crane, I find that advice patronizing, simplistic, sophomoric, and in all candor, expected. The real surprise here is that they pay you to dole out this balloon juice.

FRASIER: Ethan, where are you calling from?

ETHAN: Home.

FRASIER: Well, if any of Ethan's classmates are listening, you know where he is and he can't stay in his house forever. Thank you for calling. Well, that's all the time we have today. This is Dr. Frasier Crane, KACL talk radio.

THREE

CHEERS AND FRASIER

Besides deviating from the *Cheers* history in that both his parents were dead (this, of course, after Nancy Marchand guest-starred as Dr. Hester Crane on a *Cheers* episode in which she came to visit Frasier and Diane) and that he was an only child, several references to Boston and Frasier's old hangout have been mentioned several times on *Frasier.*

To recap what the old gang is doing:

- Sam still owns and operates Cheers. He almost got married to a woman named Sheila, but changed his mind after he discovered that she had slept with Cliff Clavin.
- Rebecca married the plumber she was dating on the final episode of *Cheers.* He got a patent on a low-flow toilet, became really rich, and then dumped her. She's back at the bar.
- Woody and Kelly had a baby boy. They sent a cigar to Frasier with no note or return address. Unlike his parents, said Sam, "He's smart."
- Norm's still sitting at the bar. Sam had his barstool

Frasier meets up with his ex-wife Lilith, to his horror, in Bora Bora.

recovered for the ten-year anniversary of him being out of work.

♦ Carla was walking toward the Commons and a Beacon Hill stockbroker in a Mercedes ran over her foot. She could be set for life.

♦ Cliff stopped coming into Cheers. He read an article about that flesh-eating virus and he hasn't come out of his mother's house since.

♦ Lilith has remarried, to an MIT scientist named Brian.

♦ Diane was working as a staff writer for *Dr. Quinn, Medicine Woman* until she set Jane Seymour's hair on fire.

Meanwhile, Other *Cheers* Memories, from the Gang at *Frasier:*

Explaining Diane to Daphne:

FRASIER: She's a one-time Boston barmaid who had a nervous break-down and ended up in a sanitarium where I met her, fell for her, and was so mercilessly rejected by her that to this day there is a sucking chest wound where once there dwelled a heart!

Diane recalling her first impressions of Maris:

DIANE: Niles, remember the last time I was in town, when we all dined together? You were just starting to date this woman—she was the queerest little creature. I remember she ate everyone's sorbet, then had to lie down in the ladies' lounge while the coat check girl massaged her abdomen. I hope I haven't put my foot in it—you two didn't get married and live happily ever after, did you?

NILES: No, can't say as we did.

Sam came to Seattle because the Mariners needed a pitching coach and he interviewed for the job.

ROZ: This is the Sam Malone you've always talked about? The one who has no respect for women and treats them like dirt? [*To Sam*] Do you need anyone to show you around Seattle?

FRASIER: The two of you face-to-face—I imagine wild animals all over the Northwest have just lifted their heads, alerted to the scent.

When Lilith came . . .

LILITH (*to Frasier*): I'm here for a convention and I happened to hear your voice on the radio. I kept hoping you'd introduce Pearl Jam's latest hit, but much to my chagrin you were doling out worthless little advice pellets from your psychiatric Pez dispenser.

Said Niles when he heard Lilith was in town . . .

NILES: How strange—I usually get some sign when Lilith is in town; dogs forming into packs; blood weeping from the walls.

Boston's most famous womanizer meets Seattle's man-hungriest producer.

Frasier starts to fall for Diane again when he sees her again.

FRASIER: She's not like the old Diane—convinced the whole world re-volves around her. And I'm not the same Frasier. The last few days have drained me of all my old animosities. People do change, Dad.

MARTIN: You're right, they do. Take me for instance. The old Martin would have said, "You're out of your mind. I'd rather see you go gay and shack up with the punk who shot me than go off with her. I'd rather see you sewed inside the body of a dead horse. But the new Martin says 'Viva l'amour.'"

FRASIER: The new Frasier resists the temptation to correct your French.

Sam comes over for dinner and learns that Frasier hadn't told the truth about his history. He wasn't an only child, and his father was very alive.

SAM: I didn't know you had a brother. This is freaky. He looks just like you did when I first met you. What happened?

FRASIER: That wasn't exactly a health club you were running, Sam.

MARTIN: What did he tell you about me, Sam? His father, the ol' cop?

SAM: Oh, you I remember. You're dead.

(Martin glares at Frasier.)

FRASIER: You had called me a stuffed shirt and hung up on me. I was mad.

SAM: You're a cop. You told me he was a research scientist.

(Martin gives Frasier a dirty look.)

FRASIER: You were dead. What did it matter?

Niles is still mad at Lilith.

NILES: At our wedding ceremony, while Maris was reading her vows that she herself wrote, words of love from the heart, I distinctly heard snickering. I glanced behind me and there was Lilith with her fingers pressed hard against her lips, her body shaking like a paint mixer.

Later, Lilith asks where Maris is. Niles says she has a cold.

LILITH: Oh. I thought she was perhaps sailing up the transplendent river of your love.

Upon meeting again, Lilith and Frasier get together again for a few minutes. In a hot kiss.

FRASIER: Come to me, my white hot flame.

LILITH: I was insane to divorce you.

FRASIER: You're on my mind every waking hour.

LILITH: You're the only man I've ever loved.

FRASIER: So are you.

Diane comes to Seattle to produce her play, a thinly veiled slice of life about this little bar in Boston.

LILITH: Take me, Doctor.
FRASIER: Yes. Yes. Yes!

Frasier, explaining his tryst with Diane to Daphne:

FRASIER: I met a lovely, if somewhat loquacious, barmaid, fell madly in love, and got engaged. Of course, she left me standing at the altar. But the point is I didn't give up. I took my poor, battered heart and offered it to Lilith who put it in her little Cuisinart and hit the puree button.

A radio interlude. . . .

FRASIER: Go ahead, Tom. I'm listening.

TOM: Hi, Dr. Crane. Uh, it's about my girlfriend. My problem is I don't know if I love her for herself or because things are so great between us physically.

FRASIER: Well, Tom, distinguishing between passion and lasting love isn't easy, especially in the initial stages of a relationship. How long have you been together?

TOM: Six years.

FRASIER: And the sex is still that good?

TOM: Man, Dr. Crane, every morning, night, and three times a day on weekends. But I'm not sure we have much else in common.

FRASIER: Well . . . sharing common interests is the foundation of . . . three times, you say?

TOM: Is that abnormal?

FRASIER: No, it's not abnormal. It's not fair, but it's not abnormal. Maybe you two share more interests than you think. Tomorrow why don't you bring home a catalog from the local university and see if you can't find a couple of classes in which you'd both be interested.

TOM: That's a good idea. Thanks, Doc. Have a great weekend.

FRASIER: I'd wish you the same but that hardly seems necessary.

FOUR

THE CHARACTERS

Everything you ever wanted to know about Frasier, Niles, Martin, Roz, Daphne, and Bulldog, and the men and women who play them.

The Dr. Frasier Crane File

Frasier Winslow Crane, forty-one, was born and raised in Seattle. He lives at the stylish Elliott Bay Towers, on the nineteenth floor, the same building where many top Seattlites reside, including Dave Hendler, the head of the Seattle Psychiatric Board. Frasier has refined tastes in furniture, with a Corbusier lamp, Eames chair, and a sofa that is an exact replica of the one Coco Chanel had in her Paris atelier.

Frasier speaks Spanish fluently, likes to weary fancy Italian loafers (his shoe size is ten), and is quite the pianist, with a repertoire that ranges from arias and classical to a blistering rendition of "Great Balls of Fire."

For breakfast Frasier likes to have coffee, a bran muffin,

and some yogurt. His favorite coffee is the Kenya blend from Starbucks, and at Café Nervosa his usual after work is a double kona with cream. He also enjoys a glass of sherry after work.

As a kid he hated sports, took clarinet and piano lessons, and had a skin condition, pityriasis, on his butt when he was young. Frasier received his first tetanus shot when he was five or six, and recited the names of Puccini's operas to keep his mind off the pain.

He used to sit on his mother's davenport in his tweeds and tams, listening to the *Texaco Symphonic Hour* on the radio as a child. Other boyhood memories include a dachshund named Pavlov, membership in a chess club, and the Boy Scouts. And he starred as Conrad Birdie in a high school production of *Bye Bye, Birdie.*

Frasier did his undergraduate work at Oxford and graduate studies at Harvard, where he graduated with honors in psychosocial behaviorism. His specialty is adult relations. The doctor is the author of more than twenty-seven magazine articles, including one for *Redbook* entitled "Psychotherapy: Is it for You?"

Dr. Crane moved to Boston in 1984 after he met Diane Chambers at the Golden Brook sanitarium, where he was a staff psychiatrist. Diane had checked herself in, and Dr. Crane fell in love with the Cheers barmaid and would-be novelist. When she left, he followed her to Cheers. They eventually became engaged and flew to Europe to be married, but Diane jilted him at the altar. Frasier followed Diane back to Cheers, and even hung around the watering hole after she quit her job to concentrate on her writing. He married the former Lilith Sternin in February 1988, and together they once wrote a series of articles on the keys to a successful marriage. (It was his second union. He was earlier wed to a woman named Nanny Gee, a Raffi-like children's entertainer. And attention, trivia buffs: Gee was played on one episode of *Cheers* by Emma Thompson.) Frasier and Lilith divorced in 1992, and since then, Frasier has dated such Seattle lovelies as Miss SeaBea 1994, Tawny Van Deusen, Madeline Marshall, a designer of her own sportswear line, feel-good self-help author Dr. Honey Snow, and Frasier's own hard-driving agent, Bebe Glazer.

Frasier and Lilith have a son, Frederick Crane, born November 1989. Dr. Joyce Brothers is the boy's favorite psychiatrist, and *The Sound of Music* is his favorite movie. He lives in Boston with Lilith and her new husband, Brian, a scientist at MIT. Frasier and Frederick talk often on the phone, and Frederick came to Seattle in 1995 to visit his dad at Christmastime.

Frasier drives a black fuel-injected BMW around town and into the KACL offices, located in downtown Seattle near the Pike's Place Market. He has hosted the *Frasier Crane Show* since 1993, opening every program by saying "This is Dr. Frasier Crane. I'm listening," and ending by wishing "good mental health" to his listeners. Some of Frasier's radio colleagues, besides his producer and confidant Roz Doyle, include Gil Chesterton, the food critic; Chopper Dave, the traffic reporter; Bonnie "the Auto Lady" Weems; Ray "The Green Grocer"; and, of course, gonzo sports jock Bob "Bulldog" Briscoe.

Frasier's favorite city: Paris. Musical: *Candide*. Politically he's a Democrat, and as for his jogging frequency . . . "Once in a dark parking lot when a truck backfired."

"The doctor is in and he's listening"

To a caller:

FRASIER: And while I agree that washing his hands twenty to thirty times a day would be considered obsessive-compulsive behavior, bear in mind that your husband is a coroner. Thank you for your call, Jeanine. Whom do we have next, Roz?

Frasier is very picky when he's sick.

DAPHNE: Try this homeopathic tea. It'll flush out your system and also make your hair more shiny and manageable.

FRASIER: Thank you, but I'll pass on your voodoo brew. Just bring me another ginger ale. But this time make it shaved ice, not cubed. And I don't like these straws. I only like the bendy kind. And these Saltines are too salty. I want low sodium.

DAPHNE: Anything else?

FRASIER: Yes, these pillows are hot. I need some cooler ones.

DAPHNE: Should I put them in the fridge for you?

FRASIER: Thank you. Not too cold. About the temperature of a glass of chardonnay.

Frasier on his morning routine:

FRASIER: I am not a morning person. I need to ease into my day slowly. First, I need my coffee. Sans eggshells or anything else one tends to pick out of the garbage. Then I have to have a light low-fat, high-fiber breakfast. Finally, I sit down and read a crisp, new newspaper. If I'm robbed of the richness of my morning routine, I cannot function, my radio show suffers, and, like ripples in a pond, so do the many listeners who rely on my advice to help them through their troubled lives. I'm sorry if I sound priggish, but I've grown comfortable with that part of myself. It is the magic that is me.

Frasier on shopping, to Niles at the shopping mall on Christmas Eve:

FRASIER: Dear God, shoppers are marauding through here like packs of feral dogs. Did you see that woman? She practically knocked me over to get to the escalator.

NILES: How about that woman near the cosmetics counter who tried to Mace me?

FRASIER: That was a cologne sample, Niles. That's what they do.

"We'll be right back after these messages with more of The Dr. Frasier Crane Show. *Your port in the storm in this turbulent world—an oasis of peace and tranquillity."*

Frasier in the waiting room:

MARTIN (*to Frasier*): I remember taking you in for your first allergy shots. You were about five or six. God, you were so scared. I remember holding your hand. You'd bend over the table and drop your little drawers, and as the nurse gave you the injection, you'd take your mind off it by reciting the names of all of Puccini's operas in chronological order.

FRASIER: Now I know why I always get a sharp pain in my buttocks whenever I hear *Turandot.*

Frasier is attracted to a roadside cop who pulled him over for speeding.

NILES: Frasier, it's patently obvious what was turning you on. The gleaming jackboots, the dangling night stick, the glint of her handcuffs hanging from her belt. . . . You were off on some lurid little disciplinary fantasy.

Why Frasier decided to become a psychiatrist:

FRASIER: I guess it all started in the womb. My mother was a psychiatrist. I suppose subliminally I was a part of her sessions. She swore when I disagreed with her, I'd give her a good, swift kick in the placenta.

Frasier on relationships:

FRASIER: Once a woman has dipped her toe in Crane Lake, dry land is never the same again. They don't fall often, but when they do, they fall hard.

To his son Frederick on the phone:

FRASIER: Now son, calm down. . . . Listen to Daddy . . . it was just a dream. . . . No, I promise you. Senator Thurmond is not in your closet. Now go back to bed . . . I love you too. See you this weekend. (*Beat*) No, you may not stay up to watch *Crossfire* tonight. Good night.

On the concept of a focus group commenting on his radio show:

FRASIER: Imagine Freud being hauled into a roomful of Viennese laymen offering comments like "Hate the Oedipal thing. Love the penis envy."

The origin of "I'm listening . . ." in a conversation with Martin:

FRASIER: I'm looking for a phrase that's a little familiar, yet not a cliché. Something that can be remembered, but not gimmicky. Still at the same time—

(Martin turns the TV on.)

FRASIER: Dad, it's difficult to have a conversation with the TV on.

MARTIN: I just want to check the score.

FRASIER: But I'm trying to tell you about that phrase I'm looking for—

MARTIN: Oh, all right. (*Turns off TV.*) I'm listening. Are you happy? I'm listening.

FRASIER: (*Jumps up from the couch.*) That's it! "I'm listening."

Another radio interlude . . .

MADMAN MARTINEZ: I don't understand it, Doc. I'm a successful guy. I have my own car dealership. But still I'm depressed. You've probably heard of me, Madman Martinez.

FRASIER: What seems to be the source of your depression, Madman?

MADMAN MARTINEZ: I guess it's just that business is down. I don't know why. I slashed prices this week. Right now I got an '88 Olds Cutlass on the lot in rare turquoise metallic, Cordova roof, leather, factory air . . .

FRASIER (getting dubious): Madman . . .

MADMAN MARTINEZ: And that's nothing compared to the six brand-new Supras I got in. They're priced to sell with a twenty percent discount to all your listeners. People say to me, "Madman, you're crazy," but I say, "Hey, I deal in volume, so . . ."

FRASIER: So do I.

(Frasier slides the volume down and Madman Martinez fades out.)

FRASIER: This is Dr. Frasier Crane. We'll be back after these paid commercial messages.

The Kelsey Grammer File

The son of professional musicians, Kelsey Grammer was born in St. Thomas, U.S. Virgin Islands, and raised by his mother and grandfather in New Jersey and Florida. At the age of eleven, the death of his grandfather propelled him into a new direction—theater.

His first performance was a high school production of *The Little Foxes.* This experience, along with encouraging words from his English and drama teachers, convinced him to pur-

sue an acting career. After two years of training at the Julliard school, he was accepted into the Old Globe Theater in San Diego. Grammer spent three years performing the classics of Shakespeare and George Bernard Shaw, like *A Midsummer Night's Dream* and *The Winter's Tale*.

"The stage," says Grammer, "is my first love. It is, I think, what establishes you as an actor." From San Diego he went to New York, where he performed in off-Broadway productions like *Sunday in the Park with George*, *A Month in the Country*, and the Obie Award–winning *Quartermaine's Terms*.

He did *Othello* and *Macbeth* on Broadway and also appeared on several daytime soap operas (*One Life to Live, Guiding Light*, and *Another World*) as well as the prime-time series *Kate and Allie, The Tracy Ullman Show*, and a *Star Trek: The Next Generation* episode ("Cause and Effect") as Capt. Morgan Bateson.

The actor joined the cast of *Cheers* in its third season, in 1984, and was Emmy-nominated for his performances as Dr. Crane three times before *Frasier* began—twice for *Cheers* and once for his guest spot as Frasier on *Wings*. (He's the only actor to be nominated as the same character in three different shows.) During the *Cheers* era he also appeared in the television miniseries *Kennedy* and *Washington*, and has filmed several TV movies, including *The Innocent* and *Beyond Suspicion*. He lent his voice to the 1995 Walt Disney Mickey Mouse short "Runaway Brain" as Dr. Frankenollie and the upcoming animated feature *Anastasia*, and appeared in the film *Galaxies Are Colliding* (1992). His first big-screen starrer, *Down Periscope*, opened in 1996 and his autobiography *So Far . . .* was published in 1995.

I interviewed Grammer in his dressing room at Paramount, which is decorated with pictures of Jack Benny and Sideshow Bob, the animated character he sometimes plays on *The Simpsons*. An accomplished pianist who plays music that can be best described as a cross between jazz, new age, and classical, Grammer has a piano right outside his office door.

JEFFERSON GRAHAM: There was something about that *Wings* episode you were on that made you want to work with Angell, Casey, and Lee. What was it?

KELSEY GRAMMER: It had absolutely nothing to do with it. Dan Fauci, an executive at Paramount, mentioned to me that they had a deal with these Grub Street guys, and that I should talk with them about my show. So I did. Their years on *Cheers* was more significant as far as understanding who they were and how they worked. I set up a meeting, said, "Guys, I have a deal with Paramount to do a new show, I was wondering if you'd be interested in working with me?" They said yes. I felt fairly certain we could work well together.

JG: At what point during the *Cheers* run did you make your deal with Paramount?

KG: The eighth year, three years before the show ended.

JG: In developing the *Frasier* show, I remember you were pretty adamant that Frederick not be a weekly part of the show. Were there any other concerns as well?

KG: Frankly, any show that has a child who is growing up, by definition, becomes the focus of the show. I knew the name of the show was *Frasier* and I wanted it to stay that way.

JG: You also didn't want a British nanny.

KG: Yeah, well, the British nanny seemed like such a copout, a sterile comedic character, but as it turned out, it's worked out just fine. I also didn't want any scatological humor. I always believe in playing up to the audience. That was one of the tenets of our credo. Always play up, don't make it dirty, make it intelligent, and don't make it stupid.

JG: Could you describe the Frasier of *Cheers* versus the Frasier of *Frasier*?

KG: Well, the Frasier of *Cheers* was a man who operated in what I call "hit-and-run" comedy. That was my obligation to the show. To get in and out as quickly as I could with a joke. Like a SWAT team. For *Frasier,* I am the glue of the show. The action takes place around me. The other characters are really responsible for the hit-and-run aspect of it, and I give it a center, some reason to be. I'm sort of the canvas of the show, whereas before, I was one of the bright spots of color.

JG: Does this Frasier feel very different from the other one?

KG: Not really. I am the guy who plays Frasier, so I am pretty familiar with him, and myself, at the same time. Although I don't think I really behave like him. He's like my alter ego. There are many things he gets away with that I'd love to do, and there are many things that he does that I think are absolutely ridiculous. But I'm terribly fond of him, and we have a sort of peaceful coexistence.

JG: What do you like about him?

KG: I like his kindness, his dedication to do good if he can. We're very similar in that regard. We'd both like to save the world. He's chosen that world in which to do it and I've chosen my world, in which I attempt to do it. But on that level, we pretty much share the same basic philosophy.

JG: Anything you'd like to see Frasier do in the next couple of years?

KG: Well, you can do almost anything with Frasier. You can accept anything he's decided to do. He could climb Mount Everest or learn to fly a plane. He could get away with it—and fail miserably. That's the beauty of him. Is there anything I'd particularly like to see him do? No. I sort of enjoy stumbling through the adventure of discovering Frasier week to week. I do things in every show that I've never done in my life. Or thought of. Like last night [at the filming]. I've never fallen backwards on a chair. There's a great delight I get to take at discovering these moments that Kelsey gets to go along for the ride with, and that's really fun.

JG: Frasier lives so well. How much money you think he makes at KACL?

KG: I don't understand what the radio station is paying this guy. I think he must have done very well in the divorce or saved his money. He must have some other source of income than simply this local radio show. He only works three hours a day. I can't imagine KACL is paying him more than $100,000 a year. Frasier has obviously put some money away. He lives really well, better than I do, and I think I make more money. . . . He probably bought Microsoft stock just as it was coming out, and lots of it.

JG: How did a blue-collar cop like Martin get Niles and Frasier as sons?

KG: Everyone always wonders that. I think it's completely obvious. They're [Niles and Frasier] both equally opinionated, they have narrow viewpoints, but they're universally good. They are fraught with fault, yet there's a real commitment to doing the best that can be done, and they got that from Martin. They got the style from Mom, but the substance from Dad.

JG: When *Frasier* first debuted, Moose got so much publicity. Tell the truth. How did you feel about his ascension?

KG: Moose is just a dog. He's a funny dog. I've had no objection to him at all. When it works, I'm very pleased. I only feel sorry for him at times because he doesn't really live the life of a dog, he lives the life of a child in a sweat factory. "Will work for food." And does. Originally, all he was going to do was stare at Frasier. Then the Christmas show came up and we put the antlers on him, and he jumped up on the table, and we thought, that's pretty funny. So then we got really silly and started writing little adventures for him. But he is a dog. He can't really retain these things in his head and it's time-consuming for all of us, so that we've made a conscious decision to bring him back to the world of staring, primarily. There's only so much the dog can absorb. I'm really fond of animals as a rule. But it's been fun to fan the flames of the rumors about me being the W. C. Fields of my generation.

JG: Do you have dogs at home?

KG: I have five dogs. Cats, birds, fish, I have them all.

JG: David Pierce also received a lot of the early acclaim.

KG: The better the performer, the better for all of us. David's extraordinary. It wasn't a surprise to me that he would pop up, because he's so good.

JG: I've seen you not be able to get through scenes with David because you two were laughing so much.

KG: Oh, I've been doing that for years. That's just something that happens.

JG: Is there somebody on *Cheers* you used to do that with?

KG: George [Wendt, "Norm"] used to crack me up a lot. It just happens, it just does. It's part of the deal.

JG: How does the *Frasier* experience compare to *Cheers*?

KG: It's completely different, except for the name. I like filming it on the same stage because it feels like home to me. That's the reason I wanted it. Before we started the pilot, I called [former Paramount TV president] John Pike and said, "John, we've got to keep Stage 25." I just didn't want to move. And also, there's a great energy here. A heritage of success on this stage that I wanted to take advantage of. [*Mork and Mindy, Taxi, Happy Days,* and *Here's Lucy* were filmed on Stage 25.] That has turned out pretty well.

J G : So this is a totally different experience?

K G : Yeah. It's my show. That's a pretty big difference. I have a lot more power. I call the shots pretty much as I see fit. What's good is that I don't pull that kind of nonsense. I believe in a collaborative effort and I also believe in staying out of people's hair if they're doing their job. I work with the writers on stage, during the rehearsal process. That's a collaborative thing. I've come up with many a line in my day. That's because I walk around with Frasier all the time. I know how he's going to talk. I invented him. People always ask me what's coming up next season. I don't know, because that's up to them [the writers]. And I don't want to intrude on that or be part of it. I want to be surprised, week to week. I really enjoy that. Once in a while they'll consult with me on a possible story for *Frasier.* They asked me if I thought Shelley Long coming on the show was a good idea, and I did.

J G : Did you mention to them the things you had written about her in your book?

K G : They may have actually read it. What I wrote about Shelley, is, from my point of view, fact. There's nothing vicious or bitter about it. I think Shelley and I have come to a burying of the hatchet . . . things change . . . but in the early years, there was some difficulty. [She wanted to get rid of the Frasier character on Cheers.] That's pretty simple, isn't it? There are people who can tell you they heard her say it, so it's pretty silly to deny it. It just wasn't a very comfortable feeling for a while.

J G : How do you feel about the *Frasier/Cheers* reunion shows?

K G : The only one I thought was really good was the one with Diane, because it put some demons to rest for Frasier, and parenthetically, for Shelley and me. It was really great. I loved the show. It was wonderful working with her, and it was wonderful moving on. The one with Sam, unfortunately we didn't hit anything that was important, and I don't know why. We did hash this one around quite a bit. Jimmy Burrows directed and he was of the same footing that I was. I hoped there would be something vital between us that would have to be settled. A fight, an argument, a bitterness, something about Diane, possibly. "You stole my girlfriend." "Yeah, well you stole *my* girl-friend." Something that would help them come to a new peace, a new understanding about each other. But instead it became about some girl he was going to marry who was a nymphomaniac. I was not happy with that episode.

JG: The Lilith shows?

KG: By definition, you have to have her around once in a while. She's Frasier's ex-wife. Those shows don't count as *Cheers* reunions.

JG: Would you like to do more *Frasier/Cheers* shows?

KG: If there's some growth involved, then yeah. It's kind of fun to revisit those people from time to time. They were all so quirky.

JG: Let's talk about Seattle coffee. What kind of coffee do you drink?

KG: I drink organic coffee. My favorite coffee is Jamaican, but I have different tastes from Frasier. I don't drink that much coffee. I used to when I was in the theater. I drank so much that I realized I had to quit. So I stopped drinking coffee at all for about five years. Over the last decade, I'll have a cup about once or twice a week.

JG: So that's not real coffee you're sipping at the Café Nervosa?

KG: Sometimes it's water, sometimes it's Postum, or just very weak cof-fee. Watch me closely. I usually just fake a sip.

His favorite episode is . . .

"There's so many I'm really proud of. I love the one from the first season where the doctor dies and Frasier goes to the shivah to find out why he died at my age [number 21 "Forty-something"]. I was very fond of that one. The ones I like the most tend to be the episodes that resonate over Frasier's rela-tionship with his father. I loved the one we shot last night [number 71 "You Can Go Home Again," a prequel to the pilot that takes place right after Frasier moved to Seattle]. I enjoyed the show where I found out my mother had an affair on Martin, and I always thought it had been the other way around. I also enjoyed the episode where we went to Bora Bora [numbers 32 and 33, "Adventures in Paradise"] and I ripped the bed apart. I never had the opportunity to do anything like that before."

The Martin Crane File

Martin is sixty-three years old, was born and raised in Seattle, and his best friend is Eddie, a loyal Jack Russell terrier. In fact, he feels so close to Eddie that he carries a picture of his pooch sitting in front of the Space Needle in his wallet. Martin worked thirty years for the Seattle police department before retiring in 1991 when he was shot in the hip by a punk robbing a convenience store.

Martin lives with Frasier at the Eliott Bay Towers, up on the nineteenth floor, and spends most of his time on a twenty-five-year-old BarcaLounger, watching TV and drinking beer (Ballantine's, of course). When not watching TV, he enjoys listening to the Bulldog sports show on KACL, much to Frasier's chagrin. Martin also spends his days doing physical therapy with Daphne every day, such as stretching exercises and leg extensions.

Frasier and Niles's dad was married to Dr. Hester Crane, a psychologist, for thirty-five years. He met her at the crime scene over the chalk outline of a victim, and they were married six months later. The boys took after Hester, who enjoyed the finer things in life, and at home, it was always three against one. Martin doesn't get along with Niles's estranged wife Maris, saying she's too strange. Which is nothing new. He also thought Frasier's ex-wife Lilith was "weird."

When Frasier and Niles were kids, Martin would always dress them in matching sweaters, put them on the hood of his old Packard, and take their picture. This was the Christmas card the family would always send out. He would also take the kids down to the police station often as kids and play a game of locking them in a cell and losing the key.

A life lesson, per Martin: "You sleep with dogs, you get fleas."

On living at home with Frasier:

MARTIN: It seems like I'm always being told to get my feet off the furniture, put a coaster under my beer, turn the TV down. I used to make the rules, now I've got to follow them. Is any of this making any sense?

FRASIER: From a psychological standpoint, it's making perfect sense. Slowly, over the years, your responsibilities have been taken away from you and, in a way, you feel symbolically castrated.

MARTIN: Why does everything with you shrinks start in the crotch?

On his days on the beat:

MARTIN: I was on a stakeout once for fifteen hours without ever leaving the car. We used to have a contest to see who could last the longest. The winner was Canteen McHugh. His bladder was the size of a canteen. You could have slung his bladder over your shoulder and gone on a twenty-mile forced march through the desert.

On Frasier and Niles's mom:

MARTIN: Hester was a psychiatrist. From time to time the department would ask her to work up a profile on a suspect. The first time I saw her was over the chalk outline. One look at her in those rubber gloves and I was a goner. Her hair silhouetted against the flashing blue light of the coroner's wagon . . . She drew a little smile on the head of the outline and I drew eyes. Before long we were laughing like schoolchildren. Six months later we were married and I never regretted a day of it.

On his dispute with his former partner Alex, a fight that involved a large keister and a crying fit for Martin after watching Brian's Song:

MARTIN: "His wife had a gigantic rear end. Enormous. I mean, this woman must have had to get in the bathtub facedown. For twenty years I avoided any mention of it—and you couldn't miss the thing. It looked like she was shoplifting throw pillows."

(Then one morning Alex came into the station.)

MARTIN: "He said hi and I said hi and he said how's the wife? And I said at least she doesn't have an ass the size of Albuquerque."

Martin, with help from Frasier and Niles, finally finished writing a song for Frank Sinatra.

The lyrics:

"She's such a groovy lady.
She makes my heart go high-di, hey-di.
She is the chick I spend my nights dreaming of.

Her lips are as red as ruby.
She makes my heart go scoobie-doobie.
She is the broad who makes me coo-coo with love.

She is a nifty cutie
She sure knows how to shake her bootie
She makes me want to shout
Hey, baby, you're fine.

She's got the whole world swingin'
She makes my heart start ringy-dingin'
That hubba-hubba groovy lady of mine."

The John Mahoney File

Born in Manchester, England, the fictional home of Daphne Moon, Mahoney immigrated to the United States after high school and joined the army, where he worked on losing his British accent. After college and a series of unfulfilling jobs (including medical journal editor, college professor, and hospital orderly) Mahoney—at age thirty-seven—enrolled in classes at Chicago's St. Nicholas Theater, where he performed opposite John Malkovich, who invited him to join the esteemed Steppenwolf Theater. Mahoney went on to appear in more than thirty Steppenwolf productions, and won a Tony award for his performance on Broadway in *House of Blue Leaves*.

Mahoney has appeared in over thirty-five films, including *In the Line of Fire, Say Anything, The American President, Moonstruck, Barton Fink, Reality Bites, Tin Men, The Manhattan Project, Suspect, The Hudsucker Proxy*, and *Eight Men Out*. On television, he starred as a physician at an inner-city hospital in the short-lived medical series *The Human Factor*, and the fearless battalion chief in the *H.E.L.P.* (1990, ABC) cop show. He's also appeared in several TV telefilms, including *Favorite Son, Will, The Killer Floor*, and *The Water Engine*. He appeared on an episode of *Cheers* as Sy, a jingle writer Rebecca hired. The joke was that all his jingles were set to the tune of "Old MacDonald."

I met with Mahoney in the Frasier conference room, after the table read of episode 71, "You Can Go Home Again." Unlike Martin, Mahoney didn't walk to the table with a limp, and he didn't drink beer during the interview. Instead, he opted for a bottle of Evian water.

JEFFERSON GRAHAM: Is it true that you commute from Chicago to LA?

JOHN MAHONEY: I don't do it every weekend, but we work three weeks and get a week off, so I go home every fourth week, two weeks at Christmas, and I try to spend my four months hiatus there, in between the seasons. I have a house in Chicago, and in LA, I just sort of crash wherever I can. I've had about four places here so far.

JG: Do you have a family back in Chicago?

JM: None at all. It's just me. But Chicago's home. I didn't start acting until I was thirty-seven, so most of my friends are not in the business. They're old friends from my previous life, and they're all in Chicago. I don't hate California by any means. It's a lot of fun to come out here, but home is where the heart is, and that's where mine is. Chicago.

JG: What do you like about Chicago?

JM: Everything. The first time I saw Chicago I just absolutely fell in love with it. I was going to Quincy College in downstate Illinois, and I had a lot of friends in Chicago, and the first time I went to visit, I saw that city and just said, "This is it. This is where I have to be." So after I finished college and graduate school, I moved there. That was in 1970.

JG: You decided to change careers at age thirty-seven. Tell me about that decision.

JM: It was pretty radical. I was working at the time as an associate editor for a medical journal called the *Quality Review Bulletin* and I was just going through a period of my life where I thought—is this what I really want to do? Write about cataracts and hemorroids for the rest of my life? I didn't go home and bash my head against the wall every night, but I just felt dissatisfied. I examined what I had done in my life to give me joy and I thought back to growing up in England. I had worked as a child actor and loved it. So I enrolled in an acting class at the St. Nicholas Theater in Chicago, which had just been founded by David Mamet, and I was cast out of the class into a play. The second play I did—while I was still working as a journalist—was with John Malkovich, and he invited me to join his theater company, Steppenwolf, and that was when I quit my job. I was making $75 a week, in good weeks. As a medical editor, I had been pulling in around $35,000 a year. I don't know where I ever found the guts to do it then, because I come from a very poor family. I was making good money, I had a good education and I always had a fear of being a burden or not wanting to have to ask anybody for anything. I guess I was just so desperate with the way my life was going that I took that chance. I went through all my savings. I sold my furniture to pay my rent, sold my records, my books, but I was still incredibly happy.

JG: What did your family say about your move?

JM: My brothers and sisters and parents told me I was out of my mind. But now they're very happy.

JG: You made the switch in 1977. How long did it take until something really good came along?

JM: In about three years I was making commercials and industrial films, and by then, I was probably making around $12,000 a year, and that was no problem—I could live on that. The big breaks came when I went to New York. I was doing a play with Steppenwolf called *Orphans* and it was transferred from Chicago to New York and it was a huge hit. When you do a play in New York, especially a hit, it's full every night with agents and writers and casting directors, and so we were sort of the toast of the town. We had the agencies lining up to sign us. [Director] Marshall Brickman came to see the show one night and offered me a part in a movie. That one play got me the part in *The Manhattan Project,* which I did for Brickman. It led to me going on Broadway the following year, because people in New York now knew me. When I got through with *Orphans,* I went back to Chicago to do a play called *House of Blue Leaves.* It went to New York, and when I won the Tony award for that, all of a sudden, I wasn't auditioning anymore. I was going on meetings and being offered roles and that led to a lot of films—*Tin Men* and *Suspect* and *Moonstruck.*

JG: Your resume lists over thirty-five movies. What are the highlights for you?

JM: The top three would be *Say Anything* with John Cusack, *Moonstruck,* and *Tin Men*. They were all great parts, complex characters, and they appealed to such different people. With those three films, I pretty much encompassed everybody. When women come up to me and talk to me, it's usually about *Moonstruck*. When men talk to me, it's usually about *Tin Men*. And when kids approach me, it's usually about *Say Anything*. They were all terrific movies, critically well received and all three in Siskel and Ebert's top 10, so they're my three favorites.

JG: Hopefully people come up to you and mention *Frasier* occasionally too.

JM: Oh, yeah.

JG: Do you think that after three years, Martin's hip should be showing some signs of improvement?

JM: You would think so, wouldn't you? It might be time for him to re-break it again or something.

JG: What are your thoughts about Frasier and Martin's relationship.

JM: It was terrible when they first started to live together. The first two or three episodes was just screaming and yelling, but then they settled into an uneasy truce and now it's sort of settled into a friendship. Frasier's a very smart guy for all his pomposity, so I'm sure he probably realizes that Martin could probably make it on his own. But I think he's just become very comfortable. For the first time in his life, he's getting along with his sons and he doesn't want to do anything to jeopardize that. Frasier and Martin have also come to the realization that although they've disappointed each other, it wasn't all one-sided. Martin originally felt sorry for himself in that he never had kids he could watch playing Little League and the kind of boys that Martin would want. I think gradually over the last couple of years, Martin has come to realize that it's just as much of a disappointment for them, that they weren't able to give Martin that. They would have loved to have Martin be proud of them, but it just wasn't in their makeup. I think now their relationship isn't based on physical disability, I think it's probably discovering each other and things they have in common, and everyone's making up for all those years of misunderstandings and disappointments.

JG: What do you enjoy about playing Martin?

JM: Everything. I like having sons, I like discovering them, I like, through them, discovering parts of myself that I didn't know existed. Feelings I didn't know I had. Knowledge about myself and them. I love his straightforwardness, I just think Martin is a great character. He's a complex man. He doesn't seem to be, but he is. He lived his whole life three against one. A wife who was a psychiatrist, two sons who were psychiatrists, kids who took after their mother, the incredible independence that he has, that he's learning to temper with the need for companionship and love from his kids. It's interesting to see him work his way through this.

JG: I understand that unlike Martin, John Mahoney is a major opera buff. True?

JM: Oh, yeah, I'm a real culture vulture. I have a master's degree in English, I'm a great reader, I love classical music and the opera. That's another great thing about playing Martin. It's so much fun to go outside yourself. That's where the challenge is, and that's where the fun is. That's the way it is with Martin too. He's just very very unlike me. There are a few similarities. He's very loyal and so am I. I'm very loyal to my friends. I don't suffer fools very easily, and I'm very quick to try and deflate pomposity. But there are other things about Martin that are not me.

JG: I assume you've been known to go to a French restaurant or two.

JM: I can't boil water myself, so I eat virtually every meal of my life out. When I couldn't afford it, I went to greasy spoons. And now that I can afford it, I go first-class. I deny myself nothing!

JG: What kind of coffee do you drink?

JM: There I'm a Martin person. I'm a regular black coffee drinker. I've never ever been in a Starbucks. It's not my bag.

JG: How is it working with Moose?

JM: Let's see. Moose is like working with another actor. It's not like working with a dog. He's the most un-doglike dog that I've ever known, inasmuch as he's been trained all his life to only do things when he's ordered to do them, when he's rewarded, so he has no spontaneity, except around his trainer, whom he loves. But with us, he just sort of puts up with us. If you want to pick him up, that's fine, if you want to scratch his belly, that's fine, but he would never think of licking you. He would never think of wagging his tail. If you want him to wag his tail—you give him a piece of liver. That's how it works. It's like he's never really had a dog's life. He's always been an actor. He won't do anything unless he's paid for it. He's like a colleague who doesn't talk. He's different from the rest of my colleagues in that with my human colleagues, we feel like we've known each other all our lives. I'd do anything in the world for them. Moose is just a colleague. I don't dislike him, I'm not crazy about him, he's just something I work with.

JG: Since he's Martin's loyal dog, does he know you?

JM: Not really. If Moose were over there [other side of the room] right now and I said "Hey, Moose," he wouldn't even look. You'd never see his tail wag. But if [Moose's trainer] Mathilde [DeCagny] said it, he'd jump up and run and kiss her and lick her and everything. Or if Mathilde told him to come over to me and wag his tail, he'd do it, knowing that he was going to get a reward for doing it. It's been three years and we've done a lot of shows together, but he's remote. He's a one-person dog, and that's Mathilde. The rest of us, he tolerates us.

JG: Are you ever jealous of his success?

JM: Oh, no. That I would never be jealous of. We've all made cracks about him being on the covers of magazines, but we all know where our bread is buttered and a lot of people watch the show to see Moose, and they always ask about him. There isn't a person who I meet on the street or in a restaurant who doesn't ask about Moose. It's either—"Where's your cane?" or "Where's Eddie?" If we're in a restaurant, I usually say "I think you're eating him." If we're somewhere else, I say, "He's renegotiating his contract."

JG: Other actors say he's hard to work with.

JM: I do get angry sometimes. He's hard to work with when he doesn't get his trick right. I work and work all week long rehearsing and getting these lines down, you concentrate on your character, try to remember your lines, and Eddie screws up, and you get a half hour of waiting for Eddie to get it right, at which point, all the work you've done on your character has gone out of your head, and you can hardly remember what lines you're supposed to say. Sometimes it's a little irritating.

JG: Ever think that Martin should run off one day with Daphne?

JM: (*laughs*): No. But I think he should have an affair with Roz. I've pitched that a couple of times. But not with Daphne. I don't think she would go for it. I would love to have Martin have a lady friend. He's had a few dates, I'd like to see him have some more.

JG: Who cracks you up the most on the set?

JM: If I'm watching the show, it's David. Some of us are more like our characters than others, and David couldn't be more different from Niles. When I watch David being so fussbudgety and playing that character and I know what he's really like, I find it very very funny. Kelsey amazes me at how big he can go and still be real. But he knows exactly how far he can go, and not one step further. He makes me laugh an awful lot. He's totally irreverent. Everybody else works pretty hard on their lines. Kelsey just likes to wing it, so during rehearsals we'll get Frasier Crane as played by James Mason . . . we'll get Frasier Crane as played by Richard Burton . . . Frasier Crane as played by Bette Davis . . . and it's very very funny. He plays around a lot and keeps everybody very loose. Hard to say which one makes me laugh more. They both make me laugh a lot.

JG: I understand you're the joker of the set.

JM: We're all jokers, but I have the reputation of taking things a little too far. I always take things one step beyond where they should be, I think. If we start getting a little risqué, I go a little further and if we get a little bitchy, I go too far. I don't hold too much back and I let it out and people get a kick out of it. That's where the joker comes from.

JG: Are you a practical joker?

JM: Sure. I do them a lot during rehearsals, not during our performances. I'll mouth other people's words, I'll correct them in a funny way if they say something wrong. I like to keep it light and fun.

JG: What does place mat mean?

JM: I don't know, it must be my age. I have these little synapses, and strange words come out of my mouth. The wrong words, and that was one of them, and it was very funny. I was talking about a woman and how fat she was, and I was supposed to say she looked like she was shoplifting throw pillows, and it came out place mats instead. It's like last night, I was supposed to say "I can't tell you the truth because of my Indian heritage, I'm afraid your magic box will rob me of my spirit," and it came out, "I'm afraid your magic box will rob me of my dreams." Those things happen. But place mat has become a running joke around here. I hear about it all the time. It was on *Bloopers,* and our end-of-the-year wrap party gag reel. Now, when any of the cast can't remember someone's name, it's automatically just place mats.

John Mahoney's favorite episode is . . .

"The Winnebago show (number 23, "My Travels with Martin"). I loved that one. The only thing that could have made it better was if Roz had come along too. But it was such a wonderful concept, it was great to have us all trapped together in that little space. When people come up and talk to me about *Frasier*, that's usually the episode they all like the best. It's extremely popular. I had a lot to do, I was able to be forceful and get close to my sons, and the whole Daphne riff with not being able to speak American was very funny, so yes, it was my favorite.

The Dr. Niles Crane File

Dr. Niles Crane was born and raised in Seattle, and like his famous brother Frasier, he's also a psychiatrist. In fact, his Mercedes E 320 has SHRINK on his vanity license plate and he serves on the board of the local psychiatric association. He attended Yale and Cambridge and was a National Merit Finalist. He is a Jungian (as opposed to Frasier's expertise in Freud) who looks down on Frasier's radio show and the field of pop psychiatry. Niles has written several important articles, including one for the *Journal of Psychiatric Medicine* entitled "Gestalt Therapy: Probing the Subconscious."

Dr. Crane conducts workshops and groups for fear of abandonment, sexual addiction, fear of intimacy, multiple personality disorders, healing with humor, and compulsive spending. Not that he's in perfect health. Niles has a congenital heart condition and weak kidneys.

Niles's usual at the Café Nervosa is a latte with nutmeg and a brush of cinnamon. His favorite drink is a Stoli Gibson with three pearl onions. His vegetable of choice is carrots. And he is obsessed with expensive Italian shoes with tassels. He once announced that he was wearing $400 Bruno Maglis loafers, with tassels, and another time bought his dad new shoes with tassels that were "handmade by an artisan toiling

in a hilltop village above Florence. It's an event when he completes a pair of shoes. They ring the cathedral bell and the whole town celebrates.''

Dr. Crane has been married to his Maris for seven years. He met the queen of Seattle society when she was locked out of her estate. She was banging on the electric gates with a tire iron. The mansion, which has gargoyles on the outside, has been in Maris's family for four generations. Niles and Maris were married three years later and went to Zurich on their honeymoon. Niles's bedroom is across the hall from Maris's. He once dressed up like a pirate to perk up their love life, which wasn't successful. What did work was buying Maris a new Mercedes. After that present, they had sex twice in one session. You never know what will hit Maris's love button. She once got aroused when Niles called to tell her he was performing manual labor.

Maris and Niles are currently separated.

Niles is infatuated with Daphne. He helps Frasier pay her salary, videotaped her once while sleeping, had Daphne try on a sexy cocktail dress he bought for Maris, and says that Daphne stirs in him a passion he's never known before. The two of them danced the tango in 1996.

Frasier and Niles didn't have the typical childhood of Little League, soccer games, and pizza parties. Niles once mentioned going to one of Martin's friends' house for a weenie roast, where Niles shocked the host by requesting a salad Nicoise instead.

His earliest childhood memory is of Frasier climbing into his crib and jumping on him. And that wasn't the only childhood torture he had to endure. A neighborhood bully named Danny Kriezel also used to shove his head in the toilet and give him a ''swirlee.'' In junior high, Niles's clothes were once stolen after gym and hung on the goalpost. After that incident, he was nicknamed ''Jingle Bells'' and ''Peachfuzz.''

At a steak house:

NILES: I'd like a petite filet mignon, very lean, not so lean that it lacks flavor, but not so fat that it leaves drippings on the plate, and I don't want it cooked, just lightly seared on either side, pink in the middle, not a true pink but not a mauve either, something in between, bearing in mind the slightest error either way and it's ruined.

Niles Exit I:

NILES: Well, this has been kind of fun, but I must really run. I'm conducting a seminar for multiple personality disorders and it takes me forever to fill out the name tags.

On his patients:

NILES: . . . and then she said she's been seeing someone else, that she couldn't live a lie anymore. I was dumbfounded. What about everything we'd gone through together? Didn't that mean anything to her? I'm devastated, just devastated.

FRASIER: Niles, a patient has a right to change therapists.

NILES: Yes, but this is the third one who's terminated this year. I've used up two bottles of whiteout on my appointment book.

On marriage:

NILES: Love's a funny thing, isn't it? I mean, sometimes it's exciting and passionate, and sometimes it's something else. Something comfortable and familiar. That newly exfoliated little face staring up at you across the breakfast table, or sharing a little laugh together when you see someone wearing white after Labor Day.

Ordering coffee:

NILES: I'll have a double cappuccino, half-caf, nonfat milk, with enough foam to be aesthetically pleasing, but not so much that it would leave a mustache.

Niles's first meeting with Daphne:

FRASIER: Daphne, this is my brother Niles.

NILES: You're Daphne?

DAPHNE: Why, yes I am.

NILES: You're Daphne?

DAPHNE: Right again.

NILES: When Frasier mentioned he'd hired an English woman, I pictured someone a little more . . . not quite so . . . You're Daphne?

DAPHNE: Three's the charm.

NILES: What a lovely accent. Is it Manchester?

DAPHNE: Yes, how'd you know?

NILES: I'm quite the Anglophile. I'm sure Frasier and Dad have already told you.

DAPHNE: No, they didn't mention it.

Later on, over coffee at the Café Nervosa:

FRASIER: Are you in love with Daphne?

(*Niles does a spit-take.*)

NILES: That's preposterous. I refuse to dignify that question with an answer.

(*Niles proceeds to stir his coffee while Frasier stares at him.*)

NILES (*snaps*): I don't know! There. I've said it. Are you happy? Oh, why couldn't you have just hired some beefy, Eastern European scrubwoman who reeked of ammonia instead of Venus herself?

FRASIER: I asked, but it was an Olympic year. The agency was fresh out.

NILES: I can't get her out of my mind. You probably haven't noticed, but sometimes, just to be near her, I make up silly excuses to come over to your house.

FRASIER: Yes, I began to suspect that when you dropped by yesterday to remind us to always buckle our seat belts.

On the post–Maris separation blues:

NILES: Ever since the separation I've been paying women to touch me.

FRASIER: You can't mean . . . ?

NILES: Manicurists, pedicurists, facialists . . . Whenever you see a man who's well groomed you can bet he's not getting any.

On his nephew, Frederick:

NILES: It always cheers me up when Frederick calls me Uncle Niles. Hold my hand, Uncle Niles? Read to me, Uncle Niles? Recommend a wine, Uncle Niles? They grow up so fast.

Niles Exit II:

NILES: Oh dear, look at the time. I have a session with my multiple personality. Well, not to worry. If I'm late, he can just talk amongst himself.

FRASIER: How would you explain Niles, Dad?
MARTIN: I usually just change the subject.

Niles and Daphne walk into the living room together, apparently adjusting their clothing:

FRASIER: What were you two doing back there?
NILES: Maris lost her earring at the party last night. Daphne was good enough to crawl under the bed to look for it while I . . .
FRASIER: Yeeess?
NILES: . . . searched the credenza!

Is Niles ready for fatherhood?

NILES: To tell you the truth, no. One minute I'll be thinking there isn't a chance in hell I'd ever be able to handle all the stress. Then, suddenly, I'll find myself daydreaming about taking my son to the museum for the first time, or listening to him pick out his first feeble "Für Elise" on the piano, and I swear there are tears in my eyes.

Niles once had a crush on his dental hygienist Jodi.

MARTIN: He had his teeth cleaned so much his gums hemorrhaged.

FRASIER: Hello, Niles. Thanks for coming over on such short notice.
NILES: No problem. I welcome the chance to sneak out of the house for a while. Maris fell asleep doing her needlepoint and she's snoring like Bluto. . . . Hello, Dad. Hello, Daphne.
DAPHNE: Hello, Dr. Crane.
NILES: Actually, I was just in the middle of my workout, but I can always pump iron later.
FRASIER: Pump iron? Niles, you've never even pumped your own gas.

NILES (*sniffing Daphne's perfume*): Is that "Forbidden"?
FRASIER: In every sense of the word!

Niles, looking for Daphne at "Mom's" saloon after he heard she went out on a date with an ex-con:

NILES (*to bartender*): Excuse me. Has there been a young woman in here this evening approximately five foot nine and three-quarters with skin the color of Devonshire cream and the sort of eyes that gaze directly into one's soul with neither artifice nor evasion?

Niles and Frasier watch as Daphne orders two pounds of the Kenya blend in the Café Nervosa:

ERIC: Some people find that blend too intense.
DAPHNE: I like something that holds its body on my tongue.
(*Niles spills the cream all over the table.*)

After Niles and Daphne get into a rare fight over daytime talk shows:

NILES: Oh, mama, it was glorious—blood-pounding, sarcastic zingers flying . . .
FRASIER: You enjoyed fighting with Daphne?

NILES: Every exhilarating moment. It was pure unbridled passion. I think I still have some of her spittle on my forehead. Why did Dad ever tell us not to fight with girls? It's wonderful.

On why Niles didn't listen to Frasier's radio show that afternoon:

NILES: Oh, I'm sorry. I meant to, but I had a crisis with a patient. One of my multiples had a new personality emerge—a one-hundred-and-ten-year-old Frenchwoman. It would have been too risky to put off his therapy. Plus I would have missed out on a wonderful recipe for bouillabaisse.

On KACL for a day:

NILES: Hello, Seattlites. This is Dr. Niles Crane, filling in for my ailing brother, Dr. Frasier Crane. Although I feel perfectly qualified to fill his radio shoes, I should warn you that while Frasier is Freudian, I am a Jungian, so there'll be no blaming mother today. Roz, who's my first caller?

The David Hyde Pierce File

David Hyde Pierce was born and bred in Saratoga Springs, New York. He attended Yale University, where he received his degree in English and theater arts. In 1981, with degree in hand, he moved to New York City to take the city by storm, and got a job selling ties at Bloomingdale's. He also studied acting in the evening, and got his first professional acting job in *Beyond Therapy* (a prophetic title) on Broadway, followed by stints off-Broadway and in regional theater. Between 1983 and 1985 he worked in various productions at the Guthrie Theater in Minneapolis before returning to New York to appear in *Hamlet* at the New York Shakespeare Festival. He then traveled to the Soviet Union and Japan to perform in the stage production of *The Cherry Orchard* from 1988 to 1989.

His first feature film role was in *Bright Lights, Big City,* and he has since appeared in other films like *Little Man Tate, The Fisher King, Crossing Delancy, Sleepless in Seattle,* and *Wolf.*

Pierce picked up guest spot roles in *Crime Story* and *Spenser: For Hire,* and got his first series in 1992 on NBC's *The Powers That Be.* He played Rep. Theodore Van Horne, the little-known congressman and suicidal son-in-law of Sen. William Powers, played by John Forsythe. After *Powers* was canceled in 1993, Sheila Guthrie, an associate of *Frasier* casting director Jeff Greenberg, came across Pierce's photo and suggested to the producers that if they were ever thinking of perhaps giving Frasier a brother, they should consider Pierce, since he's a dead ringer for the younger Kelsey Grammer.

The rest is show business history.

I met with David Hyde Pierce in the *Frasier* conference room, again after a table read, this one for episode 70, "Frasier Loves Roz." The actor was dressed very casually, in non-Niles-type attire of tan Dockers and a blue button-down shirt, with the two top buttons open.

J G : In reading all of the *Frasier* scripts, one can't help but notice how the lines for Niles just jump right off the page.

D H P : There's just something about that character that the writers tapped into. A combination of whimsy, intelligence, and there's also the whole Maris thing. She's such a great thing for the writers, because they have so much fun with this horrific person. I'm not an actor who loves to do a lot, but my favorite thing is to get a perfect line. It's magical, and they do that again and again for Niles.

J G : What do you think Maris looks like?

D H P : I think she is rail thin, and very short, and tightly pulled in every

Niles speaks for the prosecution in "Crane vs. Crane."

way. I think she probably dresses extremely well, but she's so thin you wouldn't be able to tell. I'm not sure what color her hair is. At one point it was blond, but I think it changes. And I have a feeling she has very pointy teeth. She favors riding boots a lot. Her hair probably appears to be short, since she wears it in a bun. I don't picture it hanging below chin level.

JG: Why do you think Niles is so much in love with Maris?

DHP: I think he sees a little bit of his mother in her. He finds her beautiful. I think in a way he finds her helpless. As demanding as she is, she also seems incapable of functioning without him, until the separation. That's what's so devastating about the separation. She's on her own and seems to be doing fine. But while they were together, her constant cravings and demands and her difficultness tapped into that therapist part of him that wants to take care of her.

JG: Why do you think Niles hasn't acted upon his feelings, in a real way, for Daphne?

DHP: I think it's because he's a moral person. That's what makes Niles bearable, because he's so stuck-up. But he's also very ethical. He's not quite as ethical as Frasier is, but he has a very strong moral center that he certainly got from his dad and maybe their mom, so I don't think he would consider seriously having an affair and cheating on Maris. He wouldn't consider it fair to Maris or to Daphne.

JG: He's clearly obsessed with Daphne.

DHP: Head over heels in love with her. She's the opposite of Maris. Where Maris is tight, Daphne is loose. Where Maris is short, Daphne is tall. I think she's just such an exotic flower to him, and she's so beautiful and it's so unusual for him to be treated by a woman with such friendliness that he's overwhelmed by that openness because Maris is so manipulative and difficult.

JG: Does David Pierce enjoy opera?

DHP: I listen to classical music. I'm not a big opera fanatic, but I do have a few that I listen to occasionally. Not on the level of Niles, but I don't object to them.

JG: How do you like your coffee?

DHP: Black. The most elaborate I'll get is, if I'm staying up late, I'll have a decaf espresso, but that's as far from the cup as I'll stray.

JG: How different are you from Niles?

DHP: We have the same education. We both went to Yale. We both like classical music. I have an older brother, who's thirteen years ahead of me, and he was older enough that I didn't know him that well growing up. When we first started doing the show, I felt very strongly about how different I was from Niles, and now that we've completed three seasons, it's harder for me to draw the line between him and me. We don't dress alike, we have very different tastes. I'm not a suit person. I have to borrow from wardrobe when I have to go out and attend something. I'm single and not obsessed over any maids. Although I will add that on *The Powers That Be,* my character had an affair with the maid. There must be something in there that I'm tapping into, but I don't know what it is.

JG: What do you think about psychiatry?

DHP: I think psychiatry is like religion. In the right hands, it can be incredibly helpful and in the wrong hands it can be pretty destructive.

JG: Kelsey Grammer sees a therapist. How about you?

DHP: I never have. Many of my friends recommend I do, and probably I'll take them up on that at some point.

JG: Have you learned anything about yourself from Niles?

DHP: Yes. When you play a character, you learn how much you're actually like that person. Everybody has all kinds of people inside them, and when you play a character over a long period of time like this . . . I can certainly be pretentious, and I can be obsessive, and I can certainly be as myopic as Niles can be, and by playing him, I'm more aware of those aspects of myself when they come up in real life.

JG: I've heard that people used to stop you on the street and say, "You look like that psychiatrist guy from *Cheers*."

DHP: The first time I met Kelsey, he and I were doing plays together at the Long Wharf Theater in New Haven. I was doing *Holiday* and he was doing *The Common Pursuit*. We had our meals in the same place and I went in to have dinner and he was sitting at the table and I looked at him and thought I was already eating. Because we looked that much alike. And if you see pictures of him in his twenties in New York, he looks like me in my twenties. It's amazing. We still have a certain resemblance, but when we were both younger, we really looked alike. I'm going to be thirty-seven in 1996 and he's forty-one.

JG: How did you thank Sheila Guthrie for getting you the job?

DHP: She's the one who brought the picture to Jeff Greenberg, the casting director, so both of them really get the credit, but she's the one who found my picture in the first place. I sent her Harry & David food-of-the-month club for a year. It wasn't a car, but it's amazing what came out of that. It is an example of how when someone is good at their job, and is creative about it, and can say "What about this?" she set the whole ball into motion for this character. There wasn't going to be a brother, so it wasn't like anybody was looking for one.

JG: How were you as a tie salesman?

DHP: Terrible. I'm not a good salesperson, I'm not good at convincing people to buy things. I found the whole experience overwhelming. The automated cash registers were completely beyond me. However, I was only on as temporary Christmas help, and when the season ended, they passed on making me permanent, and I was so upset. Even though I hated every minute of it, I was still hurt.

JG: What kind of ties did you sell?

DHP: It was the era of jelly-bean ties, because Ronald Reagan had just become president. It's really hard to tell someone they needed to wear a jelly-bean tie. And it was a scary place to work, because on Christmas Eve, people that come into a store to buy neckties are very angry people who haven't been able to find what they really wanted, or they forget to do their shopping.

JG: What did you do to support yourself after you gave up tie sales?

DHP: I went to work for a temp agency that sent me to this law firm as a paralegal. There was a computer fraud case that went on for several years, and I'd work on this case and be familiar with the paperwork, and then I'd get these acting jobs, and quit. The play would run and close, and then I'd go back to the temp firm, and they'd send me back to the law firm, because I knew everything about the case. By the time I finished with the law firm, I started to work consistently enough, and also started to go out of town for theater work, that I didn't need to go back.

JG: Who cracks you up the most on film days?

DHP: It's between Kelsey and John. John makes me laugh because he's just completely silly and Kelsey makes me laugh because a lot of times we're doing stuff in each other's faces and he's just funny. So it's hard to keep a straight face.

JG: Let's talk about some of your films. Let's begin with *Nixon.*

DHP: I loved doing that movie. It didn't end up doing that well at the box office, but I think down the road people will look back at it and say it's a very good movie. But the box office performance doesn't really matter to me. The film was a very fulfilling thing for me to be a part of. I loved the people I was working with, the historical subject matter, and the fact that I got to meet a lot of the actual people who were involved, including John Dean, who I played.

JG: *Wolf?*

DHP: *Wolf* was the first time I felt a director [Mike Nichols] really took care of me. I was in scenes with Jack Nicholson and I was completely prepared to walk into the theater and see nothing but the back of my head. That happens a lot. That's not uncommon. Consequently, what was a pretty small part didn't feel that way. He got the value out of it that was there.

JG: *Sleepless in Seattle?*

DHP: I got to spend some time in Seattle, which was great, even though my scenes took place in Baltimore, which didn't matter. It was a small part, but I was married to a woman very much like Maris. I played Meg Ryan's brother.

JG: *Bright Lights, Big City?*

DHP: My first film. It cost me more to join the union than they paid me. I had to borrow the dues from my agent. I had the line, "I'm sorry, the bar is closed" and I said it to Michael J. Fox. I had been acting for five or six years by then, and I was scared stiff, because I had never been on a movie set. The director said, "You pour your drink, you hit your mark and say the line." I was panic-stricken. How do you hit the mark without looking down and seeing the mark? Suddenly it was like starting all over again. But it worked out. Nobody fell over or died.

JG: *Crossing Delancey?*

DHP: I got that part because the director Joan Micklin Silver came to see me in a play, and my bio in the program said, "Film and television audiences will have no idea who I am." She read that and said, "They should have some idea," so she brought me in to read for the part.

JG: *The Powers That Be.*

DHP: That was a great experience. Norman Lear produced it, and Marta Kaufman and David Crane (the executive producers of *Friends*) created it. They wrote incredible scripts. It was a great cast of theater actors, we had a terrific ensemble and loved playing off each other. I adored the character. He was a suicidal congressman who muttered all the time. Sometimes they'd let me come up with my own mutters, and sometimes they'd write me some wonderful mutters. The show wasn't treated very well by NBC. It was a political satire which they took off for the entire election season, and put back on a week after the election was over. And when that was done and not picked up, I thought, "Well, OK, I won't do another television show. Certainly not for NBC." I was so angry and hurt. I'd been in plays that closed before. I knew what that experience was like. But because this was a whole new event for me, I didn't see the warning signs, which now, being on a successful show, I see how the network treats you. They weren't behind the show. For whatever the motives, they weren't behind it. There's only a select number of good time slots, and the shows they like, they push. And that leaves the rest of us. I figured I'd go back to the theater. And then a few weeks later, I ended up meeting with the producers of *Frasier* about playing Niles. I never saw a script on this. It was based on knowing Kelsey's work, knowing the producers were from *Cheers*, that John Mahoney might be involved, I thought it was worth the chance.

His favorite episode of Frasier . . .

"That's tough. For someone who hasn't seen the show before, I'd always begin with the pilot, because it's one of the best written pilots ever. They did such an incredible job of introducing all the characters. Otherwise, it wasn't the flashiest show, but I loved "My Coffee with Niles" (number 24), in which Frasier and I sit at the Café Nervosa and talk for twenty-two minutes. It was so well written and unusual for sit-com TV, very ballsy for the writers to do, and a lot of fun to act because it was really, even more than usual, like we were back in the theater. And of course, the fencing episode (number 44, "An Affair to Forget") and the tango episode (number 63, "Moondance"), they were the flashiest things. I also loved the episode where Frasier and I attempted to fix the plumbing (number 35, "Seat of Power"), where we open up our own restaurant (number 43 "The Innkeepers"), and the Winnebago episode (number 23, "My Travels with Martin"), and all for different reasons."

The Daphne Moon File

Daphne Moon grew up in Manchester, England, and came to the United States in early 1993. She lives in Frasier's study and was hired as a home-care worker to cook, clean, and help Martin with his physical therapy. Daphne is a bit of a psychic and her powers are strongest during her time of the month. But she is occasionally subject to psychic headaches caused by a clawing at the cosmic continuum. In fact, she got such a headache when Frasier's ex-wife Lilith came to visit.

Like Dr. Crane, Daphne has also been involved in show business. She starred in a British TV series at age twelve called *Mind Your Knickers.* As she puts it, "It was about a group of high-spirited, ethnically diverse twelve-year-olds in a girls' private boarding school. I played Emma. Of course, I was sixteen by the end of the series, five foot ten, and they had me boobies bound up tighter than a mummy."

Daphne's famous saying on the show: *"Don't get your bloomers in a twist."*

Ms. Moon has many, many relatives—eight brothers and many, many uncles and aunts. She used to care for her younger brothers when they were growing up. Her grandfather, father, and brothers all work on the docks. It's a family tradition.

Grandfather lived to be ninety-three. He took a nap every afternoon and died in his sleep. Grammy Moon thought he was just napping. Speaking of Grammy, she used to make her famous sticky buns on Sunday. She'd add a pint of rum to the batch and wind up loaded in the garden in her wedding dress, facedown in the birdbath. And speaking of Granddad, he used to take out his teeth and chase the kids around the room until his mood changed and they all ran for their lives.

One of Daphne's aunts owns a little tearoom, and she has an uncle who's a political writer for a London tabloid. Her brother Billy—Mum's favorite—is a ballroom dancing teacher.

During the day, when she can wrestle the TV remote away from Martin, Daphne likes to watch soap operas and daytime talk shows. In the evenings, she enjoys poker, darts, pool, and occasionally has a couple of pints with her girlfriends.

Daphne has gone out on friendly dates with both Niles and Bulldog as well as Eric, a waiter at Café Nervosa, who dumped her to stay focused on his band and music. She has been seeing Joe, a carpenter she met when he came to work on Frasier's apartment, for six months.

Daphne seems oblivious to the fact that Niles is mad about her. Even after they danced the tango and Niles called her a goddess, Daphne thought Niles was putting her on.

On love:

DAPHNE: There's nothing quite as exciting as a first date. You're both so full of questions. What's your favorite food? Do you have brothers and sisters? If you came back as an animal, what sort of animal would you be?

Frasier and Daphne on love II:

FRASIER: Sexual mores being what they are in America, the third date is often the point at which two healthy adults decide whether or not to . . . take it to the next level.

DAPHNE: Excuse me? First date, second date, whoops, let's all drop our knickers?

Niles on love III:

DAPHNE: There's never been anyone serious in my life.

NILES: You? I find that hard to believe. I can only imagine a long line of suitors vying for that silky auburn hair, dew-kissed complexion, and bee-stung lips.

At a cocktail party, a man tries to pick up Daphne.

MAN: I've got a catamaran moored in the harbor. Why don't we ditch out of here and you and me go for a midnight cruise?

DAPHNE: Oh, well, thank you, but I think I'd rather be stripped naked, oiled up, and thrown into a South American prison.

MAN: Hey, I'm flexible.

Niles to Daphne:

NILES: Someday a man worthy of you will come along, just as soon as the gods create him.

Daphne on Grammy Moon's famous plum duff. It was a flour pudding boiled in a cloth bag. She'd soak it for hours in rum, then ignite in a blinding flash.

DAPHNE: As soon as she came out of the kitchen with no eyebrows, we knew dessert was ready. To this day, the smell of burning hair puts me in the holiday spirit.

On Granny Moon's buns:

DAPHNE: I decided to prepare you a traditional English breakfast. We have eggs and bangers, or as you call them, sausage. And to finish it off, a batch of Granny Moon's famous sticky buns. Granny made these every Sunday. Of course, she always added a pint of rum to the recipe. Nobody liked these more than Granny herself. Many's the Sunday I'd head over to her house after church, only to find her out in the garden in her wedding dress, facedown in the birdbath.

On Granny Moon's passing:

DAPHNE: Me brothers had been off on a three-day bender. They were all pissed as newts; couldn't even stand up, but they crawled to that funeral on their hands and knees.

On her granddad, who used to nap every day:

DAPHNE: He'd lie there on the sofa and you couldn't wake him for the world. Grandmum would say "He might as well be a dead man." Then of course one day we couldn't wake him because he really was a dead man. Poor Grandmum. For weeks she kept insisting "He's napping, he's napping."

Daphne's relatives, part II:

MARTIN: I think I need more comfortable shoes. My dogs are killing me.

DAPHNE: Pardon?

MARTIN: My dogs. My feet. What do you call 'em in England?

DAPHNE: Well, we mostly call our body parts by their rightful names. Except my uncle Harold. He named parts of his anatomy on the Queen's Pins, he sat on the Duchess of Kent. He was quite a jolly fellow. That is until Aunt Kate caught him introducing the Prince of Wales to a cocktail waitress.

Frasier, on Niles's Daphne dreams:

FRASIER: I don't know what sort of twisted fantasy you've concocted about your future with Daphne. I suspect it involves a comet hitting the earth and the two of you having to rebuild the species, but trust me, it's not going to happen. She needs a man. One who's in a position to do more for her than just smell her hair.

Frasier on a bad day, to Daphne:

FRASIER: The day I give a fig what you think is the day England produces a great chef, a world-class wine, and a car with a decent electrical system!

DAPHNE: I have reached the end of my tether with you, Doctor. You are by far the most ungrateful, disagreeable, self-centered, whiny fusspot I've ever had the misfortune of caring for. I've had patients on their deathbeds who were more considerate than you and a damn sight more jolly too! Mother Teresa would be hard-pressed not to slip a dose of arsenic in your soda and be done with you. As far as I'm concerned you can lay in those sweaty sheets till you're one giant bedsore!

On British dates:

DAPHNE: My girlfriends in Manchester used to set me up all the time. And it was always some gangly bounder with a boarding house reach. And he wasn't going for the Coleman's hot mustard, if you know what I mean.

Niles lets Daphne try on an emerald necklace he has purchased for Maris, but while he is undoing the clasp, he lets it drop down the front of her blouse.

DAPHNE: Can you see them?

NILES: Oh, yes! Thank you.

(*Frasier enters during this encounter*)

FRASIER: Hello, Niles. Whatever are you doing here?

NILES: I bought an emerald necklace for Maris, and I needed some place to hide it.

FRASIER: May I see it?

NILES: Not at the moment, no.

DAPHNE: It's down me blouse.

FRASIER: Well, I'm sure Maris will never think of looking for it there.

Daphne dances the tango with Niles at a society ball, in a bid to help him make Maris and her friends jealous:

DAPHNE (*while dancing*): I feel you're holding back.

NILES: I am.

DAPHNE: This is no time for inhibitions.

NILES: I know.

DAPHNE: Let it out, Niles. Let everything out.

NILES: Oh, Daphne, I adore you.

DAPHNE: I adore you too.

NILES: What?

DAPHNE: I adore you too.

NILES: Oh, how I've longed to hear those words.

DAPHNE: How I've longed to say them.

NILES: You're beautiful. You're a goddess.

DAPHNE: I don't ever want this moment to end.

NILES: Then let's not end it.

(*But, later, when the moment ends, when the dance is over and they're sitting at a table . . .*)

NILES: I'm a new man. Do you have any idea what I'm feeling?

DAPHNE: Of course I do. Your friends look positively dumbstruck. From now on there'll be no more of that "Oh, poor Niles" attitude.

NILES: Far from it.

DAPHNE: I knew you were a good dancer, but I had no idea you were such a good actor. "I adore you, Daphne." "You're a goddess, Daphne." We fooled everyone, didn't we?

NILES (*sadly*): Oh yes, we did, didn't we?

The Jane Leeves File

Jane Leeves was born in London and raised in East Grinstead, Sussex, England, the daughter (along with two sisters and a brother) of a contracts engineer and a nurse. Her first dream was to be a ballerina, but that career was cut short by an injury when she was eighteen. She bounced back with modeling and less strenuous dancing in commercials and rock videos.

She moved to Los Angeles to break into acting in 1984, and soon got a job in the syndicated series *Throb* (1986–88) about the record business. *The Complete Directory to Prime Time Network and Cable Shows* describes her *Throb* character of "Blue" as "a flighty young English girl who was more punk than most of the groups that paraded through the office." After *Throb* was canceled, Leeves guest-starred on many series, including *Murder, She Wrote*, *My Two Dads*, *Blossom*, and *Who's the Boss?"* She had a recurring role on *Murphy Brown* as Audrey Cohen, the girlfriend of *F.Y.I.* executive producer Miles Silverberg, but was probably best known for the *Seinfeld* episodes in which she played Marla, the "virgin" who seduced John F. Kennedy Jr.

Her feature-film credits include *To Live and Die in L.A.*, *Monty Python's The Meaning of Life*, *The Hunger*, *Mr. Write*, and *Miracle on 34th Street*.

I spoke with Leeves in the bleachers at Stage 25 during rehearsals for the "Frasier Loves Roz" episode. She wore a gray "Lucky" T-shirt, black sweater, and jeans.

Daphne visits the station.

JEFFERSON GRAHAM: I understand that you know everything about Daphne, even more than the writers.

JANE LEEVES: It's true. I have quite an extensive background of her. In 1982 she was at beauty school. It hasn't been talked about in the scripts, but I know that she tried her hand at many things. For Daphne, it's always been about taking care of people and helping them feel better. She has eight brothers and comes from a very working-class background. The little house she grew up in was just like the one in *My Left Foot,* with four to a bed. She had to contribute to the running of the household by bringing home what she made and giving a bit for Mum.

JG: When did she come to Seattle?

JL: Three years and six months ago. Her brother Billy, the ballroom dancer, told her to go out and make a life for herself before she ended up like her mum, so she went to San Francisco and stayed with her

Uncle Jackie, who's a transvestite. She stayed a few months, and then hopped on a train to Seattle, because she heard it was a nice place.

JG: Do the writers appreciate that you know so much about your character?

JL: It helps them and me. They'll often say "Why do you think she'd do this or that" and since I come from England and knew people just like Daphne, I can offer my views. Before she got the job at the health care agency, she was living hand to mouth, doing what she could. For Daphne, living with Frasier and Martin, she's in a mansion as far as she's concerned. She has her own room and all these gentlemen who treat her nicely.

JG: Why do you think Niles is so obsessed with Daphne?

JL: Because she is the complete opposite of anything he's ever known. She's grounded and down to earth, and that's just not the sort of person he's used to. She's not out for herself like everybody else, she's there to help others. And it turns him on to see her rooting around under the sink and fixing things.

JG: Is she truly unaware of his desires?

JL: I don't think so. It's just one of those things that's scary to deal with. Also, there's a certain amount of denial. Somebody that wonderful and cultured couldn't possibly be interested in a little guttersnipe like me, could he?

JG: Are they showing *Frasier* in England yet?

JL: Yes, it's on Channel 4 and it's very well received there. The critics and the audience love it.

JG: Tell me about your accent.

JL: I have a standard British accent and Daphne has a Mancunian accent, since she's from Manchester. It's like the difference between a traditional American and a southern accent. A Mancunian accent is more working class. I'm so used to slipping in and out of it, but sometimes my accent has gotten us into trouble on scripts because the words don't come out the way the writers envisioned. For instance, I was supposed to say a joke once that ended with the word duck, but with the accent, it didn't sound funny, so they changed it to elephant.

JG: If people used to stop you on the street and say "You're the virgin!" after *Seinfeld,* what do they say now?

JL: They go "Daphne, we love her, she's so sweet." She's a great calling card because she's such a good person and so likable that people relate to her and immediately embrace me.

JG: What are your memories of East Grinstead?

JL: It was just a very small town in the middle of the countryside. Everybody knew each other, you felt safe there, you didn't have to lock your doors.

JG: Do you ever get back to England?

JL: At least once a year. My parents, sister, and brother are still there, as well as many friends.

JG: How do you look back at your *Murphy Brown* experience?

JL: It was great. It gave me an opportunity to work with my best friend, Faith Ford [*FYI* reporter Corky Sherwood], which I never thought was possible, because we're so different.

JG: How did you become friends with her?

JL: We moved here at the same time. We met in an acting class and then became roommates for six years. I came to visit her at *Murphy Brown* a few times, and [producer] Diane English had seen me on *Throb,* so they wrote the part of Audrey for me.

JG: Tell me about the *Seinfeld* experience.

JL: It was so much fun but it was so fast and it happened so quickly. When I did the first "Virgin" episode they didn't know what the following week's show would be or whether I would be back. We shot "The Virgin" on a Wednesday, I went home, and they called me on Friday and told me to be back at rehearsal on Saturday. I came in and asked what happens to my character. "You end up losing your virginity to JFK, Jr." "No," I said, "what really happens?" Again, they told me. I thought, well, that sounds hilarious and great, but how will they handle it on TV. Luckily, they came up with all those great sayings like "Queen of my castle" and "Master of my domain."

JG: You've been in five movies. Take me through your highlights.

JL: The best one is the latest, *James and the Giant Peach,* and you don't see me in it because it's animated. It's just my voice, but I get to sing and play this wonderful character, and it looks great. I'll also be doing *The Lion King* sequel for video, playing a little bird who is friends with Simba.

J G : And the live-action films?

J L : I liked the scenes I had with Paul Reiser in *Mr. Write.* We had a fun time and a neat little chemistry. *Miracle on 34th Street* was fun, but grueling. And it was great fun meeting the Monty Python guys on *The Meaning of Life.*

Her favorite episode of *Frasier* is . . .

"I have so many, it's hard to choose one. The pilot (number 1, "The Good Son") was a good episode for me, and I also liked the one where Daphne had to buy Bulldog in an auction (number 12 "Can't Buy Me Love"). Then we rode home in a limo, I got drunk, and turned the tables by giving him a horrible time. "The Matchmaker" (number 28) was wonderful, and so was (number 41) "Daphne's Room" and the Tango episode (number 63, "Moondance"). I wasn't in (the fencing show) much (number 44, "An Affair to Forget") but I loved the swordfight.

The Roz Doyle File

Roz Doyle is the producer of *The Dr. Frasier Crane Show,* approves all his guests, screens the incoming calls, and occasionally offers advice as well. She's been in the radio business since 1983.

Roz grew up in Wisconsin, where her mother is the state attorney general, and the family occasionally meets for family reunions at her uncle's dairy farm.

Roz is quite the lady about town. She has season tickets to the Sonics and once bought T. J. Smith, a linebacker for the Seahawks, at a bachelor auction. She's best known for her

experienced ways in male-female relationships. Roz loves sex and isn't shy about saying so. Roz once dated an older man and was afraid she'd overexcite him in bed and he'd die. During college, Roz had sex in an elevator, a phone booth, an airplane, and even a merry-go-round.

Roz on men:

ROZ: If you want to know if a man's cheating, you offer him two choices for dinner. One that's really rich and fattening and one that's light and sensible. If he picks the one that's calorie packed, he doesn't mind turning into a bloated pig, which mean he's happily married and you're in the clear. If he chooses the diet plate, it means he's staying in shape for his main squeeze, and you should get yourself a lawyer who can sue the sweat off a racehorse.

Roz on sex:

ROZ: Gary? I dumped him three weeks ago. The sex was okay, but he was kind of limited. . . . It's not that Gary was bad in bed. I mean, he knew where all the parts were. Unfortunately, most of them were his.

Roz and Bulldog:

BULLDOG: May I say you're looking pretty tasty today, Roz.
ROZ: If you plan to put the moves on me, Bulldog, I'll need to see an updated shot record.
BULLDOG: Anytime. I'll even show you the injection marks.

Niles on Roz:

NILES: She's had more men serve under her than General Schwartzkopf.

Roz and Bulldog II. Bulldog asks Roz to be his producer, and Frasier thinks he has ulterior motives.

FRASIER: Come on Roz, don't you think there's just the tiniest possibility that the reason Bulldog asked you to be his producer was because he . . . you know, maybe he wanted to . . .
ROZ: Wanted to what?
NILES: Dip his biscotti in your latte.

On dating:

ROZ: My typical date's idea of a gourmet evening is take-out, make out, and home by Letterman.

FRASIER: Niles, you'll never believe what thriving Seattle night spot is closing its doors.
NILES: Roz, you're moving?

At KACL, Noel put out a joke petition for the producers of **Star Trek** *to add a new character, Rozalinda, the four-breasted queen of the Planet Rozniak.*

ROZ: It's the joke of the station. When I come in in the morning, the guard used to say "Morning, Roz." Now it's "All hail, Rozalinda."

(Later on, Frasier needed to leave the show early. Could Roz handle it without him?)

ROZ: If I can nurse quadruplets and still find time to rule Rozniak, I can do anything.

Roz on a guy she met on the bus:

ROZ: We're all crowded in there when suddenly I smell Lagerfeld and I look up into these big brown eyes and they were looking down into mine.

FRASIER: I hope you mean eyes.

ROZ: We got to talking. His name's Gary, and we're really connecting. You know, I'm starting to believe in kismet, and all of a sudden, a bunch of people want to get off, and I'm in their way, so I get off just to let them out and before I can get back on, the damn bus drives off. Out of my life forever!

FRASIER: I'm sure another one would've come along in ten minutes.

ROZ: I'm talking about the guy.

FRASIER: So am I.

Roz and Bulldog II, after he invites her to a Sonics game:

ROZ: Sorry, Bulldog, but I'm already going. I have season tickets.

BULLDOG: We could still get together afterwards.

ROZ: Only if I smash into your car in the parking lot.

BULLDOG: Why is it the ones that want it the most put on the biggest struggle?

ROZ: Because when I do finally give in I want us to enjoy it all the more. That is, if I'm not too distracted by the fact that every other man on earth has died and the earth is hurtling toward the sun.

On animals:

ROZ: I'm a cat person. I mean, it's not like I'd ever buy a cat mug or a cat calendar, but I had a cat when I was growing up. We were practically inseparable. "Muffles" or "Scruffles"—something like that.

FRASIER: Well, is it possible that there's a dog person inside of you who's just dying to get out? Come on, Roz. Maybe a puppy will awaken your maternal instincts.

ROZ: Sorry. I had them surgically removed.

Roz on callers:

ROZ: We've got a couple of jilted lovers, a man who's afraid of his dog, a manic depressive, and three people who feel their life is going no-where.

Roz on dates, IV:

ROZ: I had the most hellacious date of my life. First, he doesn't drive. So he asks me to pick him up from work. I paid for the parking. Then I stop for gas, he doesn't move a muscle. I have to pump it myself, while he just sits there reading the sports section. So, I take him back to my place to make my famous sweet-and-sour shrimp. I'm in the middle of cooking and I ask him to hand me the honey. He gets this freaked-out look on his face, and tells me he can't because he has a deathly fear of touching anything sticky. I told him it was a new jar but he didn't want to take the risk.

FRASIER: Where do you meet these people?

ROZ: I answered his ad.

FRASIER: Maybe you should take a sick day and call in sometime.

ROZ: At nineteen a man is just reaching his sexual peak, whereas I won't reach mine for another (*checks watch*) twenty minutes.

The Peri Gilpin File

Peri Gilpin was born in Waco, Texas, and raised in Dallas. She began her professional acting career at age nine, appearing in numerous television commercials. As a child, she used to accompany her late father Jim O'Brian, a nationally known broadcaster, to the Dallas radio station where he worked. In addition to having a father who was in show business, her stepfather is a commercial performer, her mother is an actress, and her two sisters and one brother have also ventured into acting.

While in school in Dallas, Gilpin studied acting at the Dallas Theater Center, where she performed in various stage productions and was inspired by the Center's house manager, Chantal Westerman (now a reporter at *Good Morning, America.*) After high school, she continued her acting studies at the University of Texas at Austin and the British-American Academy in London, England.

Returning to the States, Gilpin found work in Dallas as a makeup artist, and then headed east, where she became an apprentice at the famed Williamstown Theater Festival in Massachusetts.

Her stage credits include the off-Broadway productions of *Lucky Lucy* and *The Fortune Man* and many regional theater productions, including *The Crucible* and *A Midsummer Night's Dream.*

She moved to Los Angeles and began picking up guest spot roles on such series as *21 Jump Street, Max Monroe,* and *Matlock.* She appeared on Grub Street's *Wings* ("Four Dates That Will Live in Infamy") as Brian's date as well as one of the final episodes of *Cheers* as a reporter who interviews city council candidate Woody ("Woody Gets an Election").

Her first series role was on *Flesh 'N Blood* (1991) at Paramount, from the executive producers of *Cheers,* Glen and Les Charles and James Burrows. The series was about a con man named Arlo Weed (David Keith) who moved in with the sister neither he nor she knew they had. Gilpin played Irene, the sister's secretary and best friend. Gilpin also worked in the successor to *Flesh,* called *Local Heroes,* that featured much of the same cast and producers. However, NBC canceled it after five episodes, and they never aired. In 1995 she costarred in the NBC-TV movie *Fight for Justice: The Nancy Conn Story.*

I met with Peri Gilpin in the Frasier ''green room'' at Stage 25, near the actors' dressing rooms. The ''green room'' is a lounge for the actors and guest stars, decorated with more than a hundred wall photos of great moments from *Frasier*, along with cards and notes on a bulletin board. Gilpin wore a black-and-white-striped sweater and black pants.

JEFFERSON GRAHAM: How did you get the name Peri?

PERI GILPIN: My parents thought I would be a boy, because my mother was so big. I weighed ten pounds at birth. They were thinking strictly boy names and thinking of naming me Peter or Petry, which is the Yugoslavian version of Peter. I came out a girl, everybody was shocked, and nobody knew what to name me. My mother decided on Beth, but I had a different last name at the time, and it would have made my initials BO, and she thought that was terrible, so she gave me the name Peri after the Walt Disney character Peri, the squirrel.

JG: Tell me about your life in Texas.

PG: I was born in Waco, but grew up in Houston and Dallas. My mom and dad were at college when I was born, and my sister was born after me. I only lived there until I was three, then we moved to Dallas, my parents broke up, and my mom and sister moved to Houston. We lived there till I was nine. My mom remarried and then we all moved back to Dallas. My real father, who left Waco, was a traveling broadcaster. He left Texas and went to Cincinnati and did the radio station thing where he went to a different station every two or three years. His name was Jim O'Brian, and he died in 1983 in a parachuting accident. He was in Philadelphia at the time and he'd been there for many years. At the time of his death, he had the top morning show in the country. He was a real big-time DJ. He also did the weather on TV and anchored the news.

JG: Did you get to spend much time with him?

PG: No. From the time I was four till the time of his death when I was twenty-two, I probably only saw him four or five times. They were in Philadelphia and we were in Texas.

JG: In talking with you, I detect a southern twang that I never hear on Frasier.

PG: I'm from Texas. There are some episodes where I can hear it so loud and clear, but I try to speak in a normal American dialect, and I try to take the Texas out. She's supposed to be from Wisconsin, which would be much more of a midwestern accent.

JG: How was your year in England at acting school?

PG: That was probably the year I did the most growing emotionally. The students at the school were expected to find our own lodging. There was no dorm or meal plan. I really learned for the first time how to take care of myself. Thank goodness they spoke English. Other than that, there were no similarities between London and Texas. It dawned on me the day I arrived in this country, I didn't even know how to get a cab, and no one helped. Nobody cares who you are, where you're from, you're going to have to do it on your own.

JG: Professionally you started as a makeup artist.

PG: I always did commercials. I studied acting since I was eight years old. I did lots of plays in school, but then I went to school in London and when I came back, I was broke. I had no money and I didn't know what to do. I knew it was time to embark on a professional career, but I didn't know where to go—NY or LA, so I started working that summer as a makeup artist with a friend to make money. A friend of mine had become a makeup artist, but not only that, she also opened up an agency that represented makeup artists and wardrobe people, stylists, all kind of support people. I did that for about a year and a half, but when I finally worked on a movie, I finally realized I'm never going to be happy doing this. I couldn't be on that side of the camera. I needed to be an actress if I was going to be in this business. So I went to Williamstown, then to New York, got an agent, and five years later, moved to LA.

JG: Tell me about the *Wings* audition.

PG: I had never met Jeff Greenberg before [the head of casting for Grub Street]. I went in to read for him. After I read, he said "It's Spo-can, not Spo-cane, and can I ask you a personal question?" What? "Can you look better than this?" When the script said an immigrant's daughter who owns this diner in Nantucket, I went very literal on that, and he said, well, "Maybe don't go so literally." I came back, met with him again, looked a lot better, and he took me to several auditions. I met with the producers, the studio, the network, and I was the only one until the network audition. They definitely had other ideas. It was my first experience to go that far. Eight auditions over six weeks. It was nerve-racking to get that far and I never knew what the next step would be. They're making a crucial decision, and that's hard, but when you come from the theater, it's hard to walk into a room with thirty people and do a scene. Now that I've been through it, I get it, and I can rise to the occasion, but it's still tough.

JG: Had you done any series before?

PG: Just guest spots on single-camera shows like *21 Jump Street* and *Max Monroe.* I had never worked on a four-camera sit-com.

JG: What happened after *Wings?*

PG: I produced a play at the Tiffany Theater in Los Angeles. Jeff came to the play and we got reacquainted and by the time the play closed, Jeff got me on another Paramount TV show, *Flesh 'N Blood.*

JG: How did your guest spot on *Wings* come about?

PG: After *Flesh 'N Blood,* I did another show at Paramount, *Local Heroes.* While I was doing that one next door, Jeff asked if I wanted to come over and do the *Wings* episode. Jeff is my lifeblood in this business and responsible for my last six jobs. I love him.

JG: You were also on *Cheers?*

PG: Yes, the fourth-to-last episode. I played a reporter in "Woody Gets an Election," where he runs for city council. I had been begging Jeff to be on *Cheers* in the last season, and Jeff said "You and everyone else." I read for the part that Sharon Lawrence ended up getting [which was the next-to-last *Cheers* episode, written, incidentally, by Casey, Angell, and Lee, in which Sam goes to a support group to deal with his sex obsession] didn't get it, was bummed out, but then, I came in to work on the *Frasier* audition with Jeff before I did it for the producers. While we met, he told me about what a hard time he was having casting this part on a *Cheers* episode. Did he have anyone I could recommend? After I read it, he said, "It's yours." And I just cried. It was such a sweet way to do it.

JG: Tell me about the *Frasier* audition.

PG: The year before, I didn't even have to audition for *Local Heroes.* Same network, same production company, but they wanted me to come in and read for Roz. But like *Wings,* I went in for the producers, went in for the studio, went in for the network, screen-tested, the whole thing.

JG: Did you meet Lisa Kudrow?

PG: Oh, yeah. We ran into each other every time I came in. We got very friendly during that process. One day we're at Paramount with five other women, and the next day it's just us. What are you going to say? She was so gracious and sweet. We both wished each other luck and then she got it. Lisa and I went to lunch at the Daily Grill after she got it and we fought over the bill. She said, "I'm employed, I'm paying." They called and told me I didn't get it. Then, two weeks go by, and I was sitting at a restaurant with my agent, and Jeff called me. I was so flipped out we walked out without paying the bill.

JG: What did you like about the Roz role?

PG: It was wide open. She could be so many different things, and much to their credit, they were very honest about it from the beginning. They said they weren't sure who she was, and that they were going to play [with the role]. I loved that Roz was not a stock character, I didn't have to slip into some kind of slot and say, "Oh, here's how I deliver my lines and here's what my function is." They really took it slow and let somebody come out of that booth.

JG: Who is Roz now?

PG: Roz is very good at what she does and very happy doing it. She's needed, she's appreciated, she has a great time at work, she's in just the place she wants to be, she's ambitious and wants to move up at the station, but it's so good where it is now that she's very happy. She's also happy running around and meeting guys and going where the wind blows. I don't think she's ever had one judgment about a guy. There's no one who hasn't been good enough. She just wants to sample them all. But now I think she sees other women settling down, and even though that never looked good, it's starting to look better.

JG: I know this is highly personal, but is Peri more successful at love than Roz?

PG: No. Peri never went through most of the phases that Roz went through.

JG: What do you think of psychiatry?

PG: I'm a big fan of psychiatry. As long as it's used right. It can be amazing if you see the right person.

JG: Do you see a therapist?

PG: Occasionally. Not all the time.

JG: Do you talk about the show?

PG: No. We discuss issues around my own insecurities in this business and my own talent, but not *Frasier*. That's too bizarre.

JG: Why does Roz hate Niles so much?

PG: Niles is a much more exaggerated version of Frasier, who she can barely tolerate when he gets pompous and pedantic. Niles is that much of a hard-core snob, and that's offensive to her. But I think that she sees he has a vulnerable side, so the swipes are acceptable. He usually gets her too. Somebody has to jump in before it gets violent.

JG: What kind of coffee do you drink?

PG: I don't drink coffee. I gave it up several years ago. I drink tea like a nut.

JG: Who makes you laugh the most during filming?

PG: Everybody's pretty even, but the ringleader of this whole cast is John. He loves to crack you up. He will do anything to make that happen. Especially on tape night. He is so funny. He has this weird mind blip, where he'll lose a word and replace it with the funniest stuff. One time he was very angry and in talking about the person, instead of saying the person's name, he said "place mat." He replaces nonsequitur words with others. Now, when anyone can't think of the word, they just say place mats.

Her favorite Frasier episode . . .

"I loved the season ender for year two (number 47, "Dark Victory") in which Roz comes to Frasier's house for a party, because I got to be in the living room with everybody. I also loved "The Matchmaker" (number 28), which was brilliant. It was the funniest episode. And Roz's best was from the first season, called "Oops" (number 10), where I start gossiping and cause Bulldog to lose his job. It's early on, and where a lot of pennies dropped for me on who Roz was."

The Bob "Bulldog" Briscoe File

"All right folks, it's time to pop a cold one and loosen up that belt buckle, 'cause you're in the doghouse with you-know-who."

The host of KACL's *Gonzo Sports Show*, Bulldog is KACL's highest-rated on-air personality. He's been on the air for fifteen years, has been nominated for the SeaBea award four

times in a row, and is known for the different and unusual sound effects he employs on his show, like gongs, donkey brays, and duck calls, along with the frequent sayings "droppa your pants" and "You're in the dog pound with Bulldog."

Bulldog loves to humiliate Frasier and Roz on the air. For instance, Roz once had the misfortune of walking into the booth when Bulldog was on the air. She was introduced as Martina Navratilova's new girlfriend. Martin is one of Bulldog's biggest fans, and while most sports players respect Bulldog's opinions, not everybody agrees with what the opinionated sportscaster has to say. Mike Ditka, for instance, once rammed Bulldog's head into a locker when he tried to interview him.

KACL's sportscaster has the hots for Roz, and is never shy about letting her know about his heat. He once hired Roz to work as his producer, but she quit during a meeting at his apartment, when he got more comfortable by stripping down to just a towel. Daphne "bought" a date with Bulldog at a celebrity bachelor auction, but she got so drunk in their limo that Bulldog was, for once, turned off.

BULLDOG: I love weddings. I've never been to a wedding where I didn't bag at least one bridesmaid.

After Frasier's show ends:

BULLDOG: Blah blah Frasier Crane Show happy health good-bye. All right, sports fans, we're going to clear all the nutcases off the lines now and make room for some real Americans. . . . All right folks, it's time to pop a cold one and loosen up that belt buckle 'cause you're in the doghouse with you-know-who.

After telling Frasier about winning three SeaBea awards:

BULLDOG: I've been a symbol of broadcasting excellence in Seattle since 1991.

FRASIER: You know, I've visited your place a couple of times, but I've never seen your statuettes. Where do you keep them?

BULLDOG: Let's see. Numero uno went to my mom. The second one's still rolling around in the trunk of my car. And the last one I gave to a babe in a bar.

FRASIER: How could you?

BULLDOG: Hey, I got the trophy I wanted.

Later, at the ceremony, he runs into Mrs. Littlejohn, a large woman in a red dress near the bar:

BULLDOG: Hey, Mrs. Littlejohn . . . I remember you. You're the head of the nominating committee. Let me just say that you get lovelier every year.

MRS. LITTLEJOHN: The winners have already been chosen, Mr. Briscoe.

BULLDOG: Oh, in that case, you're showing a lot of white meat, aren't you, toots?

The Dan Butler File

Dan Butler grew up in Fort Wayne, Indiana, and made his performing debut in a local production of *The Music Man.* He joined a theater group in high school and after graduation he received a grant for acting studies endowed by the late Irene Ryan (who played Granny on *The Beverly Hillbillies.*)

Butler made his Broadway debut in the American premiere of Harold Pinter's *The Hot House,* and also starred in several other plays, including *Biloxi Blues* on Broadway, *Much Ado About Nothing* at Joseph Papp's New York Shakespeare Festival in Central Park, and *The Lisbon Traviata* at the Mark Taper Forum in Los Angeles. *Frasier* casting director Jeff Greenberg saw the play and sought him out for the role of Bulldog.

The actor has been seen in the films *The Fan, I Love Trouble, Dave, Rising Sun, Captain Ron, Manhunter, The Silence of* the Lambs, *The Long Walk Home*, *Longtime Companion*, and the TV movies *A Jury of One* and *Country Gold*. He appeared on three episodes of *Roseanne*, played the role of a deranged head of a witch coven who gets eaten by a twenty-foot python on *The X Files*, and had a spot on a 1995–96 episode of *Caroline in the City* as a gay art gallery owner. He also wrote and starred in his autobiographical one-man show, *The Only Thing Worse You Could Have Told Me*, which consists of numerous characters in fourteen vignettes.

I met with Butler in the *Frasier* conference room, after he completed rehearsals for his scenes in the "Frasier Loves Roz" episode.

JEFFERSON GRAHAM: Is Bulldog infatuated with Roz, like Niles and Daphne, or just all women?

DAN BUTLER: I think it's like an impulsive response. It's not infatuation. He's like a dog. I love that Bulldog is sort of a jerk, not maliciously, but it's just easy for him to do the locker room stuff. It would be nice to see him smitten with someone. He just doesn't know how to communicate other than sexually. He's always got to say something crass. It's a constant knee-jerk response to any babe. There's the mountain. Climb it.

JG: How did you get involved with *Frasier?*

DB: I had never met Jeff Greenberg before. He called me into the initial reading for the character. It was very sketchily drawn. The material wasn't great at that time. I don't think they really found the character. I didn't hear from them for three weeks. I guess they had this big search and it didn't pay off. Then I was called back for a final callback. They had this great scene where he went ballistic and lost his temper. I thought it was hilarious. I went in there and thought I had it, and acted as if they'd be stupid not to cast me. I had fun, and I got it.

JG: You've been with the show for how long?

DB: Since the second episode. Show number 2.

JG: How many episodes did you do that first year?

DB: Five. Then I was hired as a regular, to do at least thirteen out of twenty-two a year, on a four-year contract.

J G : You were in both *Manhunter* and *Silence of the Lambs,* which are both based on Thomas Harris's novel *Red Dragon.* How did that come about?

D B : It was a fluke. It's a great trivia question, since I am the only actor who was in both films, but I played different characters. I was an FBI fingerprinting expert in *Manhunter,* and in *Silence* I was an entomologist, a bug scientist. I had a bigger role in *Silence.* We scientists were the only comic levity in the whole thing.

J G : Tell me about the play.

D B : It's called *The Only Thing Worse you Could Have Told Me,* and it's about being gay. I take on fourteen different characters and come back to autobiographical sketches. It's about what the hell does any label mean and how we seem to be drawn to just specifically talk about gay, but that's because it's safe to type and define it. We don't have to let the whole person in or have our own authentic experience of what a person is. I wrote the play four years ago, premiered it in Los Angeles, took it to Broadway last season and got great reviews, and now Kelsey has optioned it for his production company. Hopefully it will be on cable by the time this book comes out. I'm real proud of it. It sticks with people, and it pisses some people off, but that's what you're supposed to do in theater. You're supposed to challenge yourself.

J G : Do people come expecting to see Bulldog?

D B : I don't know, but anything that gets people in the door to see theater is okay by me. I think the play has enough press behind it now that people know what they're getting. But we've had some people surprised and angry and demand their money back. One guy saw the reviews but hadn't really investigated it, and brought his bride there for an anniversary present. He demanded his money back because it was about homosexuality. And I said, "Why'd you stay for the whole play?" He didn't get a refund.

J G : Do you find it ironic that an openly gay man plays a womanizer on *Frasier?*

D B : Oh, yeah. It's funny. What I really would like to do—it would be more challenging now to see Bulldog with a woman, and let him have love scenes. Shake up the whole thing we have about sex, that it could be sexy and hot, and you buy it, knowing that the actor playing him is gay.

JG: There are many gay writers at *Frasier*—have you ever discussed the possibility of Bulldog being gay, and that he perhaps uses his bravado as a shield?

DB: No. I think that would be an easy out. A lot of critics, I heard, felt I was making some statement about heterosexuality by playing Bulldog this way. No, it's the part. It's the part. A lot of people, when I came out, said, "You spoiled the character." I think it's time for all of us to grow up a little about sexuality.

JG: What do you like about playing Bulldog?

DB: He's just fun. He shoots from the hip and says what he wants to. He doesn't know he's being crass. I think it's an outlet for the writers to say every sexist thing they want to and get away with it. Matched up against Niles and Frasier, who measure everything in their head, it's nice to just have someone who says what's on his mind. It's a kick. We can get too serious about acting sometimes, so it's nice to have an outlet where you feel like you're shot out of a gun and you trust your instincts and you just go.

His favorite episode of *Frasier* is . . .

"The one where Bulldog hires Roz to produce his show (number 36, "Roz in the Doghouse"), and the one where Bulldog thought he was going to be fired (number 10, "Oops"). When I stripped down for Roz (in "Doghouse"), that was a great farce and a lot of fun. We got to see a lot more of Bulldog in that one.

More from Frasier and Niles on Their Brotherhood, Their Childhood and Other Stuff

FRASIER: If you were stranded on an island, what would you choose as your favorite meal, aria, and wine?

Frasier and Niles attempt to write a book on sibling rivalry.

NILES: The Coulibiac of Salmon at Guy Savoy. "Vissa d'arte" from *Tosca*. And the Cotes du Rhone, Chateau Neuf du Pape, '47.

FRASIER: You're so predictable.

Martin on Niles and Frasier as kids:

MARTIN: If one of you had something, the other one always had to have it too. I had to buy two Balinese lutes, two decoupage kits, two pairs of lederhosen. . . . When you finally left home that was one embarrassing garage sale.

On the differences between the Crane boys and their father:

NILES: When you stop and think about it, we are quite a sociological study, aren't we? Outside of our last name and abnormally well-developed calf muscles, we have nothing in common with the man.

FRASIER: It doesn't take a Louis Leakey to figure out that we took after our mother. She's the one who exposed us to the finer things in life.

FRASIER: Remember you once thought the 1812 Overture was a great piece of classical music?

NILES: Was I ever that young?

At a party:

FRASIER: I'm Dr. Frasier Crane. This is my brother Dr. Niles Crane, the eminent psychiatrist.

NILES: My brother's too kind. He was already eminent when my eminence was merely imminent.

The name of the restaurant that Niles and Frasier run, Les Frères Heureux, which means the Happy Brothers in French.

NILES: It's homey and just hard enough to pronounce to intimidate the riffraff.

At a baseball game with Dad:

FRASIER: By the way, Niles, it's just as you feared . . . communal urinals in the men's room.

NILES: Oh, fine. What am I supposed to do about my shy kidneys?

FRASIER: Cross your legs and go easy on the chardonnay.

NILES: I'll have a decaf, nonfat latte.

FRASIER: Make that two.

COUNTER PERSON (*yelling to espresso operator*): Two gutless wonders!

Frasier and Niles both had problems with school bullies.

Billy put Frasier into a locker wearing a girl's field hockey uniform. Half the school saw them cut off the lock and pull him out in his little plaid skirt. He stuck a fire extinguisher down his pants. Called it a jet pack. Billy's brother Danny dunked Niles in the toilet, saying "There goes Crane, down the drain." He also made Niles wear a jockstrap like a tiara.

FRASIER: I remember a car trip we took when I was nine. We drove from Seattle to Spokane and the only thing Dad said to me was "I think we've got a problem with your brother, Frasier."

NILES: I still remember those awful family driving vacations. Dad insisted on covering as many miles a day as possible. The two of us, tiny hostages in the backseat, clutching our car-sickness bags, straining to see something out the window as the landscape whizzed by. I was thirteen before I realized cows weren't actually blurry.

NILES: So we decided to play a little prank on the president of the wine club. At last night's tasting when he thought he was tasting a Chateau Petrus, he was in fact sipping Forcas Dupre. You see, we'd switched the labels.

The gang takes an ill-fated vacation in a classy RV.

FRASIER: Niles, when you someday go up to heaven and you have to justify your life to St. Peter, don't tell him that story.

NILES: We were just trying to be funny. But as so often happens, roughhouse leads to tears.

FRASIER: What happened?

NILES: He didn't notice the difference.

FRASIER: Between a Forcas and a Petrus? The president of the club?

NILES: Impeachment proceedings begin next week.

When Niles got the initial interview to join Seattle's exclusive Empire Club:

ROZ: It's eating you inside, isn't it?

FRASIER: Like a carnivorous bacteria.

Niles and Frasier rarely had friends as kids. Just themselves.

MARTIN: The two of you always holed up in that damn garage. At least until you burned it down.

NILES: With Frasier and his Bunsen burner and me and my mosquito repellent, well, in retrospect it was unavoidable.

NILES: You know, sometimes I wonder if I'm not just in psychiatry for the money.

FRASIER: Oh, I wouldn't say that's true. If you were, well . . .

NILES: What were you going to say?

FRASIER: No, no, I'd rather not.

NILES: Well there's no need to, actually. I think I know what you were getting at. You've been wanting to ask me this for years—Did I marry Maris for the money? I resent that. I did not marry Maris for the money. It's just a delightful bonus.

FRASIER: So, you really do love her?

NILES: Of course I love her, but it's a different kind of love.

FRASIER: You mean, it's not human?

FIVE

Moose and Mathilde

Frasier to Eddie, who can't stop staring at him.

FRASIER: What is so fascinating about me? What is it? In your eyes, does my head look like a large piece of kibble? Am I some kind of doggy enigma? What is it? (*Eddie continues to stare.*)

FRASIER: Think about it. Get back to me.

In the fertile imagination of the *Frasier* writers, Martin's loyal dog Eddie can stare and sneeze on cue, run across the apartment whenever the word "walk" is mentioned, hide when he hears the word "bath," and do such abnormal dog tricks as listening to the answering machine or burying his head under a couch cushion.

Some of Eddie's greatest tricks:

♦ Got his head stuck in a tub of ice cream.
♦ Trotted around the apartment once with a pack of cigarettes in his mouth.
♦ Ran into Daphne's bathroom and drank from the toi-

121

Moose and his
trainer, Mathilde
DeCagny

let. Has also been known to parade around the apartment with Daphne's bra in his mouth.

* Hopped up and down for a muffin.

In real life, Eddie is known as Moose, and his loyalty goes
not to actor John Mahoney but to a woman named Mathilde
DeCagny, who quite simply has taught him everything he
knows.

Moose is a long-haired Jack Russell terrier and a classic overnight success. He was the first "breakout" star of *Frasier*,
finding his mug on the covers of such magazines as *TV Guide*,
Entertainment Weekly, and *Life* during the show's first season.

He is four years old and was born and bred in Florida, as one of ten pups. But life in Florida was short and sweet. His previous owner dumped him after he tore up the place with his intense doglike energy. Moose eventually found his way to a man named Gary Gero and his company Birds and Animals Unlimited, which rescues dogs from the pound and adoptions and puts them to work in show business.

Moose first started acting when he auditioned at Universal Studios Florida in Orlando and became a featured player in their *Animal Actors Showcase*. When *Frasier* was seeking a dog for Martin, Gero sent Moose to Los Angeles, to his associate DeCagny, and she arranged the audition for the producers. She drove up to a park in a van with ten dogs. They saw his face, thought a small, scrappy dog would be perfect for Martin, and the rest is show business history.

Moose lives with DeCagny and six other dogs in Venice, California, where he spends his off days by hanging around the house and taking walks by the sea. His roommates include Einstein, who was seen in *Back to the Future II* and *III*, Barney, seen in *Outbreak*, and Cody, Moose's puppy, who has yet to break into show business.

After Angell, Casey, and Lee selected Moose as their dog, the first order of business for DeCagny was teaching Moose how to stare. They thought the idea of a dog who stared at Frasier was a hoot. "You have to get him so focused on you that they won't notice any other distraction," says DeCagny. "We worked on that for about a week." As Moose's reward, he gets an East Coast specialty called a "Billjack," a liver treat that she imports to the West Coast. That's how good it is. "The food is a nice reward, and obviously dogs are food oriented, but there's a lot more that goes into it besides that," she says, "because obviously, I can't give him food in the middle of a scene."

Her job is all about bonding with the dog, showing them over and over again how to do the trick, and working with a dog who is "friendly and outgoing."

"You can't do this with just any dog," says DeCagny. "A dog who is shy or independent won't do. I can pick the right dog out of any crowd right away. The ones that have their tail wagging, excited eyes, and come right up to you are the kind I look for. The ones who say 'Me, Me, Me!' when you look at a group of dogs. When I pick an animal, I never go wrong."

DeCagny is on the set all the time with her animals, and helps entertain audiences on Tuesday nights, when they come to watch *Frasier* being filmed, by taking questions and showing off Moose and his greatest tricks. In an interview in the "Frasier" conference room, she showed off the various hand signals she uses to show Moose what to do.

- *Sit:* One finger pointing down.
- *Stay:* Flat hand.
- *Speak:* Finger moves back and forth.
- *Lie Down:* Hand down.

But sometimes things don't work out as planned. One night at a filming, Moose was supposed to run across the stage and hide under the pillow of Frasier's couch. But Moose couldn't remember what to do. So when Moose's cue came up, DeCagny was forced to run across the stage, out of camera sight, to remind Moose of his professional duties.

"It's back to square one at times like that," she says. "You just have to start over again and retrain him. That night was very rare. We were blown away by it. He's usually really good. But he's on his own out there. Everybody else is an actor, but Moose is a dog. I'm orchestrating the whole thing, and I have to remind him what to do."

The original idea was to have Eddie do nothing but stare at Frasier. "We got a lot of mileage out of that," says David Lee.

"But there was an uprising across America. People wanted to see him do more. We didn't want to just do a show about a cute dog, but we couldn't resist, and so we started giving him more and more to do."

Additionally, the tricks also began to multiply because the producers simply got tired of the Eddie-stares-at-Frasier routine. "The stare was funny for the first ten shows, but we couldn't milk that one forever," says Christopher Lloyd. For the first Christmas show, they put antlers on Eddie, and the audience ate it up. Then they had him carry in the newspaper. Ever since, the writers have been brainstorming for more creative stunts. DeCagny meets with the writers occasionally to clue them in on new tricks she's teaching Moose, and that gives them ideas for new bits for Moose.

No script is complete unless there is something to do for

every major character in the show. After all, they're getting paid whether they work or not, so the studio wants to make sure they participate. And that goes for Moose too. No script goes before the camera without at least one great Moose stunt.

But the writers try not to get too fancy. "Nothing can hold up a filming more than an elaborate stunt," says coproducer Joe Keenan. "Moose gets confused and we all sit around forever, waiting for him to get it right."

Keenan recalls one episode where the joke was that Eddie would walk into Café Nervosa and sneeze. DeCagny taught him how to sneeze, but on film night, Moose just couldn't do it. The producers decided not to keep the audience waiting and moved ahead with the show, figuring they could do Moose's scene over again. It was the final show of the season, and when it was over, everybody was set to go to the Paramount commissary for a late-night wrap party.

But before they could get started, they had to do the sneeze scene again. They worked on it for a half hour, but finally gave up. Eddie just couldn't sneeze on cue that night. "Such are the perils of writing for a dog," says Keenan.

Lee says they'll be toning down Eddie's tricks in the fourth season. "We were asking him to do ridiculously complicated things, and making the actors wait a long time. They work very hard to pump it real hard and get it just right, and they have to do it again because the animal isn't doing right. That wasn't fair."

DeCagny hails from Paris, France, where she raised horses and worked as an assistant trainer. She moved to Los Angeles in 1984 and began volunteering her services at training companies. Eventually she was hired, and got her first paid job working on an episode of the *Alfred Hitchcock Presents* revival, in a scene with thirty cats. She's also worked with animals in *The Bodyguard, Steel Magnolias, The Man Without a Face*, and the TV series *Tequila and Bonetti*, which featured a large French mastiff named Tequila who could supposedly comment on the show's proceedings.

DeCagny concedes that Moose is easily the biggest star she's ever worked with. She has to be careful when she goes out with him in public, "because sometimes he gets mobbed."

People will come up to her and say her dog looks just like the one on *Frasier*. Sometimes she'll smile and agree with them. Other times, if she's wearing her green *Frasier* jacket, people know immediately, and they pull out their cameras and ask to pet him. Luckily, Moose doesn't mind being photographed. Paramount took him twice to a huge TV convention in Las Vegas, where Moose graciously agreed to sit and pose with TV station managers. He even barked on cue.

Moose prefers working to sitting around at home, says DeCagny, which she says bores him. "He's a hyper dog. Terriers are very hyper and overwhelming dogs. You need to keep them busy or they'll destroy your house in a hurry. That's why his previous owners got rid of him."

The big question everyone always asks is how much Moose gets paid. ("We talk about that all the time," says Keenan. "He probably makes more than we do.")

But the salary is confidential, and DeCagny refuses to give any hints, saying "that is not to be discussed." She will reveal that owner Gero, who pays the food and vet bill, is the one who reaps the financial rewards for Moose's performance skills. (DeCagny is paid separately by Paramount.)

And if Moose has a million-dollar trust fund, enough money to live on "Billjacks" forever, we'll just probably never know.

Much has been written about the actors' supposed jealousy over Moose, especially in the first year, when he received so much press. The actors say that's all just a trumped-up tabloid rumor, but they do admit he can be tough to be around. "We don't hate Moose, even though it makes a good story," says David Hyde Pierce. "The thing about Moose, is Mathilde. The dog isn't great, it's the person making him do these things who's great. Moose is a wonderful dog, but it's Mathilde who makes him so great on the show. He's so smart and he's such a terrier that if he learns a trick too soon, he gets bored with it, so Mathilde knows how to just balance things so he almost knows it by the time we shoot, so when he's in front of the audience, he'll perform it. The irony is that his kind of dog has a temperament that's totally opposite to what Eddie is supposed to be. The last thing a Jack Russell terrier does is stare at someone. They bounce off the walls. So she really has to work to get him to do what she needs him to do, and that's why you get such a great personality from that dog."

Leeves, who since her character is home all day, does more stunts with Moose than the other actors, admits that working with the pooch can be a pain sometimes. "He's a dog and sometimes doesn't want to do what he's told, and it can be frustrating," she says. "I get the brunt of it because I tend to be in most of the Eddie scenes and nobody else has the patience for working with him. Personally, I do think he's a cute dog, but there's something independent about him and he doesn't thrive on affection like most dogs."

Leeves did get to bond with Moose, however, when the cast went to New York City together to appear on *Donahue* during the first season of *Frasier*. She took him for a walk in Central Park, and they got to know each other.

"It was the weirdest thing you ever saw," she recalls. "You wouldn't believe how many people recognized him from four hundred yards away. I'd say "I'm here too," but they were so busy fussing over Eddie they hardly noticed me."

So is she sorry that Moose is on the show? "No way. A

lot of our success is attributed to him. People love that damn dog. There's not an event that we go to where they don't bring him up. So what are you going to do?''

Peri Gilpin admits that not having to work with Moose has made her life easier. She's never done a scene with him. Not that she doesn't love her costar.

''I remember one thing he did backstage one night that just knocked me out,'' she says. ''As an actor, you're back-stage on tape night, and about to go out onstage, and you catch your composure, and I looked over, and there was Moose, waiting for his entrance. Like another actor. Totally focused. That was so cute.''

FRASIER: Eddie, what are you staring at? Didn't your mother ever tell you it's rude? How would you like it if I stared back at you?

SIX

THE EVER MYSTERIOUS
MARIS CRANE

DAPHNE: If I may ask, why does Maris take the train instead of flying?

NILES: She almost had a fatal accident.

DAPHNE: Her plane crashed?

NILES: No, she choked on a honey-roasted almond and a flight attendant had to administer the Heimlich maneuver. All the way to Aspen she could hear them giggling back in coach.

Who is this mystery woman? From where does she come?
   Read on . . .

The Maris Crane File

- *Age:* Forty, on more than one occasion. Maris is five years older than Niles.
- *Children:* None.
- *Father:* A yachtsman ("the Commodore") with only months to live.
- *Other family:* Has a sister who lives in Dallas and Aunt Patrice from Washington, D.C. An entire branch of her family tree was slaughtered by the Huguenots.
- *Household income:* Filthy rich.
- *Appearance:* Small and slender, with a pale complexion. Or, as Frasier once put it: "Bleached, 100 percent fat free, and best if kept in an airtight container." Maris is small. Very small. In fact, once Niles said to Frasier that Maris and Daphne are about the same size. To which Frasier replied: "Give or take a foot." And her hairstyle is quite severe. Niles once described "air" conducting along with his Brahms recording, using one of the gilded chopsticks that Maris wears in her bun. She has a $25,000 face-lift, cosmetic surgery on her lips, cheeks, and eyelids. She flies to Switzerland once a year for goat placenta treatments.
- *Demeanor:* Frosty.
- *Hobbies:* Sensory deprivation, plastic surgery, fencing, interpretive dance, and the Women's Senior Yoga Group ("old money in bodystockings," per Niles). She kept several prize topiaries until Yoshi the gardener emasculated them during a drunken trimming spree. Maris always dreamed of being a ballet dancer, but according to Niles, "The poor dear could never get her weight up enough." Maris plays the autoharp, collects

eighteenth-century antiques, speaks German, and loves to trot out "G-speak" with Aunt Patrice at parties (where you add a G to ever syllable of a word).

* *Clubs:* Won election as wine club president when her photos from rival Matthew Pym's wedding showed the label on the champagne he served. Worked tirelessly in a failed attempt to get Niles into Seattle's prestigious Empire Club by cultivating relationships, rumor-mongering, and accidentally dumping crabmeat into the cleavage of another candidate's wife.

* *Medical history:* Hypoglycemic, allergic to roses, and unable to produce saliva. Unusually rigid vertebrae, and quadriceps so tight she can't straddle anything larger than a Border collie.

* *Views on romance:* Does not trust unconditional love. Requires proper motivation (as in a nice new Mercedes) to get in the mood.

* *Defense mechanism:* A pearl-handled revolver she keeps under her pillow.

* *Appeal:* "Maris is a wondrous distillation of many essences," says Niles's alter ego, actor David Hyde Pierce. "It's as if you could take a great French cathedral, a painting by El Greco, and the upper third of Norway and magically transform them into one tiny woman with ferret eyes and disturbing hair."

* *Shoes and cars:* Maris was driving through Seattle one day when she passed a shoe store with a "stunning pair of Ferragamo pumps" in the window. "I can't tell you what effect a Ferragamo sighting can have on Maris's hand-eye coordination," says Niles. "She drove right onto the sidewalk." The police ran her name through a computer and discovered she'd neglected to pay 112 parking tickets.

* *When Maris met Niles:* In the middle of the night. "When I was just a young intern, I used to drive

through these hills never dreaming that one day I would live in one of these great mansions," recalls Niles, "and then, one day, there was Maris banging on the gates with her little fists and a tire iron."

* *The manor:* Has a morning room, a koi pond, a music room where Maris and her music group rehearse, an east wing, and eighteenth-century antiques. The mansion has been in her family for four generations.

* *Transportation:* Maris has been afraid to fly since the harrowing incident where she was bumped from first-class. She still wakes up screaming.

* *Servants:* Maris has several trusted assistants who work for her, like Marta, her seventy-eight-year-old Guatemalan maid. Maris rings a bell when she needs her. Yoshi is her gardener. She once dug up her camellias so Yoshi could put in a Zen garden. She also has a topiary garden because she's unable to have pets.

* *What kind of Frau is she?* Gunnar, the fencing instructor who had a crush on Maris, once described the object of his affections as a *"nicht eine menschliche Frau,"* which translated means "not quite human woman."

* *Self-defense:* Niles's estranged wife always calculates the nearest escape route in case of fire or urban unrest.

* *Sense of direction:* Maris wandered into the kitchen accidentally once and didn't know where she was or how to get out. She had to call Niles for directions.

* *Food problems and allergies:* She can't eat shellfish, poultry, red meat, saturated fats, nitrates, wheat, starch, sulfites, MSG, dairy, or nuts. She cannot produce saliva, can't eat candy because she's hypoglycemic, perfume gives her hives, and she's allergic to roses.

According to Niles, his estranged wife is subject to "episodes." For instance, she once had a run-in with a rude directory assistance operator, and that shattered her calm. Every time her aunt Patrice visits, Maris dives under the duvet with a two-week migraine. More examples:

- She exhausts easily under the pressure to be interesting.
- She had an episode once after catching a glimpse of herself in a mirror.
- She sulked about not being important enough to need a bodyguard.
- She was despondent after being kicked out of the cast of *Cats* for forgetting the words to the song "Memory."
- After Frasier questioned the political correctness of her serving veal, Maris locked herself in the garage with the engine running on her golf cart.
- She won't trust porters with her makeup case.
- She makes an annual pilgrimage to the holy land (Dallas), the site of the first Neiman-Marcus.
- When she gets angry, her eye twitches like a frog in a science experiment.

And where oh where is Maris? Why hasn't she joined the party? Let's let Niles answer that popular musical refrain:

- "While dressing for the evening, she suddenly slumped down on the edge of the bed in her half-slip and sighed. I knew then that dinner was not to be."
- "She's on your bed asleep under the guests' coats. She exhausts easily under the pressure to be interesting."
- "She stayed in the Mercedes practicing her vivacious giggle."
- "The last I saw, she was apologizing to one of the other candidates' wives. Apparently Maris bumped an entire chafing dish of crab meat into the poor woman's décolletage."

Finally, to answer that age-old question, will we ever see Maris? Not in our lifetime. Originally, the plan was to talk about her, and then eventually introduce her, because the producers were worried about comparisons to Norm's never-seen wife Vera on *Cheers*. But once they got started, there was no turning back. "With all this buildup," says Lee, "it would be a letdown. We don't really want to see her."

Adds Grammer: "It would be an injustice to people's imagination. Everybody has their own carved-out identity for this woman."

Niles exit:

NILES: That's enough excitement for one evening. I'm going home to Maris.

FRASIER: I thought she wasn't speaking to you?

NILES: She's not, but she grows weary of being frosty to the help.

Frasier on Maris:

FRASIER: I like her from a distance. You know, the way you like the sun. Maris is like the sun . . . except without the warmth.

Niles on why Maris won't be attending the SeaBea awards:

NILES: This time it's a good one. She's very upset about her manicurist. The woman's been doing Maris's nails for years now, and, sadly, she's just been taken critically ill.

DAPHNE: Oh dear. How bad is she?

NILES: Oh she'll be fine when she finds another manicurist. Until then she's curtailing all public appearances.

Exit II:

NILES: Well, I guess we should get going. I promised Maris I'd brush her hair. Ta.

At a party, Maris went to look through a telescope.

NILES: Apparently she heard a nasty rumor that the star I bought her for her birthday imploded.

Frasier on the fact that Maris neglected to pay 112 parking tickets:

FRASIER: What do you expect from a woman who thinks a chocolate allergy entitles her to use a handicapped space?

After making up with Maris by buying her a new Mercedes:

NILES: Nothing says I'm sorry quite like an in-dash CD player and a passenger-side air bag.

Exit III:

NILES: Frasier, I'm afraid I won't be able to stay for dinner after all. I just remembered, Maris is giving herself a bikini wax tonight and I'm on dip-and-rip duty.

Before the split, Niles and Maris played chess every Thursday night.

FRASIER: No wonder. The king remains stationary while the queen has all the power.

Maris's fencing instructor Gunnar was the Bavarian champion three years running. He doesn't speak a word of English, and wrote a love letter to Maris.

He called her "Mein Kleine Leberknödel," which, translated, is "My little liver dumpling." He went on to say that he loved her beautiful little body, as thin as his sword, and her skin as white as bratwurst.

Maris's wine club had an outing to a local vineyard. As the new president, she had the honor of being first into the stomping vat.

NILES: Imagine her humiliation as she danced herself into a barefoot fury and was unable to break even a single grape.

Niles and Maris split after Frasier urged Niles to speak up for himself. She kicked him out, but said he could stay if he apologized.

FRASIER: If you cave in now, you'll spend the rest of your life feeling weak and small, all because you lacked the courage to say "I will not let you treat me like this, Lilith . . . Maris."

After a lightning storm, the only way Niles could coax Maris out from under the bed was by tying a Prozac to the end of a string.

NILES: I was hoping Daphne could take a look at this plant. I bought it for Maris, but it unaccountably turned against her. I thought Daphne was the perfect person to nurse it back to health with her soft sensual hands and her loving manner. (*To Daphne*) I had the fervent hope that you could coax it back to life. It's one of Maris's favorites.
DAPHNE: My goodness. What did she do to it?
NILES: Nothing. Just loved it.

Maris doesn't like dancing.

NILES: She dislikes public displays of rhythm.

Niles says jockeys remind him of Maris—underweight figures in expensive silks, wielding riding crops.

Niles can't get sex out of his mind. Frasier suggests taking a cold shower.

NILES: It's obviously an old wives' tale because I'm still thinking of my old wife's tail.
FRASIER: I suppose it was ill advised. Being showered with coldness could only bring Maris more to mind.

When Maris goes into the hospital for her face-lift, Niles tells his family that she's afraid.

NILES: She hasn't had much hospital experience, just the usual child-hood things—tonsils, adenoids, force-feeding. . . ."

And to Maris he says on the phone . . .

NILES: Yes Maris, I'm sure. No, you can't gain weight from a glucose IV. No, my little worrywart. There's no such thing as a Nutrasweet drip.

Niles and love, II:

NILES: It doesn't burn with the passion and intensity of a Tristan and Isolde. It's more comfortable, more familiar. Maris and I are old friends. We can spend an entire afternoon together, me at my jigsaw puzzle, she at her autoharp, not a word spoken between us and be perfectly content.

FRASIER: I'm told it was a lot like that near the end in the Hitler house-hold.

In an effort to convince his brother that he is really happily married:

NILES: Maris means the world to me. Why just the other day I kissed her for no reason whatsoever.

NILES: I always throw out my back when I try to lift Maris's luggage.
DAPHNE: Why didn't you use a skycap?
NILES: We did for most of it, but Maris won't trust strangers with her makeup case since a ham-handed porter dropped it and broke three vials of rare lamb placenta. On the upside, the calfskin lining of her case had never been more soft and supple.

TOM (*Frasier's boss*): Wait a minute. This Maris guy he kept mentioning is a woman?
FRASIER: Well, the jury is still out on that one.

Exit IV:

NILES: Well, I better get home. Maris will be missing me.

FRASIER: I thought she's not speaking to you.

NILES: She's not. But what fun is it not speaking to someone if they're not there to not speak to?

Frasier and Martin Try to Have a Serious Conversation

FRASIER: It's no secret there's been tension between us. I think part of the problem is that we never talk. So I was wondering if we could sit down and have a conversation.

MARTIN: Right now?

FRASIER: Yes. Now would be a perfect time.

MARTIN: What do you want to talk about? Is this more of your psycho mumbo-jumbo?

FRASIER: I'm not talking about a long, drawn-out conversation. I'm talking about three minutes of your life.

MARTIN: I hope it really is only three minutes because my program's coming on.

FRASIER: If it will make you happy, I'll get out the egg timer and set it for three minutes.

(*Frasier crosses to the kitchen and comes back with an egg timer. He sets it on the table.*)

FRASIER: Now come over here and sit down.

(*Martin crosses to the table.*)

MARTIN: Can I turn the TV on so I can hear when the program starts? (*Off Frasier's looks.*) Okay, okay.

(*They sit at opposite sides of the table.*)

MARTIN: So what do you want to talk about?

FRASIER: Well, the point of this is for you and I to have an honest, normal conversation like real people do without getting on each other's nerves.

(*Frasier starts the timer.*)

MARTIN: This is stupid.

(*Frasier stops the timer.*)

FRASIER: One second. That's our personal best. Let's see if we can beat it.

(*Frasier resets the timer.*)

FRASIER: Ready . . . go.

(There's an awkward pause.)

MARTIN: So how 'bout those . . .

(*Frasier stops the timer.*)

FRASIER: No sports.

MARTIN: Three minutes, huh?

FRASIER: Maybe we're setting our sights a little too high. Let's try two minutes. It's good for eggs. It should be good for us.

(*Frasier resets the timer. There's another long silence.*)

MARTIN: Well this was your idea. You say something first.

FRASIER: All right. I'm going to tell you something about myself that you don't know. Six months ago, when things were really on the rocks with Lilith and me, I went through a period of depression so terrible I actually stepped out on a ledge and wondered if life was even worth living. But then I thought of Frederick . . .

(*Frasier stops. There's a pause.*)

MARTIN: And you didn't jump, right?

FRASIER: Good, Dad.

MARTIN: Wow, I never knew that.

FRASIER: That's the point of this exercise, to reveal something about ourselves, something vulnerable. Now it's your turn.

MARTIN: Okay . . .

(*He gathers himself before the plunge.*)

MARTIN: Well, about two months ago, I was in the basement going through some old pictures of your mother and me. All of a sudden something flew up in my eye. When I was trying to get it out, I realized I could turn my eyelid inside out like kids do at camp.

FRASIER: And?

MARTIN: That's it.

FRASIER: You call that vulnerable?

MARTIN: It hurt.

FRASIER: I'm talking about your emotions. I'm talking about your soul. I'm talking about some painful, gut-wrenching experience in your life.

MARTIN: Other than this one?

FRASIER: Aah, always the flip answer.

MARTIN: Well this whole thing is stupid.

FRASIER: Not to me. But what I should expect from you? You are the most cold, inaccessible, intractable, unapproachable, stubborn, distant, cold man I've ever known!

MARTIN: You said cold twice, Mr. Egghead.

FRASIER: Egghead? Egghead?

MARTIN: You said egghead twice too.

FRASIER: Oh, you are so infuriating.

MARTIN: Yeah, well you're no day at the beach either. You know what you are . . .

(*SFX: EGG TIMER RINGS.*)

MARTIN: I'll tell you later. It's time for my program.

SEVEN

A WEEK IN THE LIFE OF FRASIER

Like virtually all TV sit-coms, every *Frasier* episode begins with the cast sitting around a table and reading the new script aloud. This happens on Wednesdays, around 11:00 A.M., give or take twenty minutes, depending on who is late that day. The actors sit at one side of the table, while the top producers sit at the other side. (The table is that big.) Writers sit wherever they can find a spot, publicists and assistants sit in as well, with about thirty people in the conference room. The room is packed to keep the laughs going and the actors in the mood.

After the actors have read the show aloud, like a radio play, an assistant with a stopwatch calls out the time of the show—for instance, 25:40, a signal that in the five days left before the show goes before the cameras, the writers need to slice a few minutes to get it down to at least 23 minutes, which gives the producers a little flexibility in editing before handing in the 22:10 version to the network.

The actors go home after the script is read, while the writers head back to the rewrite room to work on the script and make it better. The actors return the next day at 9:00

The actors and writers gather for the first reading of a new script.

A.M. to rehearse the revised script, usually a short five-hour rehearsal to work out the blocking of the show, as in where to stand. A second rehearsal is held on Friday, and then again on Monday, where a full "run-through" is staged for the producers, network, and studio executives. On Tuesday, after more rehearsal all day long, the show is filmed in front of a live studio audience at 7:00 P.M.

I'm going to take you through the production of one such episode, number 71, entitled "You Can Go Home Again," the next-to-last show of the 1995–96 season to be filmed and the on-air season finale. Written by executive producers Linda Morris and Vic Rauseo, the episode is a flashback show that takes place six months before the pilot, on Frasier's first day at KACL. We see him showing up to work, being awkwardly pompous on the air, meeting Roz, and later, running into Niles at the Café Nervosa and going over to spend some tense time with their father, before he moved in with Frasier.

David Lee, who is directing this episode, welcomes all, congratulates everyone on a great show the night before, and announces that this script is the final one from the husband-and-wife team of Morris and Rauseo, as they had previously arranged to move to 20th Century Fox when their *Frasier* deal was up to create their own show. The two had been with *Frasier* since the first season.

"Interior, radio studio, day, day 1," says Lee, who reads the stage directions aloud and then the cast take over.

FRASIER: "Hello, Babette. You're on with Dr. Frasier Crane. I'm listening."

The assembled gathering laugh at the jokes, with an especially hearty chuckle for this line from Frasier, after he confesses that he finds the transition from Boston shrink to radio shrink quite hard, especially when he discovers his producer Roz trying to arrange a transfer after his first show. "Abe Lincoln had a brighter future when he picked up his tickets at the box office."

Big laughs, and then Grammer opines: "Abe Lincoln is finally funny."

Lee, Grammer, and several producers say, in unison, "Tragedy plus Time equal Comedy," something they've obviously uttered many times before.

The episode begins at the radio station, with Roz giving Frasier a present on their third anniversary of working together—the audiotape of Frasier's first broadcast. The action moves to Frasier's apartment for some family business with Frasier and Daphne; then we go into flashback land when Frasier begins to listen to the tape. "Good afternoon, Seattle. My name is Dr. Frasier Crane and I am a psychiatrist. If you can feel, I can heal."

Frasier does his show, and it's a disaster. Roz and Frasier go to the Café Nervosa and discuss the show, and Frasier runs into Niles, sitting alone at a table, preparing for his obsessive-compulsive group. (A subplot has Daphne on the telephone weaseling out of visiting her mother in England on her vacation.) Frasier asks if Niles heard his show, and Niles says no, telling of his disgust at how Frasier sold out. Niles plans on visiting Martin that evening and shames Frasier into joining him. At Martin's apartment, the three find they have nothing to talk about; Martin isn't happy to see his kids, and wants to cut the visit short so he can go to a bar and play darts with his friends. Frasier talks Martin into sticking around, and it's clear the three have a lot to work on. Back in the present, Martin congratulates Frasier on his three-year KACL anniversary, and the three Crane men plan to go out and celebrate over dinner.

The table reading finishes, everyone applauds, and the time is announced—"26.55." The script is at about four minutes too long. "9:00 A.M. rehearsal tomorrow."

The actors prepare to go home for the day as the writers walk across the street to the Lucille Ball building. (All the Paramount buildings are named after stars who worked at Paramount, and *Here's Lucy* was filmed on the portion of the lot that was once known as Desilu Studios. In fact, it was made on Stage 25, current home of *Frasier*.) They head into the writers' room: Angell, Casey, and Lee, Christopher Lloyd, David Lloyd, Linda Morris and Vic Rauseo, Chuck Ranberg and Anne Flett-Giordano, Joe Keenan, Steven Levitan, Suzanne Martin, Jack Burditt, and Rob Greenberg.

The writers' area is a large conference room, decorated with a cast shot of *Frasier*, several photos of the Seattle skyline and sites, and a large model of the *Frasier* logo with a neon skyline. They sit on overstuffed couches and easy chairs that face each other, as opposed to the old image of a bunch of writers crowded around a table. In the middle of the room are lots of pens and pencils, erasers, notepads, chewing gum, salt and pepper, a dictionary and thesaurus, and even a bottle of Irish Mist whiskey, presumably for the late nights when nothing is going right.

There is a large board in the middle of the room that outlines the plot for next week's script on one side, with the other devoted to a collection of story germs that might one day get fleshed out into full stories. Samples include "Roz dates Niles," "Daphne Breaks Her Leg," and "Frasier Gets Board Certified."

Number one on the list for eighteen months was "Roz Dates One of Niles's Patients." The writers always had a hard time coming up with a story for that one, but it was actually produced on March 19, 1996, the night before this table read, as number 70, "Frasier Loves Roz."

When the writers came in after the table read for "You

The creators, writers, and cast of *Frasier*

Can Go Home Again," they were happy with most of the show, except for the scene between Martin, Frasier, and Niles. They thought it was too dark, with Lee saying the scene played as if a section from Gorki's *Lower Depths* suddenly showed up on *Frasier*—"Which I happen to think would be a hoot, but America?" They also felt it could be funnier, and were concerned that Niles and Frasier both exhibited the same attitude. After talking it through, they decided to have Niles con Frasier into visiting Martin by saying it was an all-new Martin, friendlier and less gruff. The laughs would come when the audience saw that Martin was exactly the same as he always was.

Stories on *Frasier* begin out of group discussions among the writers. They talk about things that happened to them in their lives. For instance, when someone stole the parking space of a writer, others in the room had the same experience, and that turned into a script where Frasier rants about the loss of civility in the world. The show about Martin finally finishing the song he had tried to write for Frank Sinatra many years back came from a real-life experience for Christopher Lloyd. He had once worked for a messenger company, for a guy who was always trying to write songs while running the company.

"You Can Go Home Again" was on the board for a long time, as Frasier is given a tape of his show to listen to and gets depressed over his performance. Originally, it was going to be part of a show about focus groups and *The Frasier Crane Show*, but that story took a life of its own. (Twelve people give their opinions on his show, and eleven rave. One doesn't, and the dissenting voice drives Frasier crazy.) But the tape stayed alive for the story that became the prequel to the pilot. (And the focus group episode lived on in its own episode, number 72, "The Focus Group.")

"We always try to do something special for the last episode of the season, to explore how the characters have grown over the year," says writer Morris. "We view the season finales as retrospectives of the year." The first season ended with "My Coffee with Niles," a chat between the brothers at the Café Nervosa, and "Dark Victory" closed year two, in which the gang erupt at each other at Martin's birthday party. The "You Can Go Home Again" episode served to show how far Frasier has come in his relationship with Martin, primarily, but also with Roz, Daphne, and Niles.

After discussing the jokes, the story, and the hows and whys of each script nuance (how, for instance, will the producers let viewers know they've gone flashback? By a title card with the three-year-old date), the writers do a second draft of the script, which is messengered to the actors' homes by evening. (Each script is a different color. It begins as white, then it's blue, pink, yellow, and green. By the day of filming, the script

Christopher Lloyd (white shirt), David Angell (beard), and Peter Casey at a rehearsal

is multicolored, yellow, green, and white, to show the difference between the old lines and the new ones.)

The next morning the actors work with version number two while the writers continue their efforts to make the script better. At the morning rehearsal, the actors are primarily there to work out the stage directions—where to stand, which way to look, and so on.

In the afternoon, they do another run-through—the first time they've done it on their feet—for producers, and after that, the writers rewrite again. Thursday night is the biggest and longest rewrite because that is the first time the writers see the show being performed on stage, and "Something that worked around the table sometimes just doesn't work when we see it on its feet," says Morris.

Friday, the actors continue working with the director, just like a play, on the nuance of the lines and the story. And the writers do another draft after the run-through.

By Monday, it's time for serious business. The actors spend the day on camera blocking, as the camera operators practice shooting the scenes, working on camera angles and focus situations, marking the floor to get it just right. This counts as another run-through, with one last rewrite session for Tuesday's final shooting script.

The next morning, the actors arrive around noon and do a final rehearsal. One more run-through, and then a dinner break, where the actors go to "hair and makeup," working on their lines simultaneously. At 7:00 P.M., the warm-up man welcomes the studio audience to *Frasier*, the band begins playing its mix of up-tempo jazz and the very familiar "Tossed Salad and Scrambled Eggs," and soon, Kelsey Grammer will come out, welcome the crowd, and the show will begin.

The filming goes a lot slower than twenty-two minutes, as each show contains six to eight scenes, and after each scene, production personnel need to move their cameras and other equipment to another side of the stage to get to the other set.

The show is usually complete around 9:30 P.M., and the audience leaves. But the actors remain. They need to do "promos" and public service announcements, as well as the "tag" scene, where the actors do something funny silently for the segment that gets shown with the credits. These activities will keep them there for at least another hour.

Back in the writer's room, the staff worked feverishly throughout the evening to around 10:00 P.M. to cut six pages from the script and make the Martin/Niles/Frasier scene funnier and lighter. The "You Can Go Home Again" script is re-typed, copied, and then messengered to the actors' homes via a twenty-four-hour Los Angeles courier service.

The next morning at the run-through, one very important ingredient is missing. John Mahoney went out the night before and came down with a bad case of food poisoning, so he is absent. The producers watched the show minus the scene they were so concerned about. "The good news," says Casey, "is that we know that everything else did work for the most part."

Jane Leeves did express her concerns about the story, and showing how the producers take input from their cast members, they listened and responded. Earlier in the first draft, Daphne talks of going to England to visit her "mum," but doesn't want to deal with her family. Frasier doesn't encourage her to go. Leeves felt the scene was flip and too dependent on jokes. She suggested that instead, there was a perfect opportunity to give the script some weight. "There should be a reason why Daphne doesn't want to go home," she said. "Maybe her parents depress her, and they nag her. Then we see Frasier go on this journey about his own family, and it would give the story an arc. This would tie the story together nicely."

Director Lee and Grammer agreed with her and suggested that at the end of the show Frasier should walk into the kitchen and talk Daphne into making the trip, saying it's worth the investment to make the relationship work. "What that does," says Lee, "is show Frasier's growth over the last three years."

The agenda for the Thursday night rewrite is to keep on slicing the script—to cut moments that aren't imperative, so that when the run-through is held Friday, the producers will be able to see how badly not having those jokes, lines, or passages hurt the show. They also need to rewrite Daphne's scene, add the changes, and work on a few jokes that didn't "pop" as well as the producers had hoped. They won't have to work on the Frasier/Martin scene, because they still haven't seen it performed yet. Thanks to Mahoney's food poisoning, the writers had an early night, leaving the lot around 7:00 P.M., about three hours earlier than usual.

On Friday, Mahoney is back at Paramount, and after watching the actors perform the show, the writers are happy with the way the redone Frasier/Martin/Niles scene played. So are the actors. "They enjoyed the fact that it wasn't a scene full of jokes," says writer Chuck Ranberg. "that it was full of emotion."

According to director Lee, the revised scene "still had the emotional impact and darkness, but the darkness was peeking through, rather than being slathered on top."

Afterwards, the writers make a slight change. Instead of ending the show on Frasier and Martin, they make it be an exchange with Frasier and Daphne, as Martin and Niles go to the elevator, with Frasier giving her an extra week's vacation so she can go to Manchester and visit her parents. They had discovered that their Daphne/Frasier rewrite was the right idea but too "on the nose." They found a shorter way to say the same thing without, says Lee, "laying it out baldly."

The agenda for Friday night is to keep slicing at the script, which is still too long. The writers finish with the rewrite around 6:00 P.M. but have to stick around later for some late-in-the-season duties. An episode that had been filmed a few weeks earlier (number 69) suddenly needs a new scene at the end. The producers weren't happy with the way it turned out, so author Joe Keenan came up with a different one and worked with his fellow writers on perfecting it. It would be filmed on Monday, after the afternoon run-through, without a live audience, since it is a last-minute insert.

Additionally, by Monday, the writers realize they have story problems on episode 72, the final filmed episode of the season, which will begin rehearsals on Wednesday. There are

FRASIER™

The brothers Crane

Father, Sons and Eddie at Café Nervosa

Frasier and Niles compete for the last spot
in Seattle's exclusive Empire Club

Niles and Daphne

Frasier and one-time station manager Kate Costas
locked in an embrace

Frasier, Daphne and Martin share a
morning moment

Eddie

A night at the opera

Frasier and rarely seen son Frederick

so many of them, as a matter of fact, that the Monday run-through for 71 has been canceled. The producers feel the show is in good enough shape, and they need to focus their energies on 72. Actors continue to work with Lee on camera blocking and filming the new scene for 69, but the action in the writer's room concerns 72.

Tuesday, the writers are still hashing away at 72, "The Focus Group," while the actors continue working with Lee on their lines and movement. Grammer especially needs to focus on his various bits of physical business, since the episode features some great silent comedy of Frasier alone in his new radio studio for the first time. On the air, he leans back in his chair when talking to a caller, and of course, the inevitable happens—he falls backward.

Around 6:30, the audience starts to drift into the Stage 25 bleachers, as a jazz band (sax, bass, keyboards, and drums) plays music. Around 6:45, warm-up man David Willis welcomes the audience to Paramount, tells them how the show works, answers questions, and reminds all that they are there to have a good time and to laugh. The actors feed off the energy of the audience, and if they find something to be funny, he says, "Don't be shy about showing it."

At 7:00, the show is set to begin, and as always, Grammer comes out and says a few words. "It's my custom to come out and greet you," he says. "This episode will be our season finale. We're going to take you back in time to the days when I had a bit more hair."

The band launches into Paul Simon's "You Can Call Me Al," and Willis introduces the members of the troupe: Peri Gilpin, David Hyde Pierce, Jane Leeves, John Mahoney, and Kelsey Grammer, who proceeds to kiss each actor and then gives the director a hug.

"Okay, everybody," shouts Lee. "Starting places, scene A."

The man known as "Big Eddie," a tall, elderly gent,

stands in front of Frasier at the radio station and bellows "Frasier 071. Apple. Take one." He claps his clapboard, Lee yells "action," and the show begins.

This is a pretty straightforward scene of Roz congratulating Frasier on his third anniversary at the station. They exchange presents (he gets the tape of his first show) and then he leaves for home. It is played as originally written in the first draft.

Lee is satisfied and moves on to scene B, which introduces the dilemma Daphne has in not wanting to go home to see her parents (rewritten and played up much stronger than in the first version). "Oh, Dr. Crane," she says, "why is it so easy to love our family, but so hard to like them?"

"Daphne," he replies, "that's one of those questions that makes life so rich and psychiatrists richer."

The scene ends with Frasier, with Eddie by his side, listening to the tape. Moose's trainer DeCagny stands on the side of the stage, making signals at Moose to be with Frasier. When the scene ends, she comes over and drops some liver snacks into Moose's mouth, and Lee asks to do the scene over again. For one thing, DeCagny ended up within camera range. For another, he says, "the performances just weren't there yet." Most scenes are filmed twice, if for nothing else than insurance in the editing room, and to give the actors an opportunity to play a scene—or line—two different ways. "It's rare that we don't do a second take," says Lee. "Something always goes wrong. It's just as easy to do it again."

Scene C begins with Frasier meeting Roz, and then sitting down to say hello to his Seattle listeners as he tries out various catchphrases. "If you can feel, I can heal." "Put your head in my hands." "This is Dr. Frasier Crane. . . . You're on the couch."

Everything's fine until Grammer forgets a line. "Oh, poopystink," he says. Lee uses the moment to reload film in the cameras and to have the prop men put large pieces of foam on the ground to cushion Frasier's fall from the chair.

He does the bit, and naturally, the audience finds it hysterical, especially when he frantically wheels the mike up from the floor like a fisherman pulling in his catch. The scene ends with Frasier erupting at Roz for wanting to be transferred on her first day with him, as Frasier loses his temper and launches into the Abe Lincoln line.

The audience responds the way the producers did at the table read—in hysterics, and warm-up man Willis says, "Is there anybody in show business who does righteous indignation better than Kelsey Grammer?"

Act One is now complete, and the actors move backstage to change clothes for the next scene. Grammer takes off his jacket and reveals that he is totally soaked. He looks as if someone has poured a bucket of water on him. That's how hot the studio lights are. You would never know this from sitting in the studio audience, where it is freezing. (Tip: If you ever go to see a show done live, wear a sweater.)

To entertain the crowd while the actors change, DeCagny comes out and introduces them to Cody, the six-month-old pup who is the son of Moose. He looks just like his pop, and DeCagny announces that this is Cody's first public appearance. He is part of her training program, and she says that begins by placing the dog on an object, like a chair or couch, so that he or she won't come up to you all the time. "It helps them to stay and be obedient," she says.

DeCagny puts Cody on the couch and uses her hand signals to have him sit down and bark.

Scene D is ready to begin. This is the one that takes place at the Café Nervosa between Frasier and Niles, and it has been greatly redone since the table read. Now Niles, as promised, persuades Frasier into thinking that Martin is a new man and that Frasier should stop by and see him.

NILES: Our father is a changed man. Ever since he was shot, he's softened. He has a whole new zest for life.

FRASIER: Niles, I visited Dad in the hospital. He made his roommate cry, and the man was in a coma.

NILES: He was still in shock then. The change came later. As a psychiatrist, surely you've seen this—a patient has a brush with death and rediscovers his love of life. Ah, the laughs we have when I'm over there—I sometimes wonder if that bullet didn't crease his funny bone.

The action moves to scene E, where Niles and Frasier show up to greet Martin at his apartment, and again, it's been greatly altered since the table read, not as dark as originally written, and leaving a light at the end of the tunnel, because it's obvious that Frasier and Martin are attempting to rebuild their relationship.

The scene is done twice, with one moment filmed four times. Eddie stares at Niles when they enter the room, and when Niles exits, he physically turns the staring Eddie toward Frasier. "Well," he says, "the torch has been passed."

Moose's concentration waffles a few times, so they have to keep trying until he perfects the stare.

They get it, and it's time for one last scene, back in Frasier's living room, where Frasier wakes up from his flashback and feels good about how far he's come since 1993. Everything is pretty much as originally written, except for the tail end, where Frasier urges Daphne to go home to see her parents.

"There's something about being part of a family that's always worth the effort," he says.

Lee films the four-page scene twice, and when the second take is complete, he yells "Cut it."

"That's our show, ladies and gentlemen," says warm-up man Willis as the band launches into an instrumental version of "Tossed Salad and Scrambled Eggs." He then introduces the members of the cast again, beginning with Moose, and

continuing with Arlene Sorkin (Christopher Lloyd's wife, who provides many of the voices for the radio callers, only to be dubbed out later), John Rajeski, a writer's assistant who played a waiter at Café Nervosa, Gilpin, Pierce, Leeves, Mahoney, and Grammer. Once again, Grammer hugs all, and the show is finished at 9:55 P.M.

The audience files out, and the cast and crew remain to film a public service spot for the National Mental Health Association and a fun thing for the script supervisor's high school reunion.

They're out the door by 10:15, and back at work the next morning at 11:00 A.M. for the table read for show 72, "The Focus Group."

"Act One, Scene A," yells director Philip Charles Mackenzie. . . .

During the first three and a half years of Frasier's life at *Cheers*, much of the writing was done by Peter Casey, David Lee, and David Angell. Casey and Lee penned Frasier's second *Cheers* episode, and part of that show, in fact, was used for Grammer's audition when creators Glen and Les Charles and James Burrows tested actors for the role of Frasier Crane.

There's a lot of Martin in Casey's and Lee's real dads. Casey's father was a San Francisco cop, and Lee's dad grew up on a dirt farm in Texas. "A lot of the relationship between Frasier and Martin came from my parents looking at this kid who wanted to be in show business from the time he was nine years old as 'Where did we get this kid?' " says Lee. "Niles and Frasier sometimes look at Martin and say, 'How did I come from him?' " (There's a lot of Angell, Casey, and Lee in the KACL call letters—one letter for each.)

David Lee grew up in Claremont, California, the son of a bank vice-president. He decided to get into show business at age nine, when an adult cousin took him to see the national tour of *My Fair Lady*. After graduating from the University of Redlands in 1972, where he studied music composition and theater arts, he moved to Los Angeles to pursue a career as an actor. He appeared in TV commercials, but mostly worked in dinner and regional theater.

By 1975, Lee had all but given up on his acting career, which was going nowhere. He got a job working as a proof-reader for a Hollywood mimeograph company, which, in the precomputer age, typed and copied scripts for TV production companies. Lee became friendly with fellow employee Peter Casey, a graduate of San Francisco State University. Casey was hired at the mimeo firm to type scripts, while Lee proof-read his work. Neither man was impressed with the quality of the work they were inspecting. "We read these scripts all day and said, 'We could do this,'" recalls Lee. "I'd been trained as an actor and director, so I understood character. Peter's background was writing, so he knew structure."

Casey, the son of a San Francisco cop, grew up in the city by the bay and recalls wanting to be in TV all his life. During his senior year at San Francisco State, he took a TV writing course and wrote a treatment for *The Waltons*. His instructor complimented him on a job well done and sent it off to his Los Angeles agent, who encouraged Casey to come to LA and pursue a writing career.

Which is perhaps how Casey ended up in Tinseltown so soon after graduation. However, he only lasted at the mimeo company for three weeks, fired for being too slow. Still, he and Lee were able to bond and commit in that short period of time to combining their writing forces. What sealed their zeal to get cracking was watching two of Lee's friends write a spec script for *The Mary Tyler Moore Show* and then quickly sell it. Things like that don't happen every day (in fact almost never). Casey and Lee didn't know any better, so they thought they'd try their hands at writing a script on spec, which gives producers a writing sample and then hopefully an invitation to come in and pitch story ideas.

But it took Casey and Lee three and a half years to get in the door anywhere.

They began by writing dramatic scripts (two *Petrocellis* and a *Barnaby Jones*) before switching to comedy with a script for *M*A*S*H*, followed by specs for *All's Fair*, their own pilot, and a *Barney Miller*.

Meanwhile, Lee continued at the mimeo company while Casey worked a series of odd jobs—at a liquor store and as a pizza delivery man and a survey taker for a radio station. Lee eventually left the mimeo firm, and both he and Casey became sandwich salesmen at Paramount, where they would go from office to office, selling sandwiches, sodas, and chips. Casey recalls selling a turkey and rye sandwich at *Taxi* to its director, James Burrows, who would later be his boss at *Cheers* and their primary director for the first season of *Frasier*.

Anyway, the *Barney Miller* script finally opened up doors for the duo. They got an appointment to pitch ideas for *Rhoda*, but unfortunately the show was canceled before they could come in. They also received an invite from *The Jeffersons*, and it was here that they found their first success with a script assignment.

Their idea: George and Louise's maid Florence wants to find a good Christian to date, but she gets more than she bargained for when he ends up being a religious zealot. But even with their first sale in three and a half years, it wasn't like Casey and Lee had suddenly won the lottery. They split $3,200 for the script, and both had to contribute $500 each from the sale to the Writer's Guild in order to join the union.

The following year, Casey and Lee got a second assignment from *The Jeffersons*, and based on that script, they were invited to join the show as staff writers. They stayed for six years and moved up the ladder to story editors, executive story editors, and eventually producers.

"It was so exciting for us," says Casey, "because it was the first script we sold, and then the next thing you knew, we were hired as staff writers. For the first time, we had real jobs in real offices. Working at *The Jeffersons* showed us how to bear down and write a script to a deadline. It showed us how a TV show was run."

But they eventually became frustrated with the sameness of *The Jeffersons* stories and longed to move to one of TV's wittier shows, like *M*A*S*H*, *Newhart*, or *Cheers*. But with a credit like *The Jeffersons* on their resume, "Nobody would take us seriously," says Lee, who adds that *Family Ties* executive producer Gary David Goldberg wouldn't even read one of their *Jeffersons* scripts. "It's cachet was that low."

But where there's a will, there's a way.

Cheers cocreators Glen and Les Charles both attended the University of Redlands, Lee's alma mater, and the brothers and Lee were invited to attend a TV writing seminar there as former grads. Lee brought Casey along with him. "It was at the height of *Cheers* acclaim," says Lee, "and we were determined to get on that show."

Driving home from the conference, they decided to stray from industry norm and write a *Cheers* spec script, even though once you're working in Hollywood as a TV writer, you're not expected to write specs anymore.

"It was unheard of to do anything like that," says Casey. "Our colleagues at *The Jeffersons* told us we were crazy. But it was the smartest thing we ever did. It got us in the door and a job on the most respected show on the air."

Most specs are never produced. Instead, they just serve to show that the writer can capture the voice of the characters and write funny material. Casey and Lee's *Cheers* spec script had Diane starting a pen pal relationship with a guy in prison as part of a sociology course, and her nervousness when he is paroled and wants to visit.

The Charles brothers liked what they read and invited

Casey and Lee in to pitch ideas. They got an assignment to write the episode "I Call Your Name," the second episode for Dr. Frasier Crane, following his introduction in the third season opener.

In "I Call," Frasier came to see Sam about a certain problem he was having with Diane. She was calling out Sam's name when they made love, although Frasier phrased it by saying the situation concerned his two patients, Scott and Zelda (changed later to Thor and Electra).

"When we went in to pitch, Glen and Les told us about this new character they were introducing," says Casey. "At that point they knew he was a psychiatrist, but they didn't have a name for him yet. They told us that he was pompous and how he talked. We didn't know how to write for a character that we didn't know, and felt that we were writing blind, but that was the assignment, and we weren't going to turn it down."

They handed in the script, but the Charles brothers didn't read it until after they returned from vacation. Meanwhile, Casey and Lee had an offer to return for another year of *The Jeffersons*. They kept putting off a decision, hoping they'd be asked to go to *Cheers*. They stalled and stalled, but finally, they couldn't put it off anymore. They signed for one more year at *The Jeffersons*. A few days later, the *Cheers* offer did in fact come in, but they felt they had to honor their contract, and the Charles brothers agreed to wait a year for them.

Meanwhile, Casey and Lee's script was in hand before the Charles brothers and cocreator James Burrows started seeing actors for the part of Frasier. In the audition, they used the portion of Casey and Lee's script for the long speech about Scott and Zelda and their unique problem.

Not only did the script get Casey and Lee a job, it was also nominated for an Emmy.

Casey and Lee finally got to *Cheers* full-time as it was preparing to begin its fourth season. Their second *Cheers* for the producers concerned Carla (Rhea Perlman) who was despondent about her lack of dating success. So she put a personal ad in the paper, got no response, and the guys at Cheers decided to create a guy for her, Mitch Wainwright, an international airline pilot. And the angels continued to be on Casey and Lee's side. Like "You Call Out My Name," their "2 Good 2 Be 4 Real?" was also nominated for an Emmy.

At the time Casey and Lee joined *Cheers*, Glen and Les Charles and James Burrows were the executive producers. The Charles brothers oversaw the writers, who included Casey and Lee, Heidi Perlman (Rhea's sister), and a man named David Angell.

David Angell grew up in the small town of West Barrington, Rhode Island, far away from Hollywood, with little of the show business aspirations that burned inside of David Lee and Peter Casey. In fact, Angell had planned on becoming a priest like his brother, and even went to a seminary for four years, but he eventually decided that the cloth wasn't for him. For a while he thought of going into medicine, then switched to English. He joined the army after graduating college in a two-and-a-half-year stint that ended with a clerical assignment at the Pentagon until 1972. After the service he returned to Rhode Island, wrote manuals for insurance companies, and worked as a methods analyst at an engineering company.

At one point in the 1970s, while watching *The Bob Newhart Show* and *The Mary Tyler Moore Show*, Angell got bit with the same feeling that so many writers get—that he could write stories as good as the ones he saw on TV and he wanted to give it a try. At the insurance company he worked with a guy whose cousin was a friend of a friend of two producers for *Rhoda*, Geoffrey Neigher and Chick Mitchell. Angell bought various books on how to write for television, wrote a spec script for *The Bob Newhart Show*, and sent it out to Neigher and Mitchell. To his pleasant surprise, they called him and said that for a first try, he showed promise.

That was all Angell needed to hear. He and wife Lynn sold their house and furniture, bought a van, and drove across country. Angell went to see Neigher and Mitchell, who had sold a pilot to CBS, *Annie Flynn*, along with an order for four scripts. After reading another of his spec scripts, this one for *Barney Miller*, the producers gave Angell an assignment to write one of their scripts. After reading his work, they gave him another.

David Angell was now in show business. But like many starving actors and writers who wonder when and where their next job will come from, Angell didn't work again for five years.

"I took meetings, I pitched stories, but I couldn't sell anything," he says. "I did every temp job known to mankind." So why didn't he give up and go back home to Rhode Island? "I really believed I could do it."

So did a new agent that he happened to meet at a party, in one of those classic being-in-the-right-place-at-the-right-time stories. His new representative got him an appointment to pitch stories for *Archie Bunker's Place*, and Angell successfully sold a story about Archie helping his friend Barney get a new job at a shoe store. Unlike *Annie Flynn*, this script was produced, and "it was the first time I heard anyone read my lines," says Angell. "It was particularly meaningful to me, because my father was a really big Archie Bunker fan."

After *Archie*, Angell's scripts started flowing. He wrote episodes for *Family Ties*, *Newhart*, and *Condo*, and then got to meet with Glen and Les Charles during the first season of *Cheers*. They didn't buy his idea, but had their own that they wanted him to work on. It was a story about con man Harry the Hat (played by Harry Anderson, in his first appearance on the show) and how the patrons of Cheers fought back in a sting operation to stop Harry from conning Coach out of his money.

The Charles brothers gave Angell an assignment for a second script (Diane's mother comes to visit) and then offered him a job as staff writer, which began in the second season of *Cheers*.

Angell and Heidi Perlman were the staff writers, and consultants David Lloyd (*The Mary Tyler Moore Show*) and Jerry Belson (*The Odd Couple*) were also on staff as consultants. Their job: to come in one day a week to "punch" up the scripts with the other writers in the rewrite room.

"I was awestruck to be in that room," says Angell. "It was so hard to speak up and contribute that I thought they were going to fire me. In a room like that, you have to know how to perform. There's nothing like that feeling of throwing an idea out and hearing total silence, but after a while you get used to it. One day I pitched a joke softly, and Jerry said 'What?' so I said it again.

"He said, 'This guy would have his own show if he'd just open his mouth.'"

Angell went on to win an Emmy for his *Cheers* script called "Old Flames," in which Sam's sportscaster buddy (played by Fred Dryer) came to Cheers and said he could break up Sam and Diane within twenty-four hours.

By the time Casey and Lee joined *Cheers*, Angell had been there for two seasons, and he wasn't so sure about the wisdom of Glen and Les Charles's latest hire. "*The Jeffersons* was a successful show," says Angell, "but the fit didn't seem right." Angell, like other *Cheers* writers, knew they were working on TV's classiest show. *The Jeffersons* was clearly in another league, that of low-brow, formula comedy.

But after the *Cheers* writers read Casey and Angell's work, they felt differently, and all started hitting it off. Perlman worked with the trio for a year, and then left, leaving Angell, Casey, and Lee as the second-in-command under the Charles brothers, who decided they had had enough of working late nights. Their role evolved into more of a consultant, where they attended table readings and show filmings and made notes on scripts, but left the hard work of coming up with stories, making them work, and crafting the jokes as funny as possible to Angell, Casey, and Lee.

"We were at *Cheers* during the most challenging years," says Lee. "The day we found out we were going to be the producers, Nicholas Colasanto [who played Coach] died, so we had to come up with a replacement [Woody]. At the end of our second season, Shelley Long announced she was leaving, so we found Rebecca [Kirstie Alley]. And Lilith showed up during our era also."

Casey and Lee feel strongly that despite their six years of apprenticeship at *The Jeffersons*, it wasn't until arriving at *Cheers* that they really learned how to write and run a TV show.

"*Cheers* didn't just settle for second best in the writing," says Casey. "It was the kind of show where you felt that the actors respected the words more. They would try to say them as they were written. *The Jeffersons* was a nice place to work, but they were doing a formula type of show, and with a star like Sherman Hemsley, you knew exactly what buttons to push, and you pushed them week after week after week. On *Cheers*, you had so many great characters and alternatives. You could do a Sam and Diane show one week, a Woody show, a Carla show . . . there were so many different ways to go."

Adds Lee: "Glen and Les and Jimmy were patient tutors. It was mostly about staying as late as it took to get it good, in terms of the writing, and letting the humor generate from the characters rather than knowing how to write jokes. It was about letting the stage and rehearsal process be where open discussion could take place, as opposed to a place where directors only talk to actors, and producers to writers, and nobody talks to one another directly."

After overseeing *Wings* for the first three years, Angell, Casey, and Lee handed over the reins to Dave Hackel, who has since been replaced by Howard Gewirtz and Mark Reisman. At *Frasier*, the three creators have had their three names on only one script—the first one, "The Good Son." Casey and Angell collaborated on "My Dinner with Niles." But don't let that fool you. Casey, Angell, and Lee are still very involved, at least with *Frasier*. They still sit in the room with the writing staff, helping to create stories and offering notes on others, at least one of them attends every rehearsal and filming, and they are involved in the editing of the show.

"Our stamp is on every story," says Casey. But as successful creators of a smash hit, they've come to the point in their life where they don't have to work until midnight every night. "When you get to the position of creating a show, you like to go home," he says. "For the first season of *Frasier* we were there for everything. Now we're gradually easing our way out, but we don't want it to get to the point where the show doesn't need us."

Angell, Casey, and Lee are the co-CEOs of *Frasier*, owning the shop and running the show. But as owners, they have the freedom now to step back a bit. To keep the corporate analogy going, executive producer Christopher Lloyd is the general manager. He's the "show runner," who's basically in charge of stories—making them work and coming up with new ones. (By the way, he's not the Christopher Lloyd who played Reverend Jim on *Taxi*.)

The younger Lloyd began his career working on the first four seasons of *The Golden Girls*. He then produced the two seasons of *Down Home* (1990–91) for Ted Danson's production company and joined *Wings* after *Down Home*'s demise.

Interestingly, a show about a son who takes in his father to live with him is run by a son of a veteran comedy writer who now works for his offspring. David Lloyd wrote for such series as *The Mary Tyler Moore Show* and *The Tonight Show with Johnny Carson* while Chris was growing up, and has been working as a "punch-up" guy for Paramount the last few years, coming in one or two days a week to add jokes to scripts for such series as *Cheers* and *Taxi*. He writes episodes for *Frasier* as well.

"We wondered about how it could work," says David Angell. "It could be potentially uncomfortable for both of them, but I haven't seen any ill effects. It seems to be working."

Chris Lloyd was hired at the very beginning, and when Paramount suggested having the elder Lloyd continue in his on-the-lot duties as a punch-up guy, "You'd have to have a really good reason to say no," says Chris, "because he's really good at what he does.

"It is an odd situation, however, but it did occur to me that this dynamic might make writing about a father and son a little easier. Though it is a little strange to be sitting in the room questioning why a son would feel a certain way about his father, and there's my father sitting on the couch across the room from me."

One of the Frasier and Martin stories that came out of having the two Lloyds in the writing room together was "Frasier Grinch," in which Frasier wants to buy son Frederick an educational toy and Martin suggests he buy him something that Frederick—instead of Frasier—might want.

"My father's a proponent of the theory that you should get people what they want as gifts," says Lloyd, who gave his father the assignment to pen the script.

Besides writing an occasional script and coming in to punch up the lines once a week, David Lloyd also discovered the writer Joe Keenan, who wrote one of *Frasier*'s most acclaimed episodes, "The Matchmaker," which won a Writers Guild of America award for Keenan and best directing Emmy and Directors Guild of America nods for David Lee.

The elder Lloyd found Keenan after reading a review of one of his novels in the *Boston Globe*, and then went out and bought his *Blue Heaven*. An homage to the writer P. G. Wodehouse, a farce about a gay man and straight woman who marry just for the wedding gifts, Lloyd thought *Cheers* co-creators Glen and Les Charles would enjoy reading the book. They responded by calling Keenan and asking him to create a series for their Charles/Burrows/Charles Productions.

"I loved TV, but I never thought about writing for television, because I didn't want to relocate to Los Angeles and go through the long apprenticeship process," says Keenan. But the Charles brothers' offer was too good to pass up. Keenan created a series for NBC called *Gloria Vane*, set in 1930s Hollywood, about a vain, fictional Hollywood star. JoBeth Williams starred, and the pilot went to NBC after *Cheers* was completed. When NBC passed, the *Frasier* producers asked Keenan to write a script. If they liked it, they said, they'd hire him full-time.

Keenan's first script to air was "The Matchmaker," but the first one he wrote was "The Botched Language of Cranes," in which Frasier says nasty things about Seattle on the radio and the city gets furious at him.

The first writers hired at Frasier were Chuck Ranberg and his partner Anne Flett-Giordano. They are former college friends who pooled their resources and started writing spec scripts in the 1970s. Eventually one of them got to Bill Persky, who bought a script from them for his *Kate and Allie*, and then hired them on staff. When that show was canceled, Ranberg and Flett-Giordano stayed with Persky on his short-lived

Working It Out series, and when that was axed, they endured a year of unemployment.

Like Casey and Lee and *The Jeffersons*, smart shows weren't interested in reading their scripts for a family comedy like *Kate and Allie*. So they wrote specs for *Seinfeld* and *Home Improvement* and came across *Frasier* before the pilot was made when a mutual friend invited David Lee to a reading of a play Ranberg wrote, *End of the World Party*. Lee enjoyed the play, found out that Ranberg and partner Anne Flett-Giordano weren't working, read their specs, had them come in to meet with him, Angell and Casey, and gave them a job, beginning with the pilot. They won the Emmy for the second-season episode about Niles and his duel with Maris's fencing instructor.

Executive producers Vic Rauseo and Linda Morris joined *Frasier* midway through the first season. They had run the *Doogie Howser, M.D.* show and began their career writing four scripts for *Welcome Back, Kotter*. Through the years, they've also worked on *Alice, Hooperman*, and *I Married Dora*.

Rauseo and Morris have since left *Frasier* to create their own series for 20th Century Fox, but while at *Frasier*, their executive producer responsibilities involved filling in for Lloyd in the writing room if he was absent, overseeing the casting, and writing.

As far as the other writers, coexecutive producer Steven Levitan began on *Wings* and went to *The Larry Sanders Show* before joining *Frasier*. (He has since moved on.) Jack Burditt came from *Mad About You*, and has since left *Frasier* to work with Ted Danson and Mary Steenburgen (and former *Mad* boss Jeffrey Lane) on their new CBS sit-com. Rob Greenberg joined *Frasier* after a year at *Love and War*. The newest hire, Suzanne Martin, came from Grub Street's short-lived *Pursuit of Happiness* and *Ellen*. Angell, Casey, and Lee also contribute to the writing, and David Lloyd and former *Wings* executive producer Dave Hackel both come in one day a week to punch up the script.

Even though the scripts have individual names on them, the *Frasier* writers work together as a unit to ''break'' the ''beats'' of a story. Because of the massive undertaking of having to produce twenty-four to twenty-five episodes a year (twelve and a half hours' worth, with commercials), ''No one person can do this alone,'' says Morris. ''[As a writer] you have to be very flexible and be prepared to work in a communal setting.''

Adds Ranberg: ''There's no way to do this volume of work without having a lot of help. You would burn out too quickly.''

As the story boss, Lloyd has a few rules he tries to adhere to. ''Frasier should be a good psychiatrist,'' he says. ''So we shouldn't go for jokes and have him act unprofessionally, or give bad advice. He's out there enough. We also try to do things that aren't funny for funny sake, but also have some kind of emotional reality to them. Our best shows tend to yield an answer to the question—what is this show about? For instance, we did an episode where Niles finally admitted his passion for Daphne while they were dancing the tango. But the story we created was that Niles was struggling with self-doubt about whether he was an attractive man and dating material, since he was still devastated by his separation with Maris. Yes, he was dumped by Daphne at the end, but another woman came up to him at the end, so he was uplifted by the end of the episode. That makes more of a story.''

The writing staff subscribes to psychiatric journals and they read them occasionally, ''But no psychiatrist would look at our show as purely authentic,'' says Lloyd. ''We occasionally get a good story idea from one of the journals, but the jargon we use is pretty basic.''

The writers are an erudite group, and while Lloyd says

they are pretty well versed on the literary and wine references, they do have the research department look up such Crane obsessions as opera details occasionally. In the beginning, there was concern among network and studio executives about just how cultured the writers should make Frasier and Niles. Several of the jokes were referred to as "10 percenters," as in only 10 percent of the country would get it.

"Some of us were concerned, but Kelsey said, 'Let's not talk down to our audience,'" recalls Lloyd. "If only 50 percent of them get the joke, then only 50 percent will get it. So what?" When the shows were mounted in front of a studio audience, the producers found that 60 percent to 80 percent of the audience laughed at the jokes, "and we were kind of ashamed of ourselves for giving the audience too little credit. I've come to learn that the TV audience isn't as stupid as people are always saying they are."

One thing the writers of *Frasier* share with their characters is a love of fine coffee. Every day at 3:30 P.M. a production assistant runs to Starbucks and brings back exotic coffees. "It's pretentious and awful, but it's the time of the day when we get to act like Frasier and Niles," says Lloyd, who simply orders a latte at midday, while others in the room opt for a double short nonfat latte or regular ol' espressos or cappuccinos.

The writers are also adept at doing great imitations of the characters. Keenan is said to do a really keen Daphne, and Ranberg keeps the room in stitches with his Niles. "We're trying to convince Joe to take his Daphne show on tour," says Ranberg.

"When you're pitching a joke," says Keenan, "you want to make sure the joke pops, so we all do imitations of the characters. Sometimes the joke just isn't funny unless you do it in their voice."

Sometimes, however, this talent can come back to haunt you. When Ted Danson did a guest spot on *Frasier* as Sam

Malone, David Hyde Pierce couldn't be at the table reading, so Keenan was called in to read for Niles instead. "It gave new life to the term underarm perspirants," says Keenan.

David Lee began directing television on *Wings* in classic show-biz style. Director Andy Ackerman's back went out suddenly, and they needed a replacement—fast. "I'd been trained as a director, but the camera stuff to me was daunting and scary." (TV directors work off four monitors and tell the camera operators which shots they want.) "But when Andy hurt his back, there was no other choice but for me to get down there and do the camera blocking. It was horrifying at first, but I had great help from the technical staff."

Since then, he's directed five *Wings* and ten *Frasiers*, as

Director David Lee works with cast.

well as an episode of Paramount's *Almost Perfect*. "I love it now," he says. "It's quite rewarding." In fact, Lee won not only the Emmy, but also the prestigious Directors Guild of America award, voted upon by other directors, for his work helming the now classic "Matchmaker" episode of *Frasier*, in which our hero tries to set up his gay boss with Daphne.

Many, many people work on the *Frasier* show to get it on the air. Besides the thirteen writer-producers, nearly a hundred people are involved. The titles: unit production manager, production coordinator, postproduction supervisor, editor, assistant editor, first assistant director, second assistant director, technical coordinator, estimator/auditor, script supervisor, director of photography, four camera operators, four dolly grips, five assistant camera operators, a gaffer, assistant chief lighting technician, dimmer operator, lamp operator, four grips, sound mixer, two boom operators, recordist, audio/video maintenance, art director and assistant art director, set decorator, lead man, two swing men, construction coordinator, property master, assistant props, costume designer, costume supervisor, costumer, makeup, assistant makeup, hairstylist, assistant hairstylist, animal trainer, casting director and three associates, still photographer, band leader, and five stand-ins for the lead actors.

These moments, from the classic script for "The Matchmaker," the episode that won the Emmy and Directors Guild of America Award (for directing) and the Writers Guild of America award for writing. It begins with the meeting between Tom, the station *manager, and Frasier, when Frasier wants to set him up with Daphne.*

TOM: You know, I just came from London. I spent the last five years there working for the BBC.

FRASIER: Really? I love London—the theater especially.

TOM: Me too. I'm a big theater buff. I hated to leave, but . . . well, I'd just gone through sort of a messy breakup. I thought I'd sleep better with a continent between us.

FRASIER: I know the feeling. (*The idea strikes him.*) So . . . I take it you're unattached?

TOM: Yes, but I haven't given up hope.

FRASIER: Well, you may have come to the right place. So, getting back to London, were you fond of the British?

TOM: Yes, very much. I guess I've always had a weakness for people who are just a little eccentric.

Frasier and his gay boss in the classic episode, "The Matchmaker"

FRASIER: Really?

ROZ (*into her mike*): Fifteen seconds.

TOM: Well, nice meeting you—

FRASIER: Same here.

(Frasier sits and dons his headphones. Tom turns to go again.)

FRASIER: Say, Tom, I know this is short notice, but if you're not doing anything Saturday, why don't you come by my place for dinner? Nothing fancy.

TOM: Thanks. I'd like that.

(Tom crosses into Roz's booth. The on-air light goes on. Tom stands facing Roz with his back to Frasier. Tom and Roz adlib hellos.)

TOM (*to Roz*): Boy, it's the same every job I take. Word spreads like wildfire.

ROZ: What's that?

TOM: Oh, you know. You tell one or two people you're gay and before you can blink it's all over the station.

ROZ: They don't call it broadcasting for nothing.

(Frasier notices Roz talking to Tom and assumes she's hitting on him. Frasier wags a finger at Roz indicating "get away from him.")

TOM (*re: Frasier*): He seems like a nice guy.

ROZ: He's okay.

TOM: I hope he's more than okay. He just asked me out on a date and I accepted.

ROZ: Frasier? Asked you out on a date?

(Frasier begins scribbling on a piece of paper.)

TOM: Yeah, he asked me to come to his place for dinner. So I wanted to ask you is there any particular wine he likes?

ROZ: Tom, there's something you should know about Frasier—

From his booth, Frasier holds up a sign. It reads, "Hands off! He's taken!" Roz reads it.)

TOM: What?
ROZ (*to Tom*): He's nuts about chardonnay.

(Later, in Frasier's apartment.)

TOM: Niles, could I speak with you a moment?
NILES: Yes.
TOM: I was just wondering. Did I say or do anything that offended you?
NILES: No.
TOM: Then maybe it's all in my head because I sensed that you had a problem with my dating Frasier.
NILES: Well, if you must know . . . (*stops*) I'm sorry, what was the question?
TOM: Do you have some problem with my dating your brother?

(Niles starts to open his mouth to say something, then stops. He thinks some more, then:)

NILES: No. No problem at all. I'm sorry if I gave you that impression.

(Frasier enters the kitchen with the remaining dishes.)

FRASIER: Now, Niles, I didn't ask Tom to join us for dinner tonight so he'd be stuck in the kitchen talking to you. There're others who might want to have a crack at him.
NILES: Forgive me brother. He's all yours.

(Tom and Frasier exit back into the living room. Martin enters the kitchen carrying an armload of dishes.)

MARTIN: That Tom's a great guy, huh? So, what do you think, maybe him and Daphne?

(Niles starts to laugh.)

MARTIN: What's so funny?

NILES: Oh, just a little predicament Frasier's gotten himself in.

MARTIN: What?

NILES: Put down those plates and I'll tell you.

(Later on . . .)
(Frasier escorts Niles to the front door.)

NILES: Oh, Frasier, a word in your ear . . .

(Frasier and Niles exit into the hallway.)

NILES: I have something to tell you. Dad wanted to, but I won the coin toss.

FRASIER: Well, what is it?

NILES: I talked to Tom in the kitchen and he's feeling romantic.

FRASIER: That's why you're leaving.

NILES: Are you aware the object of his affection is not Daphne but you?

FRASIER: Me? That's impossible. Tom is not gay.

NILES: He seems to be under that impression.

FRASIER: There's obviously been some misunderstanding.

NILES: Well, there's a triumph of understatement. Good Lord, Frasier, what did you say to the man to lead him on so?

FRASIER: I did not lead him on. I just asked him if he was single, and then we chatted about theater and men's fashion and . . . Oh, my God!

NILES: Ah, the perils of refinement.

FRASIER: Do you know what this means?

NILES: Yes. You're dating your boss. You, of all people, should know the pitfalls of an office romance.

EIGHT

EPISODE GUIDE

1 "THE GOOD SON"

WRITERS: David Angell, Peter Casey, David Lee

DIRECTOR: James Burrows

Leaving Boston, his barstool on "Cheers," and his wife and son, Dr. Frasier Crane moves to a stylish apartment in Seattle and goes to work as the host of a radio phone-in advice program. Frasier's younger brother Niles informs him that their dad has fallen and was found by one of his buddies. They agree that he cannot live alone anymore, and Frasier has Martin move in with him, with Frasier and Niles splitting the cost of a home care provider. Daphne Moon of Manchester, England, a daffy semipsychic, gets the job.

Delivery Man · *Cleto Agusto*
Waitress · *Gina Ravarra*
Claire · *Linda Hamilton (voice-over)*
Russell · *Griffin Dunne (voice-over)*

2 "SPACE QUEST"

WRITERS: Sy Dukane & Denise Moss

DIRECTOR: James Burrows

"The Good Son, Part Two." This episode opens the morning after the pilot episode and centers on Frasier's frustration that his quest for single status has been shattered by his new arrangement with his father, his dog Eddie, and Daphne. We meet Bob "Bulldog" Briscoe for the first time here when he wants to do his sports-talk radio show in Frasier's booth. By the second act, Frasier wants to kick out Martin and move him and Daphne to their own apartment. He finally gets up the nerve to tell Martin of his plans, but Martin refuses to budge. He says the two of them will have to work at their relationship and they share a beer to celebrate their new life.

Bulldog · *Dan Butler*
Leonard · *Christopher Reeve (voice-over)*

3 "DINNER AT EIGHT"

WRITERS: Anne Flett & Chuck Ranberg

DIRECTOR: James Burrows

Frasier and Niles bite off more than they can chew when they agree to accompany Martin to his favorite eatery: the rustic Timber Mill, where the nattily attired Frasier and Niles are clearly out of place amongst the blue-collar chicken-fried-steak crowd. The hostess immediately cuts their ties off and sticks them on a wall full of ties. The three can't find much to talk about, and Niles and Frasier amuse themselves by making fun of the eatery, its food, and patrons. Martin scolds them by saying they're nothing like their mother, Hester, the psychiatrist he met on a murder case. She was too classy to make anyone feel second rate, he says, and walks out. Frasier and Niles ponder their inability to appreciate the simpler things in life, and to prove they aren't snobs, they decide to clear their plates.

Waitress · *Laurie Walton*
Hostess · *Eve Brent*
Pam · *Patti LuPone (voice-over)*

4 ''I HATE FRASIER CRANE''

WRITER: Christopher Lloyd

DIRECTOR: David Lee

A newspaper critic starts a feud with Frasier by printing an unflattering column about his radio show. Frasier takes after him on the radio, which brings another response by the critic, Derek Mann, and finally, a phone call from Mr. Mann himself to the radio show, who challenges Frasier to a fight. Frasier tries to talk him out of it, saying that two civilized men should be able to solve their differences with words, not fists. Mann calls Frasier a chicken, and Frasier caves in to the fight. Niles, Martin, and Daphne show up at the Café Nervosa to lend their support to Frasier, and when Derek Mann arrives, we hear that he's huge. Frasier exits to fight, but luckily for him, the police arrive to break it up. The show ends with Frasier feeling victorious that he didn't run away, and Martin thanking one of the cops (his pal) for doing him this favor and showing up.

Cop [Harry] · *John Brandon*
Waiter · *Dean Erickson*
Derek Mann · *Joe Mantegna (voice-over)*
Lorraine · *Judith Ivey (voice-over)*

5 ''HERE'S LOOKING AT YOU''

WRITER: Brad Hall

DIRECTOR: Andy Ackerman

Frasier and Daphne set up a telescope Frasier bought Martin as a surprise. Martin's reaction is lukewarm until they all discover the fun of spying into people's apartments. Martin finds a woman (Irene) spying back at them through her own telescope, and Frasier holds up their phone number so Irene can call Martin. But to Frasier's surprise, when she does call, he turns down her request for a date. They don't know why he did it, but learn later that Martin does truly care for Irene. What was preventing him from getting involved? Irene's middle name is Rose, and that was his late wife's middle name. He's not ready, he tells Frasier. Daphne knows that Irene's real middle name is Marie, and suggests that in truth, Martin just feels self-conscious about his hip. She tells him he has nothing to worry about, that he's quite a catch, and convinces him to go out with Irene.

Aunt Patrice · *Kathleen Noone*
Doug · *Jeff Daniels (voice-over)*

6 ''CALL ME IRRESPONSIBLE''
WRITERS: Anne Flett & Chuck Ranberg
DIRECTOR: James Burrows

Frasier has an ethical problem: After telling a caller to break up with his girlfriend, Frasier starts dating her. Niles is the voice of Frasier's conscience, telling him that no self-respecting therapist should be involved with someone who could be considered his patient. The caller, Marco, calls back the next day and says he's having second thoughts about dumping Catherine. Frasier does everything in his power to keep Marco away from Catherine. When Frasier sees her later on, he has a hard time being with her because his stomach gets queasy over his ethical breach, and she dumps him.

Catherine · *Amanda Donohoe*
Marco · *Bruno Kirby (voice-over)*
Hank · *Eddie Van Halen (voice-over)*

7 ''THE CRUCIBLE''
WRITERS: Sy Dukane & Denise Moss
DIRECTOR: James Burrows

Frasier buys a painting by a renowned local artist, and then invites her to a prestigious dinner party in her honor—but his pride turns to humiliation when she announces to everyone that the painting is a forgery. A few days later, she admits that the painting was authentic, she just forgot she had painted it.

Phillip Hayson · *John Rubinstein*
Martha Paxton · *Rachel Rosenthal*
Diane · *Eugenie Bonderant*
Ronald · *Gregory Eugene Travis*
Gary · *Robert Klein (voice-over)*

8 ''BELOVED INFIDEL''
WRITER: Leslie Eberhard
DIRECTOR: Andy Ackerman

Niles thinks that Martin might have had an affair with a family friend when Niles and Frasier were kids. Niles and Frasier discover Martin in what appears to be a clandestine rendezvous with Marion Lawlor. The Lawlors and the Cranes had a falling out many years earlier. The brothers presume that Martin is getting together with Marion to patch things up. Marion starts to sob and rushes off to the ladies' room. Niles and Frasier come to the conclusion that Martin and Marion had something going on. When Martin comes home, he admits all. At Café Nervosa, Frasier tells Niles how upset he is that his father fooled around on his mother. Later that night, Marion drops by the apartment looking for Martin to apologize to him for getting so emotional at dinner. Frasier tells her he knows all about the affair. Marion reveals that it was her husband Stan and Hester who had the affair. Frasier asks Martin later why he didn't tell the truth. Martin says it was none of his business. Martin was trying to protect Frasier's memories of his mother. Frasier admits to Martin that Lilith cheated on him. Martin asks if Frasier will ever tell Frederick about Lilith's infidelity. Probably not.

Marion Lawlor · *Pat Crowley*
Waitress · *Julie Gill*
Danielle · *JoBeth Williams (voice-over)*

9 ''SELLING OUT''

WRITER: Lloyd Garver

DIRECTOR: Andy Ackerman

A savvy agent persuades Frasier to start doing commercials, but where should he draw the line? Frasier begins by endorsing products he likes, such as a local Chinese restaurant and hot tub dealer. But when agent Bebe Glazer gets him a lucrative deal for Emery's Nuts, in which he begins by saying "This is Dr. Frasier Crane and I know a nut when I see one," Frasier is convinced he's gone down the wrong path and refuses to continue his endorsement career. His replacement for the Emery's Nuts spot? None other than Dr. Joyce Brothers.

Bebe Glazer · *Harriet Sansom Harris*
Bulldog · *Dan Butler*
Walnut · *John Drayman*
Almond · *Michael David Edwards*
Herself · *Dr. Joyce Brothers*
Director · *Paul Perri*
Roger · *Carl Reiner (voice-over)*

10 ''OOPS''

WRITERS: Denise Moss & Sy Dukane

DIRECTOR: James Burrows

Nerves at KACL are at a fever pitch, as everyone hears the rumor that someone is about to be fired in a budget squeeze. They speculate on who it might be, and conclude that it must be Bulldog after he announces that he has a meeting with the station manager that evening. After his show, Frasier runs into Father Mike, who worries that he's about to be canned, and Frasier informs him that it's Bulldog who's about to be axed. Unfortunately, Bulldog overhears the news, freaks out, and decides to go tell off the station manager. Roz immediately corrects Frasier and says that the meeting with Bulldog was about taking his show national. Frasier runs in to try and save the day, but it's too late. Bulldog calls the man's wife a fat slut and quits. Frasier feels guilty about what transpired and goes to the station manager, Mr. Miller, to try and make things whole. He tells him what happened, and that he was partly responsible for Bulldog's outburst. The station manager says he'll take Bulldog back if he'll kiss his ass and that the rumor about someone being fired wasn't false. Someone was about to lose his job, and it was Frasier. But before Miller can fire Frasier, he gets a call from the higher-ups who decide to cut the budget instead by getting rid of Miller and his high salary.

Ned Miller · *John Glover*
Bulldog · *Dan Butler*
Father Mike · *George Deloy*
Chopper Dave · *Richard Poe*
Teddy · *Wayne Wilderson*
Don · *Jay Leno (voice-over)*

11 "DEATH BECOMES HIM"
WRITER: Leslie Eberhard
DIRECTOR: Andy Ackerman

When another man his age suddenly drops dead, Frasier becomes obsessed with his own mortality. Frasier takes Martin in for a checkup, and they're kept waiting for quite some time. Reason: Dr. Newman has suddenly died of a heart attack, despite being young (Frasier's age) and in perfect health. Frasier obsesses over how such a thing could happen to a young, healthy man, and he begins to investigate. He shows up at Dr. Newman's shivah and pumps family members for any and all details about Dr. Newman and his lifestyle. Frasier sits with Dr. Newman's wife, who looks to Frasier, the famed psychiatrist, for a reason why her husband died. Frasier has no explanation. He says all they can do is live for the little joys and surprises that life affords.

Aunt Bobbie · *June Claman*
Gail · *Maddie Gorman*

Mrs. Newman · *Stephanie Dunnam*
Allan Freedman · *Murray Rubinstein*
Woman at Shivah · *Shawn Huff*
Patient · *Marion Dugan*
Receptionist · *Amy Lloyd*

12 "CAN'T BUY ME LOVE"

WRITERS: Chuck Ranberg & Anne Flett-Giordano

DIRECTOR: James Burrows

After Martin convinces him to participate, a charity bachelor auction nets Frasier an evening with a model; Roz a date with a football player; and Daphne a night with Bulldog.

Bulldog · *Dan Butler*
Kristina · *Claire Stansfield*
Renata · *Ashley Bank*
T.J. · *Brett Miller*
Stage Manager · *Shawna Casey*
M.C. (off-screen) · *Ken Levine (the Frasier and Cheers writer)*

13 "MIRACLE ON 3RD OR 4TH STREET"

WRITER: Christopher Lloyd

DIRECTOR: James Burrows

The first *Frasier* Christmas show. Frasier gets a call from Lilith and learns that Frederick will be going to Austria instead of Seattle for the holidays. Frasier decides to work at the station on Christmas Day to hide from his disappointment. The callers are all as depressed as he is, and Frasier decides to cheer himself up by treating himself to dinner at a diner, where, after he says that he left his wallet at work, they all assume that he is homeless for Christmas. The other less fortunate souls pitch in to pay for his meal. Not wanting to ruin their spirit, Frasier (on hands and knees) sneaks to his BMW only to realize his keys are in the diner. The waitress finds the keys, but Frasier is unable to say anything. He walks home in the rain.

Bulldog · *Dan Butler*
Lou · *Christine Estabrook*
Chopper Dave · *Richard Poe*
Tim · *John J. Finn*
Bonnie Weems · *Katherine Danielle*
Elizabeth · *Bette Rae*
Bill · *Hawthorne James*
Tom · *Mel Brooks (voice-over)*
Gladys · *Rosemary Clooney (voice-over)*
Jeff · *Dominick Dunne (voice-over)*
Barry · *Ben Stiller (voice-over)*
Don · *Eric Stoltz (voice-over)*

14 "GUESS WHO'S COMING TO BREAKFAST"

WRITER: Molly Newman

DIRECTOR: Andy Ackerman

Frasier must make amends after he embarrasses Martin by talking on the radio about his romantic rendezvous with a neighbor. It all begins when Frasier and Martin make an agreement to clear out of the apartment on different nights that week because they both have dates planned. Martin's date is Elaine Morris from apartment 1412. The morning after Martin's date, Frasier is shocked to find Elaine still there. Elaine is invited to stay for breakfast, but Frasier cannot stop putting his foot in his mouth with stupid things about Martin's date. Elaine leaves and Martin apologizes for not warning Frasier in advance. On the radio, Frasier talks about what happened at home that morning, and at home, a furious Martin says Elaine broke up with him because she was so upset about Frasier discussing their sex life on the radio. The next day, Frasier tries to make amends by making a romantic plea to Elaine on air for Martin. At the apartment that night, a crowd arrives to see if Elaine will come see Martin. When she exits the elevator and finds the gang, she makes a hasty escape. Frasier and Martin make it into the elevator before the doors close, where Martin apologizes and the two give it another try.

Elaine · *Linda Stephens*
Noel · *Patrick Kerr*
Marjorie · *Patricia Fraser*
Tony · *Robert Colbert*
Marianne · *Piper Laurie (voice-over)*
Al · *Henry Mancini (voice-over)*
Ethan · *Elijah Wood (voice-over)*

15 "A MID-WINTER NIGHT'S DREAM"

WRITERS: Chuck Ranberg & Anne Flett-Giordano
DIRECTOR: David Lee

The first great Niles/Daphne episode, where Frasier confronts Niles on his infatuation with Daphne. Does he really expect it to go anywhere? Is Niles's relationship with Maris in jeopardy? Niles admits they've fallen into a rut. Frasier thinks they need to spice up their love life. He asks Roz what she does when the romance starts going out of her relationships. She tells him about this boyfriend she once had. They would go to a bar and pretend to be strangers and pick each other up. Frasier summarizes: "Fantasy and role-playing." So Niles dresses up as a pirate, and is kicked out of the house for it. He shows up at Frasier's door, explaining that he was lying in wait in Maris's closet wearing nothing but an eyepatch and holding a sword in his teeth. He was going to surprise Maris, but was discovered by one of the Guatemalan maids. Maris misconstrued the incident and kicked him out.

Niles wonders how to patch things up with Maris, who flew to her favorite spa to soak in mud and contemplate the future of their marriage.

Martin tells him to plan a romantic dinner. Daphne offers to prepare the meal. That stormy night, Daphne arrives. She has just been dumped by her new boyfriend, Eric, and Niles comforts her as she cries on his shoulder. Maris calls. Due to the storm, she cannot fly home. The electricity goes out. Because of the road conditions, Martin tells Daphne to stay the night. When Frasier hears the situation, he rushes to Niles's house, afraid the scene is fraught with dangerous possibilities.

Daphne changes out of her wet clothes into a silk peignoir. Niles flees, leaving an urgent message on Frasier's answering machine. Frasier's car stalls. Niles and Daphne are about to kiss when his long defunct glockenspiel springs to life. Niles realizes that he loves Maris. Frasier finally arrives and comes upon the two of them, letting out a huge scream for them to "stop!" Daphne shames Frasier for thinking anything was going on.

Eric · *Dean Erickson*

16 "CAN'T TELL A CROOK BY HIS COVER"

WRITER: David Lloyd

DIRECTOR: Andy Ackerman

Frasier and Niles take it upon themselves to spy on Daphne after she accepts a date with an ex-con. Daphne meets the ex-con, Jimmy, at a poker game with Martin and his cop friends. He asks her out and she says yes. Although there's some debate in the Crane household over whether she should date the man, Daphne is determined to go through with it. But when Niles learns that Daphne is meeting an ex-con for a date at the seedy Topaz room, he rushes to save her. When they arrive, the bartender tells them that Daphne put her date in a headlock when he got fresh with her. She can obviously take care of herself. Which is more than you can say for Frasier and Niles, who get into a fight with a brute named Rocco when they bump into him and cause him to miss his pool shot. Rocco decides to take Frasier and Niles out back and beat the crap out of them, but Daphne saves the day when she bets Rocco she can sink five balls with a single shot. If she does, the guys are off the hook. She sinks four out of five, and the three of them hightail it out the door.

Frank · *Ron Dean*
Linda · *Katherine McGrath*
Jimmy · *Tony Abatemarco*
Rocco · *Robert Miano*
Bartender · *Ivory Ocean*
Leo · *Marco Rodriguez*
Waiter · *Dean Erickson*

17 ''THE SHOW WHERE LILITH COMES BACK''

WRITERS: Ken Levine & David Isaacs

DIRECTOR: James Burrows

The first "*Frasier* meets *Cheers*" reunion featured his ex-wife Lilith, and aired in February 1994, six months into the life of the show. Lilith turns up in Seattle, saying she came to attend a convention. The truth, however, is that she found a note that Frasier had written to her (several months earlier, before he moved to Seattle) asking for a reconciliation, and she's come to Seattle to get back together. Over dinner in her hotel suite, Lilith announces her intentions. They kiss and wind up making mad passionate love.

The next morning breakfast arrives and Lilith says, "This is a mistake." Frasier agrees. Even though sex was great, they've both moved on. Their lives have changed and they can't be together again. Lilith says she was talking about the eggs. She ordered poached, not fried. Lilith breaks down and admits her confusion over the whole situation. She's been lonely and scared. Raising a child alone has been difficult. Frasier comforts her, says she can handle it, and they agree to be friends.

Lilith · *Bebe Neuwirth*
Waiter · *Roger Keller*
Hank · *Timothy Leary (voice-over)*

18 "AND THE WHIMPER IS . . ."

WRITERS: Denise Moss & Sy Dukane

DIRECTOR: James Burrows

The show where Frasier campaigned hard to get a SeaBea award, only to feel bad about his efforts once he gets to the ceremony and meets his worthy competitor. The SeaBea is the biggest award in Seattle radio, and Frasier's agent Bebe suggests her client follow the lead of fellow nominees by putting ads in trade magazines, sending out tapes, and trying other various suck-up practices. The night of the SeaBeas, Frasier meets fellow nominee, Seattle broadcasting legend Fletcher Grey, the Susan Lucci of local broadcasting, a beloved legend who's been nominated eleven times in a row. Yet he's never won. At the dinner, Fletcher tells Frasier about how badly he wants to win. As if Frasier doesn't feel bad enough about how hard he pushed when Fletcher clearly deserved the nod, the MC makes it worse when he announces that Fletcher will be retiring at the end of the year. In the end, neither man wins, and Fletcher tells Frasier that the only thing that really matters is knowing you've done a good job.

Bebe Glazer · *Harriet Sansom Harris*
Fletcher Grey · *John McMartin*
Noel · *Patrick Kerr*
Keith Bishop · *Wren T. Brown*
Mrs. Grey · *Maxine Elliott*
Tawny Van Deusen · *Trish Ramish*
Bob Peterson · *Mark Sawyer*
Committee Member · *Aileen Fitzpatrick*

19 "GIVE HIM THE CHAIR!"

WRITERS: Chuck Ranberg & Anne Flett-Giordano

DIRECTOR: James Burrows

Frasier isn't a lazy boy when it comes to getting rid of Martin's beloved recliner, but getting it back isn't quite as simple. It all begins after Frasier watches Martin patching up his chair with a roll of duct tape. Frasier wants him to replace the old heap of junk, but Martin won't hear of letting go of his prized possession. Later on, Niles rationalizes that by replacing the chair, Frasier would be helping Martin. The chair is a transitional object and there comes a time when it's healthy to put these security objects aside. The brothers choose a modern-looking, vibrating massage chair for their dad, and they have Leo from building services move the old chair into Frasier's storage area. Martin, predictably doesn't like the new chair. When he asks for his old one back, Leo realizes he made a mistake and threw it out near the dumpster. It's up to Martin and Frasier to get the chair back. After making a personal plea to his radio listeners, the chair is traced to a high school. Frasier enters the school auditorium where the chair sits center stage as one of its props in a production of *Ten Little Indians,* but the teacher refuses to give it up. Frasier said that he was in that play years ago, and when one of the students get sick, Frasier and the teacher strike a bargain. To get the chair back, all he has to do is reprise the role he once played. So once again, for one night only, Frasier is the star of a student production of *Ten Little Indians.*

Mrs. Warren · *Valerie Curtin*
Salesman · *James Greene*
Leo · *Phil Buckman*
Joey · *Marc Robinson*
Brown · *Scotty Nguyen*
Olsen · *Brittany Murphy*
Dr. Bruga · *Malcolm McDowell (voice-over)*

20 ''AUTHOR, AUTHOR''

WRITERS: Don Seigel & Jerry Perzigian

DIRECTOR: James Burrows

Frasier and Niles as coauthors of a self-help book about sibling rivalry? Sounds like a great idea. Now, if only the two brothers could get rid of their writer's block. The project begins when Niles sells a publisher on a book idea, and then discovers that it's already been done. When the publisher meets Niles and Frasier at the Café Nervosa, he suggests the brothers cowrite a book on sibling relationships. At their first meeting, they come up with nothing. Brainstorm #1: Frasier suggests Niles be a guest on his show and they'll use the material the callers give them for the book. That doesn't work, and leads to brainstorm #2: Frasier and Niles lock themselves in a hotel room and don't leave until their task is complete. After one day, all they've agreed upon is one sentence. By day two, Frasier says its hopeless. Niles says he's tired of being in Frasier's shadow, and that the book was his last chance at some notoriety. It's been that way his whole life, and the discussion leads to a nasty fight complete with chest hair pulling, body slams, and headlocks.

> Sam Tanaka · *Mako*
> Waitress · *Luck Hari*
> Laura · *Christine Lahti (voice-over)*

21 ''FORTYSOMETHING''
WRITERS: Sy Dukane & Denise Moss

DIRECTOR: Rick Beren

Frasier is having trouble adjusting to being middle-aged, especially when an attractive young store clerk flirts with him. Young Carrie asks Frasier out for coffee, and since she's only twenty-two, Frasier doesn't think it would be appropriate. In a discussion with his brother, Frasier says he doesn't want to be another midlife crisis cliché. Niles thinks Frasier needs to decide whether he's attracted to Carrie because he's running away from his age or because he feels they have potential to develop a meaningful relationship. Frasier decides to ask Carrie out, but before he can Carrie thanks Frasier for his caution and admits her attraction to him had to do with unresolved issues with her own father.

> Bulldog · *Dan Butler*
> Carrie · *Sara Melson*
> Rachel · *Reba McEntire (voice-over)*

22 "FRASIER CRANE'S DAY OFF"

WRITERS: Chuck Ranberg & Anne Flett-Giordano

DIRECTOR: James Burrows

The one time in three years that Dr. Niles Crane went on the KACL airwaves, due to Frasier's bad case of the paranoia blues. Food critic Gil Chesterton fills in for Frasier when he gets the flu, but Frasier becomes convinced that Gil is after his time slot. So Frasier sends in someone he can trust, Niles, to do his show. Niles does a fine job, so good that now Frasier believes Niles is after his job too. Frasier's more determined than ever to get back on the air. He writes himself a couple of prescriptions and sends Daphne to get them filled. A doped-up Frasier appears at KACL. He locks Roz and Niles out of the booth and goes on the air. He's so doped up—he forgets a caller's name and tells another her problem is boring—that security comes to take him away. Frasier awakes in his bedroom and thinks that what happened was all a dream. Daphne says it was. She'll tell him it all really happened tomorrow when he's good and lucid.

Gil Chesterton · *Edward Hibbert*
Marjorie · *Mary Tyler Moore (voice-over)*
Janice · *Patricia Hearst (voice-over)*
Howard · *Steve Lawrence (voice-over)*
Lois · *Eydie Gorme (voice-over)*
Robert · *Tommy Hilfiger (voice-over)*
Louis · *Garry Trudeau (voice-over)*
Blake · *Steve Young (voice-over)*

23 "TRAVELS WITH MARTIN"

WRITERS: Linda Morris & Vic Rauseo

DIRECTOR: James Burrows

The famous Winnebago episode, when Frasier, Martin, Daphne, and Niles hit the open road in a motor home, destined for Mount Rushmore, but instead find themselves across the border in Canada—where British citizen Daphne is not allowed to tread. She doesn't have her green card yet, and after Martin slips the RV into Canada while she was sleeping, she awakes and fears she'll never get back into the United States. Martin says they'll just smuggle her back in. But they do get pulled over at the border. Niles is all business, Frasier babbles, and Daphne can only say "sure" with an American accent. They are less than convincing. Martin flashes his police badge and then confesses that Eddie doesn't have a rabies certificate. The border guard buys it and they're free.

Guard · *Don Amendolia*
Marvella · *Pamela Gordon*

24 "MY COFFEE WITH NILES"

WRITERS: David Angell & Peter Casey

DIRECTOR: James Burrows

One of the more unusual episodes of *Frasier*, and a favorite among the writer-producers, in which Frasier meets Niles at Café Nervosa upon the one-year anniversary of Frasier's move to Seattle, and they do nothing but chat for twenty-two minutes. Besides their talk about personal happiness and ethics, the comedy moments come from the waitress, who keeps bringing coffee orders to Frasier, only to have him find something wrong with them. She finally brings him a Zimbabwe, decaf, nonfat, no-cinnamon coffee. "Now . . . are you happy?" Frasier ponders this, then responds: "You know, in the grand scheme of things, yes, I'd say I am."

Waitress · *Luck Hari*

Second Season

25 "THE UNKINDEST CUT OF ALL"
WRITER: Dave Hackel

DIRECTOR: Rick Beren

The Neuter Show. When Eddie gets a neighbor's dog pregnant, the owner wants Eddie to get fixed. Martin says he'll do it, but Frasier later discovers that Martin didn't take Eddie to his vet appointment. He believes his father has a psychological block against the operation. So Niles and Frasier try to round Eddie up—using French in case Eddie is onto what they're doing—and Frasier takes him to the vet's. As Frasier and Eddie await their turn, Martin comes in, furious at Frasier. It's his dog and Frasier should mind his business. Eddie runs out the door. Martin, his cop pals, and Frasier search Seattle for the missing Eddie. At the park, Frasier and Martin have a heart-to-heart about respect and authority, and Frasier admits he wouldn't have been able to go through with the operation anyway. And Eddie returns.

> Mrs. Greenway · *Jo De Winter*
> Father · *Joel Anderson*
> Rita · *Lily Tomlin (voice-over)*

26 "SLOW TANGO IN SOUTH SEATTLE"
WRITER: Martin Weiss

DIRECTOR: James Burrows

An old acquaintance bases a *Bridges of Madison County* type novella on a long-ago fling that Frasier had with his piano teacher. After he discovers Roz reading *Slow Tango in South Seattle*, Frasier tells her he knew the author, Thomas Jay Fallow, from his Cheers days, and actually helped him through his writer's block. Fallow has taken an incident from Frasier's life—an affair with his piano teacher when he was seventeen—and turned it into a book. On KACL's *Book Chat* show, Fallow says the inspiration for the book came from God. Frasier confronts him, makes him cry, and Fallow acknowledges his debt to Frasier on the air. Still, Frasier is left unsatisfied. Niles think Frasier is looking for closure, and suggests that he make amends with his piano teacher, Clarice. Frasier goes to her house and finds a hard-of-hearing woman who appears to be in her late seventies. She doesn't remember Frasier, but after he explains, she forgives him. Then the real Clarice enters, a stunning woman in her mid-fifties, who doesn't look a day over forty. Frasier apologizes to her and she apologizes for short-changing him on his lessons. Frasier then asks her out again, but she gives him a zinger when she announces that she wasn't interested in forty-year-old men then and still isn't. She leaves, and Frasier is left with the advances of Clarice's mom.

Bulldog · *Dan Butler*
Clarice · *Constance Towers*
Mrs. Warner · *Myra Carter*
Gil Chesterton · *Edward Hibbert*
Thomas Jay Fallow · *John O'Hurley*
Amber Edwards · *Susan Brown*
Date · *David Sederholm*
Steven · *James Spader (voice-over)*

27 "DUKE'S, WE HARDLY KNEW YE"
WRITERS: Linda Morris & Vic Rauseo

DIRECTOR: James Burrows

Frasier and Niles are investors in a company that plans to tear down Martin's favorite bar and replace it with a mini-mall. Because Niles's investments are paying off, Niles comes over and suggests that he and Frasier go out and celebrate. Martin suggests the boys meet them at Duke's for a beer after dinner. They've never been invited to Duke's with their dad before and they're thrilled. Martin makes a toast to all his pals at Duke's. He is going to miss everybody. Duke's is being torn down by some rat-face bastards putting up a mini-mall. Later on, Frasier and Niles feel quite guilty about being investors, but they can't get out of it. They agree not to tell Dad about it, but later that night, Frasier can't sleep and spills the beans to Martin. Martin's not too upset, but seizes the opportunity to go back to Duke's one more time. Frasier and Martin sing "Danny Boy," swap stories and say good-bye to Duke's. Niles arrives, and says he is going to face down the bulldozers. He isn't going to let Duke's be destroyed. The wrecking ball comes crashing through the wall, and Niles wonders who is he to stand in the way of progress.

Duke · *John La Motta*
Joe · *Jack Wallace*
Leo · *Bill Gratton*

---

28 ''THE MATCHMAKER''
WRITER: Joe Keenan

DIRECTOR: David Lee

One of the all-time classic *Frasier* episodes, and certainly the most honored (Emmy, DGA, WGA, and GLAAD awards) in which Frasier tries to set up his gay boss with Daphne. It begins when Daphne complains to Frasier about her dating slump. Frasier meets his new station manager Tom, a young, good-looking guy from Britain, and he tries to solve his Daphne problem by inviting Tom over for dinner. Little does he realize that Tom is gay, and when Tom mentions his orientation to Roz, she doesn't feel like clueing in Frasier. At home, Daphne is angry about being set up, but Frasier tells her that Tom doesn't even know she's going to be there, so there's no pressure. Tom meets Martin and Daphne, and Daphne is thrilled with him. Tom gets the idea that Martin is also gay, and when he meets Niles, he's convinced that all the Crane boys are gay. Daphne goes to put on some music, and Tom asks Frasier if there could be a little one-on-one time. Frasier kicks out Martin and Niles and encourages Daphne to get ready. On the way, Niles tells Frasier he's learned that Tom is gay and there for Frasier. Once Frasier understands the situation, he comes clean to Tom, says he had no idea he was gay, and Tom goes home, asking Frasier to apologize to Daphne for him. (Trivia note: Based on his performance in this episode, Eric Lutes's first-ever TV appearance, NBC cast the actor as the costar of "Caroline in the City.")

Tom Duran   ·   *Eric Lutes*

29 "FLOUR CHILD"
WRITER: Christopher Lloyd

DIRECTOR: James Burrows

Niles's biological clock is ticking. He thinks he wants to have a child, but he's not sure he's ready. Frasier tells Niles about an experiment to demonstrate the responsibility of being a parent—carrying around a ten-pound sack of flour for a week. Niles thinks it's a good idea, and proceeds to parade around Seattle with his flour-baby. By the end, Niles decides he may want to wait a little longer for fatherhood.

Arleen   ·   *Charlayne Woodard*
Clarence   ·   *Aaron Heyman*
Mary   ·   *Linda Porter*
Putnam   ·   *Alvy Moore*
Mother   ·   *Robin Krieger*
Maggie   ·   *Amy Madigan (voice-over)*

30 "THE CANDIDATE"
WRITERS: Chuck Ranberg & Anne Flett-Giordano

DIRECTOR: James Burrows

It's liberal versus conservative and reality versus outer-space alien stories, in the episode where Frasier and Niles support the opponent of Martin's favorite candidate for local office, a hard-core conservative. Frasier even goes as far as deciding to film a TV endorsement for candidate Phil Patterson, but before he gets set to go before the cameras, Patterson admits to Frasier that he was abducted by aliens and taken to a spaceship for a kind of conference before the campaign. Frasier barely makes it through the commercial, but after discussing it with Niles, they agree that Patterson is still a better alternative to Thorpe. But the next day, Bulldog says that Patterson's thing with the aliens is all over the news. Frasier, irate at the media, storms into the booth and gets on the radio to defend Patterson and tells Seattle about his intergalactic conversation. Only problem is that Patterson's trouble was about having illegal aliens work for him. And Thorpe wins by a landslide.

Bulldog · *Dan Butler*
Phil Patterson · *Boyd Gaines*
Waitress · *Luck Hari*
Director · *Jack Tate*
Boy · *Christopher Walberg*
Holden Thorpe · *Sydney Pollack (voice-over)*

31 "THE BOTCHED LANGUAGE OF CRANES"

WRITER: Joe Keenan

DIRECTOR: David Lee

Frasier's advice to a depressed listener prompts a deluge of criticism when he puts down the city of Seattle. Martin says that Frasier should apologize, but Frasier refuses. He continues to take the same stand after fifty calls come into KACL complaining about him. But after going on the air and doing nothing but defend himself for three hours, Frasier finally apologizes and signs off. In the old "Frasier Puts His Foot in His Mouth When the Mike Is Still On" bit, Frasier complains about all the whiny crybabies in Seattle. Naturally, the negative calls build and Roz suggests that Frasier emcee the St. Bart's benefit as a chance to redeem himself in the public eye by helping sick people and telling a few jokes. Frasier agrees and calls Father Mike to get some jokes that won't offend. At the banquet, Frasier is so nervous that he leaves the room to be sick. Father Mike addresses the crowd and says that the bishop was fishing, his boat capsized, and he is missing. Frasier comes back in the room and proceeds to tell a joke about a bishop on the *Titanic*. The room is not amused.

Bulldog · *Dan Butler*
Father Mike · *George Deloy*
Sister Joselia · *Helen Geller*
Edna · *Alfre Woodard (voice-over)*
Connie · *Sandra Dee (voice-over)*

32 ''ADVENTURES IN PARADISE (PART 1)''

WRITERS: Ken Levine & David Isaacs

DIRECTOR: James Burrows

The second Lilith sighting, in a two-part November sweeps special that took place on the island of Bora Bora, where Frasier and Lilith spent their honeymoon. It begins when Frasier discovers a photo of clothswear designer Madeline Marshall in an issue of *Seattle Magazine* and asks her out. The blind date goes very well, and two weeks later, Frasier tells Roz that Madeline may be the one for him. Madeline arrives at the station and tells Frasier the time has come for them to go away together. Frasier suggests Bora Bora. They arrive at their hotel and have a beautiful room with a large bed. Frasier steps onto the balcony while Madeline undresses, and from the adjoining balcony there is a familiar woman's voice. "Lilith!" a man yells. Frasier screams. To be continued.

Lilith · *Bebe Neuwirth*
Madeline · *JoBeth Williams*
Bulldog · *Dan Butler*
Ettienne · *Pierre Epstein*
Mother · *Kirsten Devere*
Yvette · *Jessica Bennington*

Busboy · *Rick Schatz*
Chester · *Art Garfunkel (voice-over)*

---

33 "ADVENTURES IN PARADISE (PART 2)"

WRITERS: **Ken Levine & David Isaacs**
DIRECTOR: **James Burrows**

In Bora Bora, Frasier discovers that Lilith is in the next hut with her date Brian. He introduces Madeline to them and they decide to diffuse the awkwardness of the situation by having dinner together. Later they go to their huts and Frasier says he can't have a passionate week with Lilith next door and wants to leave. Madeline refuses. After dinner, Madeline is trying to get romantic, but Frasier obsesses over Lilith and Brian. He thinks they're having sex in the next room. As Madeline takes a shower, Frasier jumps up and down on the bed and groans and howls in mock ecstasy. Meanwhile, Lilith and Brian appear at the window from a walk on the beach and Madeline enters from her shower. Frasier's humiliated, and Madeline leaves. Back in Seattle, he apologizes to her on the air and she calls in and accepts. They go out for dinner and come back to Frasier's apartment, where she says she was involved with a divorced man once before he went back to his ex-wife. She doesn't want to go through that again. Frasier assures her that Lilith is out of his life. Madeline goes to the bathroom, and wouldn't you know it, Lilith shows up again. This is too much for Madeline, who leaves. Lilith tells Frasier that Brian has asked her to marry him. Frasier gives his blessing. Meanwhile, back at Bora Bora with Madeline, Frasier hears a voice on the balcony. It belongs to Diane Chambers. Frasier wakes up. He's been dreaming again. He's actually in Bora Bora with Niles.

Lilith · *Bebe Neuwirth*
Madeline · *JoBeth Williams*
Brian · *James Morrison*
Diane Chambers · *Shelley Long*
Vic · *Kevin Bacon (voice-over)*

34 "BURYING A GRUDGE"

WRITER: David Lloyd

DIRECTOR: Andy Ackerman

Maris goes to the hospital for a face-lift, and Frasier notices Martin's old partner Artie in another room. He had some tests and the results weren't good. Martin and Artie had a big falling out and haven't spoken in years. Martin doesn't want to go see Artie because he didn't go see Martin when he was in the hospital. Frasier convinces him to change his mind, and once Martin gets into the room, he and Artie start arguing. Turns out the bad blood started when Artie spread a rumor at the station house that Martin cried during the movie *Brian's Song.* Martin responded that Artie's wife had a rump the size of Albuquerque. At home, Daphne and Frasier shame Martin into going back and apologizing to Artie. Artie appreciates Martin making the first step and thanks him for coming in. They agree to go fishing together when Artie gets out of the hospital.

Artie · *Lincoln Kilpatrick*
Nurse · *Lynne Adams*
Dr. Sternstein · *Paul Kent*
Linda · *Betty Comden (voice-over)*
Walter · *Adolph Green (voice-over)*

35 "SEAT OF POWER"

WRITER: Steven Levitan

DIRECTOR: James Burrows

The "What if Frasier and Niles Became Plumbers?" episode. It begins when Martin asks Frasier to fix his leaky toilet. Frasier prepares to call a plumber, but Martin convinces him to fix it on his own. Niles arrives and the two decide it will be good practical experence for both of them. But naturally, once they're done, the toilet starts to overflow. So Frasier calls the plumber, who turns out to be Danny Kriezel, and it seems their savior is the same bully who terrorized Niles as a kid. In fact, he used to flush

Niles's head in the toilet. Frasier says Danny's brother Billy used to do the same thing to him. Old feelings come back to haunt, and Niles decides to have a chat with Danny, who doesn't recognize him. Niles gets more upset the longer he speaks to Danny, who hasn't changed much, and goes to dunk Danny's head in the toilet, but Frasier stops him. Niles and Danny go into the living room to talk, while Frasier and Billy are left in the bathroom. Billy talks about the kid he used to pick on (Frasier) and laughingly goes into every detail. Frasier moves in to dunk Billy's head in the toilet. Meanwhile, thanks to Niles's calm, rational discussion with Danny, he discovers that by being a bully, he was misdirecting anger toward his father. Danny thanks Niles, but gives the credit to Frasier for convincing him to talk things out. Billy chases Frasier out of the apartment.

Danny · *John C. McGinley*
Billy · *Mike Starr*
Elliott · *Macaulay Culkin (voice-over)*

36   ''ROZ IN THE DOGHOUSE''

WRITERS: Chuck Ranberg & Anne Flett-Giordano

DIRECTOR: James Burrows

Bulldog asks Roz to produce his sports show, but Frasier is convinced that this is just another ploy for him to get Roz into bed. Roz is offended by Frasier's put-downs of her talents and she quits. Frasier's show goes to hell, as Fraser waits for the inevitable—for Roz to return to him. But it doesn't happen overnight. Frasier begins to worry that Roz will never return. Martin suggests Frasier apologize. At Roz's apartment, Roz and Bulldog are working on their show. Bulldog pinches a nerve and Roz massages his shoulders. Bulldog gets the wrong idea and strips down when Roz is out of the room. Roz throws Bulldog out, and there standing at the door is Frasier with a huge bouquet of orchids.

Bulldog · *Dan Butler*
Gil Chesterton · *Edward Hibbert*
Bruce · *Garrett Maggart*
Ed · *Edward T. Gallick*
Marie · *Carly Simon (voice-over)*
Francesca · *Rosie Perez (voice-over)*

37 "RETIREMENT IS MURDER"

WRITERS: Elias Davis & David Pollock

DIRECTOR: Alan Myerson

Martin is obsessed with solving the "Weeping Lotus" murder, a case he has been unable to solve for years. Martin promised the murdered woman's mother that he'd find the killer. She called him recently and lit a fire under him. Frasier concludes that the trained monkey from Las Vegas did it. Frasier doesn't want to solve the case that Martin worked on for such a long time, so he arranges the evidence to let Martin come up with the same conclusion. Martin presents his theory at the police station. Frasier starts to second-guess the monkey theory and worries that Martin will be a laughingstock. Martin arrives home, and Frasier apologizes for putting the theory into his head in the first place. A detective arrives and tells Martin that they apprehended the killer. A group of cops comes to celebrate with Martin. While Frasier is in the kitchen, Martin tells how he concluded that it was the corrupt vice cop. Frasier comes back in and Martin gives some of the credit to him. Frasier pompously tells how he concluded the monkey did it and becomes the laughingstock.

Bulldog · *Dan Butler*
Frank · *Ron Dean*
Leo · *Bill Gratton*
Al · *Hal Porter*
Fan · *Randy Kovitz*
Marjorie · *Mary Steenburgen (voice-over)*

38 "YOU SCRATCH MY BOOK . . ."
WRITER: Joe Keenan

DIRECTOR: Andy Ackerman

Frasier isn't thinking straight when he agrees to pen the foreword to a new book by an attractive pop psychologist, Dr. Honey Snow, the author of the popular tome *Don't Change, You're Perfect.* Frasier meets Dr. Snow when fan Daphne asks Frasier to stop by the Book Nook at lunchtime and have Dr. Honey sign a book for her. Not only does she sign, she also invites Frasier to dinner. A few nights later, Dr. Honey asks Frasier to write the foreword to her new book. He doesn't want to, but with her looks, he can't refuse. Weeks later, Frasier is still struggling with the foreword, but has a hard time ethically because he can't really recommend it. This tears him up, because he's so attracted to her physically. At Dr. Honey's apartment, Frasier eventually confesses that he doesn't think it's a good book and doesn't want his name on it. Dr. Honey is turned on by his honesty. So Frasier pours on the put-downs until it finally gets too much, and she kicks him out, telling him he won't be getting any "honey."

Dr. Honey Snow   ·   *Shannon Tweed*
Fan   ·   *Laura Waterbury*

39 "THE CLUB"
WRITERS: Elias Davis & David Pollock

DIRECTOR: David Lee

It's another contest between the brothers as both Niles and Frasier vie for the two openings in Seattle's exclusive Empire Club. They go to the club to be interviewed and make a nice impression, and both support each other until they find out that in reality, there is only one open position. Niles tells members about Frasier's suicide attempt and Frasier tells about the time when Niles mooned President Nixon. Niles and Frasier stop speaking to each other, but Frasier apologizes. All is well until they find that Frasier got in—and Niles didn't. Frasier feels guilty, since Niles wanted it so much more than he did, and goes to the Empire Club to persuade them to take Niles instead. When Niles discovers that big brother has gone to fight his battles, he runs down to the club, where we learn that they made a mistake—they wanted the Crane who wasn't in show business. Before Frasier can correct the situation, Niles enters, calls the club boss "fuzzy," and says he'd rather spend time in a bus station than in the club. When he learns the truth, Niles grovels and apologizes, but is carried out the door by a large waiter.

Mr. Drake · *W. Morgan Sheppard*
Mr. Spencer · *Mitchell Edmonds*
Wentworth · *Jim Norton*
Sid · *Gary Sinise (voice-over)*

40 "FOOL ME ONCE, SHAME ON YOU"

WRITER: Christopher Lloyd
DIRECTOR: Philip Charles MacKenzie

Frasier's briefcase is stolen, and with it, his identity. On the radio, he pleads with the person who stole it to please return it, no questions asked. Not only does the person show up to meet Frasier at the Café Nervosa, but since his car keys are in the briefcase, he comes to the Café and drives away in Frasier's car before the two can meet. Martin calls his police buddies to help find the perpertrator. At the radio station, a woman calls who went out with a man passing himself off as Frasier, and she cancels their date. Frasier is more determined than ever to find the imposter. He finds out where they were going to meet. At the bar, Frasier makes conversation with a woman who listens to his show. But she thinks that Frasier is the impersonator and leaves. Frasier spots the real con man, Phil, and confronts him at a bar. Phil doesn't have a sob story for why he is the way he is. He's just lazy. Frasier thinks that Phil wanted to get caught, that he's not happy in his life. Meanwhile, the woman brings a cop into the bar and demands that they arrest our man Frasier for imper-sonation. Phil shows his ID and Frasier is carried away.

Phil · *Nathan Lane*
Heather · *Joan McMurtrey*
Priest · *Bernard Kuby*
Customer · *Karen Person*
Cop · *James Willett*
Waiter · *Paul Cusimano*

41 ''DAPHNE'S ROOM''

WRITERS: Linda Morris & Vic Rauseo
DIRECTOR: David Lee

Frasier is the "Shower Boy" in another *Frasier* physical comedy classic that begins with our hero going into Daphne's room to look for a lost book. Daphne suddenly walks in and an embarrassed Frasier runs out—clutching Daphne's prescription bottle of pills. At dinner, Daphne, not hiding the fact that she's mad at Frasier, takes her meal into her room. Frasier goes to apologize and says he'll never go into her room again. She forgives him. But later, Frasier realizes that he still has the prescription bottle in his pocket. While Daphne goes into Martin's room, Frasier tries to return the bottle. Daphne comes back and Frasier hides in her closet. He tries to sneak out while she's in the bathroom, but she reenters and he is forced to dive under the bed. Then, cornered, Frasier runs into the bathroom, followed by Daphne, who starts to take a shower. Daphne scolds Eddie for licking her toilet bowl, calling him "sick." Frasier thinks she's talking to him, says he's sorry, and is caught. Later, Martin tells Frasier that Daphne is thinking of quitting and that he'd better do something. Frasier agrees to pay for the redecorating of her room and promises, once again, to never go in there again. She deserves to have a place to call her own. Later on, Niles comes over and runs into Daphne's room to scare Frasier—Frasier follows to get him out. They spill sherry on the bed and knock over lacy underthings and jewelry. Martin and Eddie help them straighten it up, and Daphne walks in on them all. To make up, Frasier buys Daphne a shiny new Mercedes convertible.

42 "THE SHOW WHERE SAM SHOWS UP"

WRITERS: Ken Levine & David Isaacs

DIRECTOR: James Burrows

Cheers sighting number two—Frasier's old romantic nemesis Sam Malone. He comes to Seattle and needs Frasier's advice on getting married. Frasier thinks that Sam really wants to marry Sheila, but that he is scared. It means letting go of his old self and he's afraid to do that. He convinces Sam to take the plunge. The next day Sam introduces Sheila to Frasier, Roz, and Niles at the Café Nervosa. Frasier realizes he slept with Sheila three months ago. Frasier goes to their hotel room to see Sam, but just Sheila is there, and they have an awkward conversation about sex. She's a sexual compulsive, like Sam, she tells Frasier, but she wants to make the marriage work. They agree not to tell him about Sheila and Frasier's night together. Sam shows up and admits to Sheila that he was unfaithful to her once before and that they need to start their marriage on an honest footing. She reveals that she once slept with another fellow—Cliff from Cheers—and upon hearing that, Sam calls the wedding off. And Frasier is dumbstruck. He was with a woman who slept with Cliff?

Sam Malone · *Ted Danson*
Sheila · *Tea Leoni*

43 "THE INNKEEPERS"

WRITER: David Lloyd

DIRECTOR: James Burrows

Another must addition to the *Frasier* all-time top 10 list, when Frasier and Niles decide to go into the restaurant business together as the owners of

"Les Frères Heureux." Frasier and Niles act as hosts to their guests on opening night, and ride herd over the chefs on the proper way to prepare fine food. Through the course of the evening, Frasier and Niles mistakenly knock out two waiters, take over for the chef when he quits, and draft Daphne to work in the kitchen, Martin to tend bar, and Roz to wait tables. By the end the sprinkler system goes off accidentally, everyone gets soaked, and the valet mistakenly drives someone's car through the restaurant wall.

Bulldog · *Dan Butler*
Gil Chesterton · *Edward Hibbert*
Owner · *Mike Nussbaum*
Otto · *Nathan Davis*
Brad · *Diedrich Bader*
Maurice · *Jay Bell*
Sous-chef · *Alan Shearman*
Waiter · *Robert Lee Jacobs*
Bartender · *Tom Hewitt*
Customer · *Deborah Lacey*

44 "AN AFFAIR TO FORGET"

WRITERS: Chuck Ranberg & Anne Flett-Giordano
DIRECTOR: Philip Charles MacKenzie

The top 10 list continues with the classic (and Emmy-winning) fencing episode. It begins when Frasier gets a call from a woman who suspects that her fencing-instructor husband is having an affair with his client. Frasier is convinced the caller is referring to Maris. Frasier tells the caller to confront her husband. Off the air, Roz counsels Frasier to confront Maris. And so he does, making a long speech about the perils of having an affair to Maris in her sensory deprivation tank, only to discover that brother Niles is in there. Later on, Niles confronts fencing instructor Gunnar, telling him "You stole my wife," through Frasier through Marta the maid. (Gunnar speaks German, Marta speaks German and Spanish, and Frasier speaks Spanish and translates to Niles.) Gunnar and Niles deal with the situation by taking up swords to fight for their woman. Gunnar wins and demands that Niles apologize for saying he stole his shoes. (That's what Gunnar thought the whole thing was about.) Once all is cleared up, Gunnar reveals that he wanted an affair with Maris, but that she turned him down because her heart belongs to Niles.

Gunnar   ·   *Brian Cousins*
Marta   ·   *Irene Olga Lopez*
Gretchen   ·   *Glenne Headley*

45 "AGENTS IN AMERICA, PART THREE"

WRITER: Joe Keenan

DIRECTOR: Philip Charles MacKenzie

Frasier gets a generous 8 percent raise on his new KACL contract, but his agent Bebe urges him not to take it, saying other stations in the market will pay him much more. Bebe counsels Frasier to have a sickout until KACL comes up with more money. The station responds by painting over Frasier's parking space, cleaning out his cubicle, and auditioning replacements. Frasier begins to freak, as Bebe calls the station manager and demands they renegotiate by midnight. Minutes before the clock strikes twelve, Frasier wants to hear about the other offers. Turns out there aren't any. Bebe admits it was a bluff. Frasier thinks she has ruined him. But thankfully, the call finally does come and the negotiations will begin tomorrow. The next morning, it appears that Frasier has slept with Bebe, and he knows what he's done is wrong. He breaks it off and Bebe leaves to begin the negotiations. At the Café Nervosa, Frasier learns that Bebe is on the ledge at KACL, threatening to jump. Frasier rushes to the station and tells Bebe he's not worth dying over. Bebe confides that it is just a negotiating tactic for publicity. Frasier saves her in front of the news cameras, and the station manager lets Frasier know that they're not letting him go. Bebe has lied, seduced, and shamelessly manipulated Frasier, the news media, and the entire city of Seattle. Frasier is glad she's on his side.

Bulldog · *Dan Butler*
Bebe Glazer · *Harriet Sansom Harris*
Tom Duran · *Eric Lutes*
Mike · *Tony Crane*

---

46 "SOMEONE TO WATCH OVER ME"

WRITER: Don Seigel

DIRECTOR: James Burrows

Frasier becomes convinced a fan is stalking him and hires a pretty body-guard to watch over him when he makes an appearance as a nominee at the Seattle SeaBea broadcasting awards. It the end, it was much ado about nothing, as Kari, who professes to be Frasier's number one fan, is but a harmless elderly lady.

Bulldog · *Dan Butler*
Cindy Carruthers · *Alyson Reed*
Kari · *Renee Lippin*
Mrs. Littlejohn · *Rita McKenzie*
Madman Martinez · *John Lithgow (voice-over)*

---

47 "BREAKING THE ICE"

WRITER: Steven Levitan

DIRECTOR: Philip Charles MacKenzie

An episode about the words "I love you." Roz tells Frasier that the night before, in the throes of passion, she told her date "I love you." Her date didn't say it back. Frasier says some people just never say it—his own father Martin, for instance, never has told Frasier he loves him. At home, Martin is planning his annual ice-fishing trip with Duke. Duke calls to cancel, and Martin forgives him by saying "I love ya." Martin needs some-one else to go with him on the trip and Niles agrees to go. Later, Frasier notices Martin saying "I love you" to Eddie. Frasier wants to hear Martin say it to him. Frasier joins the guys for the trip. Out on the ice, amidst the bickering, they start drinking and singing. Frasier tells Martin the reason he came on the trip was to hear him say "I love you" to his son. Martin resists, but finally gives in.

Ranger   ·   *Rick Cramer*

48   "DARK VICTORY"

WRITERS: Christopher Lloyd and Linda Morris & Vic Rauseo

DIRECTOR: James Burrows

Daphne and Martin are at each other's throats. She wants him to do his exercises, he calls her a nag, and Frasier tries to quiet them. Roz arrives and gives Martin a birthday present—a six-pack of beer. Niles is furious at Frasier. The woman on the radio that day whom Frasier advised to think about changing therapists was a patient of Niles and she has left him. Everybody snipes at each other and Roz leaves. Martin, wanting to put the party to an end as soon as possible, blows the candle out on his cake. There is a power outage all over south Seattle. Roz can't go any-where, so she returns to the apartment. Frasier suggests they all make the best of it and play a game called "I'm the dullest person." Another fight erupts, driving Roz onto the balcony, Niles home, and Martin to bed. The people who are left at the party tell their troubles to Frasier, and after he counsels them, he comes to realize that at the end of the week, he's been helping people every day, comes home to his family and has to help them too, and now he just wants a few minutes for himself. After the blackout ends, everybody wants to go to a party downstairs, but Frasier declines the invite. He just wants to be alone. They leave for the party, and Eddie jumps up next to Frasier to have his belly rubbed.

Curtis   ·   *Josh Adell*
Caroline   ·   *Shelley Duvall (voice-over)*

Third Season

49 ''MARTIN DOES IT HIS WAY''
WRITER: David Lloyd

DIRECTOR: Philip Charles MacKenzie

Frasier prepares to give the eulogy for his great-aunt Louise, who specifically asked for her favorite nephew to do so, despite the fact that Frasier hated her. Meanwhile, Martin looks back on her life as an example of unfulfilled dreams, and tells about his shoe box full of half-finished songs that he penned, hoping to sell them one day to Frank Sinatra.

Frasier and Niles sit at the piano with Martin to help him realize his dream. The good news is that the song gets finished. The bad news is that Sinatra's people reject it. The show ends with Frasier's respectful eulogy, and a rousing rendition of Martin's new song, ''She's Such a Groovy Lady,'' backed by the congregation.

Fred   ·   *Harper Roisman*
Minister   ·   *Tom Troupe*
Eileen   ·   *Mary Elizabeth Mastrantonio (voice-over)*

50 ''SHE'S THE BOSS''
WRITERS: Chuck Ranberg & Anne Flett-Giordano

DIRECTOR: Philip Charles MacKenzie

Kate Costas, the new station manager, takes over, and she and Frasier mix like oil and water. She has several ideas on how to improve the show, and Frasier disagrees with them all. Their bickering is colored with a silly disagreement regarding the particular key of a Bartók concerto. But more importantly, for refusing her suggestions on how to improve his ratings, Kate punishes Frasier by banishing him to the dreaded 2:00–6:00 A.M. time slot. Frasier retaliates by doing nothing but talk about sex during his show, and that sparks further arguments. Finally, Frasier gets his old time slot back and they agree to see eye to eye on station business.

Kate Costas · *Mercedes Ruehl*
Bulldog · *Dan Butler*
Gil Chesterton · *Edward Hibbert*
Keith · *Tom Hulce (voice-over)*
Mark · *Matthew Broderick (voice-over)*
Phyliss · *Carrie Fisher (voice-over)*
Jill · *Teri Garr (voice-over)*

51 "SHRINK RAP"

WRITER: Christopher Lloyd

DIRECTOR: David Lee

Frasier and Niles wind up in couples' therapy after their disastrous foray into a side-by-side partnership in the psychotherapy business. An episode with several flashbacks, opening with the brothers trying to salvage their relationship at Dr. Schacter's office, continues with Frasier yearning to expand beyond his talk radio base. Niles offers Frasier the opportunity to be a real psychiatrist again and share his office space. Naturally, chaos ensues, with arguments over the placement of a plant in the office and the printing of Frasier's name on the door (he feels it's slightly smaller than Niles's). Everything comes to a head when Frasier observes Niles's therapy group. He naturally can't resist butting in, and the two of them erupt into a huge argument in front of the patients.

Bulldog · *Dan Butler*
Dr. Schachter · *Milo O'Shea*
Jill · *Blair Brown (voice-over)*

52 "POLICE STORY"

WRITER: Sy Rosen

DIRECTOR: Philip Charles MacKenzie

Frasier is pulled over for speeding by a good-looking female officer. ("I'm Dr. Frasier Crane," he says, "I'm listening," when handing over his driver's license.) Frasier finds himself attracted to the woman, and has his father, through his police connections, find out who she is. Together, they go looking for her at a police hangout, where, when Frasier leaves to get beers for the three of them, she turns the tables by asking Martin out on a date.

For seemingly the first time, Martin asks Niles for advice, and his son suggests dating her first to gauge his interest before telling Frasier so as not to hurt him unnecessarily. Martin takes the lady up on the date, and trouble brews when Frasier decides to go to the hangout in search of the cop, only to find her sharing a table with his father.

Maureen Cutler · *Jane Kaczmarek*
Waitress · *Luck Hari*
Charlotte · *Jillie Mack*
Maggie · *Denise Poirer*
Elizabeth · *Bette Rae*

53 ''LEAPIN' LIZARDS''

WRITERS: Chuck Ranberg & Anne Flett-Giordano

DIRECTOR: Philip Charles MacKenzie

Fed up with Bulldog's childish pranks and told to "get a sense of humor" by his boss, Frasier decides to retaliate. Armed with the discovery of Bulldog's paralyzing fear of lizards, he plants one in the contest prize drum from which the reptile-phobic prankster will choose a winning postcard. But when it is Kate who pulls out the winning card, Frasier and Roz watch in horror as the lizard bites her finger. She vows revenge for the unknown assailant as she vents to the presumably innocent Frasier from her hospital bed. His conscience gets the best of him, and as her pain medication takes effect, he confesses. As Kate drifts off, he thinks he's in the clear. He's wrong.

Bulldog · *Dan Butler*
Pete · *Michael Whaley*
Kate Costas · *Mercedes Ruehl*

Susan Rosen   ·   *Jodi Taffell*
Jack   ·   *Billy Crystal (voice-over)*
Rob   ·   *Ed Harris (voice-over)*

54   "KISSES SWEETER THAN WINE"

WRITER: Anne Flett-Giordano

DIRECTOR: Philip Charles MacKenzie

When Frasier enlists the services of a contractor to take a scratch out of his floor the day he is to host a wine tasting, the minor buffing job turns into a major catastrophe, when the contractor takes the entire apartment apart. Minutes before the tasting, Frasier's home is up to code but still a shambles. Martin's quick thinking and his sons' cash send the workmen into high speed and settle Frasier's rattled nerves, just in time.

Joe DeCarlo   ·   *Jon Carreiro*
Painter   ·   *Kevin Weisman*
Electrician   ·   *Kev O'Neil*
Bruce   ·   *Peter Siragusa*
Marilyn   ·   *Brooke Adams (voice-over)*

55   "SLEEPING WITH THE ENEMY"

WRITERS: Linda Morris & Vic Rauseo

DIRECTOR: Jeff Melman

When Kate nixes annual 5 percent raises, the staff is in an uproar. Frasier finds himself leading the employees' revolt, even though he and the rest of the on-air talent are unaffected by the decision. With his father's help, Frasier convinces the rest of the on-air talent to back the staff in getting their deserved raises back from the woman Roz calls the "Nazi in nylons." But negotiations take an unexpected turn when Frasier goes into Kate's office to demand decent raises for the staff and ends up in a heated embrace with his boss. By the end of the show, they've settled on 4 percent raises for all.

Noel Shempsky · *Patrick Kerr*
Kate Costas · *Mercedes Ruehl*
Bulldog · *Dan Butler*
Gil Chesterton · *Edward Hibbert*
June · *Laura Dern (voice-over)*

56 ''THE ADVENTURES OF BAD BOY AND DIRTY GIRL''

WRITER: Joe Keenan

DIRECTOR: Philip Charles MacKenzie

Part two of "Sleeping with the Enemy," in which Frasier and Kate worry about how far to take their office romance. Both agree to slow things down, but unfortunately, their animal attraction to each other takes over, and all alone in Frasier's radio booth, they engage in the sexual act. All of Seattle learns what's happening at the KACL studios when Kate inadvertently hits the mike button by mistake, and listeners hear Frasier admitting he enjoys feeling like a "bad boy" and Kate that she likes being a "dirty girl." The big question in Seattle the next day is exactly who the "dirty girl" is, but Frasier won't tell. (As noted by the local paper: "I Won't Fink, Says Kinky Shrink.") Once again, Kate and Frasier agree to cool things down, but then they get stuck on a freight elevator together, which just happens to have a bed, and things get hot and heavy again.

Kate Costas · *Mercedes Ruehl*
Bulldog · *Dan Butler*
Dierdre Sauvage · *Pamela Kosh*
Moving Man · *Harris Laskawy*
Polly · *Cyd Charisse (voice-over)*

57 "THE LAST TIME I SAW MARIS"

WRITER: Ian Gurvitz

DIRECTOR: Philip Charles MacKenzie

Maris is missing and Niles is in a panic. Martin's cop buddies discover her in New York on a shopping spree, but she neglected to leave Niles a note. Her husband is relieved, but Frasier butts in, points out how inconsiderate Maris's behavior has been, and urges Niles to stand up to Maris and tell her off. She responds by booting him out of the house. After a few days at Frasier's apartment, Niles goes back home to get his things, and is informed by maid Marta that he could stay if he would apologize to "Missy Crane," per her boss. Niles is ready to apologize, but Frasier and Martin suggest that he should do otherwise, and Niles follows them out the door.

Noel Shempsky · *Patrick Kerr*
Marta · *Irene Olga López*
Vinnie · *Paul Mazursky (voice-over)*

58 "FRASIER GRINCH"

WRITER: David Lloyd

DIRECTOR: Philip Charles MacKenzie

It's Christmastime, Frasier's son Frederick is coming to visit from Boston, and Frasier orders a Junior Astronomer set and a Living Brain from a catalog as gifts. Yet what arrives on Christmas Eve is instead a Barbie doll and Suzy Homemaker Casserole Set and Frasier is forced to go mall hopping on Christmas Eve to get a suitable present for his son. Intellectual gifts are hard to come by at that hour. Martin argues that Frasier should think about what people really want when he buys gifts for them. On Christmas Day, Frederick tells Frasier that what he would really like is an Outlaw Laser Robo-Geek that he asked Santa for. Frasier feels terrible until he opens Martin's gift for Frederick—an Outlaw Laser Robo-Geek, which he rewraps and gives to his son.

Bulldog · *Dan Butler*
Waitress · *Luck Hari*
Gil Chesterton · *Edward Hibert*
Marge · *Becky Ann Baker*
Ned · *Klee Bragger*
Jack · *Tegan West*
Frederick Crane · *Luke Tarsitano*
Bob · *Ray Liotta (voice-over)*

59 ''IT'S HARD TO SAY GOODBYE IF YOU WON'T LEAVE''

WRITER: Steven Levitan

DIRECTOR: Philip Charles MacKenzie

Frasier has been holding in his lust for Kate, but he can't get her out of his mind. He finally gets up the nerve to discuss his feelings for her at the office, and she drops the bomb that she'll be leaving the next day for a new job in Chicago. Set against a backdrop of discussion of the film *Casablanca,* Frasier drops in on Kate at home, where he arrives to find her with another man, and later she comes to see Frasier, who is with a blind date. By the end of the show, Frasier is at the airport with Kate, where both admit their true feelings for each other and spend the time before her flight talking about what might have been. As the flight gets delayed, and our lovers get more time to spend together, they realize it was all a fantasy, that they have nothing in common, and can't wait, in fact, to be apart.

Kate Costas · *Mercedes Ruehl*
Jane · *Alicia Robinson*
Tony · *Vaughn Armstrong*
Donna · *Marnie Moisman*

Flight Attendant · *Doug Tompos*
Passenger · *Jane Macfie*

---

60 ''THE FRIEND''

WRITER: Jack Burditt

DIRECTOR: Philip Charles MacKenzie

Frasier realizes he hasn't made any friends since coming to Seattle. In an attempt to find a male companion, he announces on-air that he is open to meeting new people. After receiving numerous phone calls and faxes from people hoping to become his "friend," Frasier chooses a letter from a man named Bob, who sounds relatively normal, but of course he's not—he's the friend from hell. Once they get started in friendship, Frasier can't seem to get away from wheelchair-bound Bob, who continues to pop up at work, shows up at Café Nervosa, and then announces plans to move into Frasier's apartment building. Frasier finally gets the nerve to break it off with Bob.

Bob · *Griffin Dunne*
Gerard · *Armistead Maupin (voice-over)*

---

61 ''THE SHOW WHERE DIANE COMES BACK''

WRITER: Christopher Lloyd

DIRECTOR: James Burrows.

Cheers sighting number three. After being fired from her writing stint on *Dr. Quinn, Medicine Woman,* Diane Chambers comes to Seattle to oversee the production of her play about a bunch of losers who hang out at a Boston bar. Frasier is at first aghast about seeing the woman who left him standing at the altar, but begins to develop feelings again for Diane. He even agrees to back her play, and she invites him to a dress rehearsal of her "feminist odyssey," in which all the people at the bar are obsessed with the woman they call "Mary Anne," including Stan (for Sam), Dr. Franklin Crean (Frasier), Ned (Norm), Darla (Carla), and Clark (Cliff). When Dr. Crean has trouble pinpointing his technique for portraying his upset at being dumped at the altar, Dr. Crane erupts instead and exhibits the proper way to emote, at one point referring to Diane as the devil in disguise. Later, Diane apologizes for what she did so many years ago, and they both say their good-byes.

Diane Chambers · *Shelley Long*
Mr. Carr · *Don Sparks*
Stan · *Perry Stephens*
Clark · *Danny Breen*
Darla · *Judith Corber-Wexler*
Ned · *Googy Gress*
Dr. Franklin Crean · *John Carroll Lynch*
Mary Anne · *Cali Timmins*

62 ''COME LIE WITH ME''

WRITER: Steven Levitan

DIRECTOR: Philip Charles MacKenzie

Daphne's new boyfriend Joe oversleeps and ends up staying the night with Daphne at Frasier's apartment. She tries to sneak him out of the house, but they are caught when Niles is waiting outside the door. Frasier is uncomfortable with the thought of Joe and Daphne making hay under his roof. When Frasier tells Daphne how he feels, Daphne offers to move out and only work weekdays. She and Joe go away for the weekend, and Frasier and Martin are helpless without her. By Sunday night, both men realize that Daphne is the glue that holds their relationship together.

Frasier apologizes, and Daphne agrees to be more discreet, even though, Frasier learns, nothing happened in Daphne's room except for reading poetry, as Joe's "war injury" (made up for Frasier's benefit) prevents them engaging in sex.

Joe · *Tony Carreiro*
Dirk · *Tim Choate*

63 "MOONDANCE"

WRITERS: Joe Keenan & Christopher Lloyd & Rob Greenberg & Jack Burditt and Chuck Ranberg & Anne Flett-Giordano & Linda Morris & Vic Rauseo

DIRECTOR: Kelsey Grammer

The famous tango episode, in which Niles declares his true feelings for Daphne, and the two of them dance up a storm at a Seattle high-society ball. When Niles reads about Maris's date with another man in the gossip columns, he becomes infuriated and asks another society woman to the "Snow Ball," but worries that she may want to dance. Daphne offers to teach Niles ballroom dancing. The two enjoy the lessons, and when Niles's date cancels on him, Daphne offers to go with him instead. At the dance, former friends of Niles rub in the fact that Maris is dating up a storm. This prompts Daphne to get on the dance floor with Niles. With the music pulsating and the lights low, Niles tells Daphne that she's a "goddess" and that he's crazy for her. Daphne responds in kind and they kiss passionately. They sit down, and Daphne says they sure put on a good act to fool his friends. He's crushed until an attractive aquaintance gives Niles her card and asks him to call her sometime.

Waitress · *Luck Hari*
Lacey Lloyd · *Christine McGraw*
Andrew Lloyd · *Hank Stratton*
Conductor · *Michael G. Hawkins*
Clarie Barnes · *Nancy Stafford*
Marlene · *Jodie Foster (voice-over)*

64 "A WORD TO THE WISEGUY"

WRITER: Joe Keenan

DIRECTOR: Philip Charles MacKenzie

Niles is ecstatic when Maris calls to ask for his help, thinking this is a sign that she needs him and might take him back. Maris missed her court date for 112 parking tickets (says Frasier: "What do you expect from a woman for whom a chocolate allergy entitles her to park in a handicapped space?") and Niles asks Martin if his police buddies could fix things for Maris. He refuses, but Roz knows a guy who "fixes things," Jerome Belasco. He makes a phone call, everything's taken care of, and he tells Niles he owes him nothing, except a favor in the future.

The person called to perform the deed is Frasier, and the problem is this—Jerome's girlfriend Brandy is a big fan of Frasier's radio show, she refuses to marry Jerome, and he wants Frasier to talk to Brandy on the radio and urge her to settle down with Jerome. Out of fear for his life, Frasier agrees, but when she calls the show, Frasier is so aghast at her description of their relationship that he breaks down and tells her not to marry Jerome. Later, Jerome confronts Frasier at the Café Nervosa, and things get settled when Brandy agrees to marry Jerome if he helps her get a job. Her new assignment—working for Niles.

Jerome Belasco · *Harris Yulin*
Brandy · *Faith Prince (voice-over)*
Man · *Randy Travis (voice-over)*

65   ''HIGH CRANE DRIFTER''
WRITER: Jack Burditt

DIRECTOR: Philip Charles MacKenzie

After a difficult day in which someone parks in his parking space, he is ignored in a video store, and his neighbor is continually blasting hard rock music, Frasier meets Niles at Café Nervosa to try to relax. When a rude customer steals Frasier's table after he and Niles waited patiently for it and insults the doctors Crane, Frasier flies off the handle and physically ejects the man from the restaurant.

The next day, much to his chagrin, Frasier is hailed as a hero in the local paper. Frasier, however, is uncomfortable with the attention and a bit ashamed at his use of physical force, and he decides to make amends with the man. He invites him to meet him at the café to tell him how sorry he is. The man responds by announcing that he has filed a lawsuit against

Frasier for assault. Niles calls the man a chicken. The man eventually gets fed up and pushes Niles, who falls and screams "Countersuit!"

Clark · *Mark Benninghofen*
Waiter · *Paul Cusimano*
Doug Harvey · *John Cygan*
Lynette · *Laura Robinson*
Lydia · *Joan Allen (voice-over)*
Brenda · *Katarina Witt (voice-over)*
Mitch · *Jerry Orbach (voice-over)*
Chris · *Billy Barty (voice-over)*
Chuck · *Eric Idle (voice-over)*
Rochelle · *Jane Pauley (voice-over)*

66 ''LOOK BEFORE YOU LEAP''
WRITERS: Chuck Ranberg & Anne Flett-Giordano
DIRECTOR: James Burrows

It's February 29, and in honor of leap year, Frasier suggests that everyone take a "leap" of their own. Martin goes to Montana to visit an old buddy for his birthday; Daphne gets the haircut she has always been talking about, and Roz makes a plea over the airwaves for a man she met on the bus to give her a call. And in the spirit of "leaping," Frasier agrees to sing an Italian aria for the PBS pledge drive instead of his old standby "Buttons and Bows." Unfortunately, none of the leaps turn out as excepted.

Pete · *Murphy Dunne*

67 ''CHESS PAINS''
WRITER: Rob Greenberg
DIRECTOR: Gordon Hunt

Frasier buys a new, expensive chess set and is crushed when novice chess player Martin plays along and beats him consistently. Niles tells Frasier that he is subconciously allowing Martin to win because he would feel Oedipal guilt if he were to beat his father. Nonetheless, Frasier becomes obsessed with beating his father to the point where he sets off the fire alarm to wake Martin in the middle of the night to play another game. Frasier offers Martin $1,000 if he wins, just to make sure that he doesn't throw the game to get Frasier off his back. When Frasier finally wins, he rubs it in to Martin, who is a good sport about the whole thing.

Waitress · *Luck Hari*

68 "CRANE VERSUS CRANE"
WRITER: David Lloyd

DIRECTOR: Philip Charles MacKenzie

Niles agrees to represent a client in a sanity battle, and Frasier takes on the other side, setting the stage for a courtroom showdown between the two brothers. Niles is hired as an expert witness in the "Safford Case," where a son is trying to have his rich, eccentric tycoon father Harlow Safford declared incompetent. Martin, quite obviously, is on Harlow's side, and abhors Niles's helping the son. Harlow's lawyer comes to see Frasier about helping him, saying his client is a big fan of the Frasier Crane radio show. Frasier isn't sure he wants to get involved—considering that Niles was already there—but agrees to meet with Harlow. Frasier decides Harlow may be a little goofy, but not crazy. He agrees to represent him. Niles is furious and says Frasier only took the case on because he couldn't stand to see his younger brother in the public eye for once. A fight erupts with the brothers saying they'll see each other in court. All appears to be going in Frasier's favor before the judge until Harlow starts acting up and convinces all in the room that he really is nutty. The case is dropped, and afterwards, Frasier admits to Niles that he was wrong and that Niles deserves more recognition for his psychiatric skills.

Harlow Safford · *Donald O'Connor*
Beth · *Mrs. Fields (voice-over)*
Mr. Giroux · *James Winker*

Judge · *Neil Vipond*
Bailiff · *Baron Kelly*

69 "WHERE THERE'S SMOKE THERE'S FIRED"

WRITER: Joe Keenan

DIRECTOR: Philip Charles MacKenzie

KACL is sold to Wilford S. Boone (better known as just "Big Willy") an eighty-five-year-old Texan and chief of a $600 million media empire. Turns out that Big Willy is engaged to Frasier's agent Bebe, and he instructs his new employee to help him with a little problem. He wants his future wife to be smoke-free. It's Frasier's job to cure Bebe of her nasty nicotine habit, and he has just three days to do it.

Bulldog · *Dan Butler*
Gil Chesterton · *Edward Hibbert*
Big Willy · *Richard Hamilton*
Bebe Glaser · *Harriet Sansom Harris*
Hank · *Bradford English*
Andy · *Don Took*

70 "FRASIER LOVES ROZ"

WRITER: Suzanne Martin

DIRECTOR: Philip Charles MacKenzie

What if Roz dated one of Niles's patients? That's the premise for this episode, and the patient is Ben, who goes through so many women he calls them all "sunshine" to avoid slipups. Roz, meanwhile, admits to Frasier that she's finally found the man of her dreams. Niles has told Frasier about Ben, and knowing that she'll be hurt, Frasier wants to warn Roz about him, but can't, since ethically he can't discuss another psychiatrist's patient. Frasier tries to give her hints, however, and Roz comes to the conclusion that Frasier is interested in her romantically. Ben, inevitably, dumps Roz, and Frasier drops by Roz's apartment to console her. Roz tells Frasier she knows of his feelings for her, and Frasier doesn't deny it, not wanting to hurt her feelings. Roz says that she needs time to heal, and Frasier doesn't disagree.

Bulldog · *Dan Butler*
Ben · *Michael Mitz*
Tom · *David Duchovny (voice-over)*

71 "YOU CAN GO HOME AGAIN"

WRITERS: Linda Morris & Vic Rauseo

DIRECTOR: David Lee

Roz gives Frasier a tape of their first KACL show on their third anniversary together, and as he listens, Frasier flashes back to his first day at KACL, six months before the pilot of "The Good Son" introduced us to him and his decision to take in his father. In this prequel, Frasier is quite green and concerned about his performance, as he spends a lot of time trying to come up with good catchphrases for his on-air persona. ("You're on the couch," "If you can feel, I can heal.") Frasier runs into Niles at the Café Nervosa for the first time, and Niles cons Frasier into visiting Martin, saying he's not as ornery as he used to be. Niles wants to get out of visiting duty, and when Frasier shows up, Martin is just as difficult as ever. But by the end of the show, Frasier and Martin begin to see eye to eye, and when the flashback has completed, Frasier feels good about how much his relationship with his father has improved over the last three years.

Waiter · *John Rajeski*
Angela · *Sherry Lansing (voice-over)*

72 "THE FOCUS GROUP"

WRITER: Rob Greenberg

DIRECTOR: Philip Charles MacKenzie

A focus group makes their opinions known about *The Frasier Crane Show* to KACL, and Frasier passes with flying colors. Eleven out of the twelve participants think he's terrific. One man, however, doesn't like Frasier, but doesn't say why. Frasier becomes obsessed with finding out what Manu, played by Tony Shalhoub of *Wings,* a Seattle newspaper stand owner, has against him, and he becomes a real thorn in Manu's side as Frasier searches for the truth.

Manu · *Tony Shalhoub*
Data Collector · *Cameron Watson*
Leader · *Henry Woronicz*
Paul · *Abdul Salaam El Razzac*
Cathy · *Heather MacRae*
Gary · *Pat Skipper*
Chuck · *David Breithbarth*
Anne · *Lin Shaye*
Amanda · *Marita Geraghty*
Angela · *Sherry Lansing (voice-over)*

Frasier at Work

(Frasier goes to the station manager, Kate, to demand raises for all, and she says there's no money left for the rest of the employees because Frasier and the other on-air talent have fat contracts.)

KATE: Listen, there would have been raises if you hadn't taken all the money to pay for those Armani suits.

FRASIER: And what about you? Let's not overlook that overpriced Fendi scarf.

KATE: Well, what about that expensive cologne?

FRASIER: How about those pouty lips that probably cost you a fortune in collagen injections?

KATE: These lips are mine, you arrogant windbag.

FRASIER: You intractable despot.

KATE: Blowhard.

FRASIER: Tyrant.

KATE: Ass.

FRASIER: Shrew.

(*They grab each other and kiss passionately.*)

(They spend the night together. The next afternoon, at the KACL studios . . .)

KATE: Last night was great, but I think we should slow down. Let's face it, if relationships had speed limits, we'd both be looking at traffic school.

FRASIER: I'm so glad you said that. I think we should put the brakes on too.

(They agree that what turned them on was the idea that they were doing something they shouldn't.)

KATE: You're right. Going wild that way, knowing those people were on the other side of the door . . .

FRASIER: The tantalizing possibility of discovery. The quickening of your pulse.

KATE: The butterflies in your stomach.

FRASIER: For once in my cautious, button-down life I felt like a real bad boy.

KAT: I felt like a dirty girl.

FRASIER (Turned on): What did you just call yourself?

KATE: I said dirty girl . . . you bad boy.

FRASIER: You dirty girl.

KATE: Bad boy.

FRASIER: Dirty girl.

KATE: Bad boy!

FRASIER: Dirty girl!

(They begin to kiss passionately. Frasier says he has three minutes left on the newscast, and will play commercials

afterwards to divert the audience. But unfortunately, in the middle of their passion, Kate accidentally hits the mike button and Seattle's radio listeners hear . . .)

FRASIER: Yes! Yes! I am a bad boy, aren't I, you dirty girl!

(We see Niles driving along, listening to Frasier's radio show.)

FRASIER: Come to your bad boy . . . Oh yes . . . Oh, yes . . . Oh no! Is that the on-air light?

KATE: Stop talking.

FRASIER: You must have hit the switch with your elbow while we were—

KATE: Stop talking.

FRASIER: We better hurry up and get dressed before—

NILES: Stop talking!

(And with that, Niles crashes into another car and gets taken over by the air bag.)

NINE

AWARDS

A complete list of the many awards the "Frasier" cast and crew have won over the years.

EMMYS

1993–94

- ◆ Outstanding Comedy Series
- ◆ Outstanding Lead Actor in a Comedy Series: Kelsey Grammer
- ◆ Outstanding Directing in a Comedy Series: James Burrows for "The Good Son"
- ◆ Outstanding Writing in a Comedy Series: David Angell, Peter Casey, and David Lee for "The Good Son"
- ◆ Outstanding Editing for a Series (Multi-Camera): Ron Volk for "The Show Where Lilith Comes Back"

1994–95

- ◆ Outstanding Comedy Series
- ◆ Outstanding Lead Actor in a Comedy Series: Kelsey Grammer

* Outstanding Supporting Actor in a Comedy Series: David Hyde Pierce
* Outstanding Directing in a Comedy Series: David Lee for ''The Matchmaker''
* Outstanding Writing in a Comedy Series: Chuck Ranberg and Anne Flett-Giordano for ''An Affair to Forget''

GOLDEN GLOBES

* 1994 Best Comedy Series (tie with *Mad About You*)
* 1995 Best Actor: Kelsey Grammer

TELEVISION CRITICS ASSOCIATION AWARDS

* 1994 Best Comedy
* 1995 Best Comedy

AMERICAN COMEDY AWARDS

1995

* Funniest Male Performer in a Television Series (Lead): Kelsey Grammer
* Funniest Supporting Male—Television: David Hyde Pierce

DIRECTORS GUILD OF AMERICA AWARDS FOR TELEVISION DIRECTION

* 1993 Best Comedy Director: James Burrows for ''The Good Son''
* 1994 Best Comedy Director: David Lee for ''The Matchmaker''

WRITERS GUILD OF AMERICA AWARD FOR BEST WRITING

* 1996: Writer's Guild of America, best TV comedy episode, ''The Matchmaker,'' by Joe Keenan

OTHERS

* 1994 People's Choice Award, Best Comedy
* 1994 Banff International Television Festival, Best Comedy
* 1994 George Foster Peabody Award
* 1995 GLAAD (Gay and Lesbian Alliance Against Defamation) Award for ''The Matchmaker''
* 1995 Screen Actors Guild Award, Outstanding Performance by a Male Actor in a Television Comedy Series: David Hyde Pierce.

Martin and Niles on Daphne

(Daphne offers to give Niles dancing lessons. Martin says to be careful.)

NILES: What are you implying?

MARTIN: You know damn well what I'm implying. Take my word for it. You're sticking a fork in a toaster here.

NILES: Well, my muffin's stuck. Besides, what's the harm in a few dance lessons?

MARTIN: It's nighttime, you're alone, there's music playing, you got your arms around her—you're gonna end up saying something you can't take back.

NILES: I will not.

MARTIN: You will. You're a man. Look, something happened when I was separated from your mother. There was this pretty coroner in the city morgue. I guess I always had a little crush on her. Anytime we found a dead body I'd say "Okay, boys, I'll take it from here." So one night I asked her down to the corner bar.

NILES: Coroners have their own bars?

MARTIN: No, corner, Niles. The bar on the corner. Anyway, we had a few drinks, the lights were low, Sinatra was on the jukebox—suddenly it all started pouring out. I told her how I felt. I knew the second it was out of my mouth it was a mistake. She let me down easy, but we still had to go on seeing each other all the time and it was very uncomfortable. After that the morgue was a pretty chilly place.

"The Good Son"

Considered one of the all-time classic pilot scripts, here, for the first time for the general public is the first episode of *Frasier*, "The Good Son," in which Frasier Crane's perfect life in Seattle goes off track six months after leaving Boston, when he's convinced to take in his father as his new roommate.

Written by *Frasier* creators David Angell, Peter Casey, and David Lee, the episode went on to win Emmys for best script and best direction (James Burrows). The literate, sophisticated style of the script set the tone for the series, and helped nab further Emmys for *Frasier* in year one, with statues for the show and star Kelsey Grammer.

The script also performed a neat magic trick in presenting a new Frasier Crane, transporting the pompous wiseacre from *Cheers* into a slightly more humane, caring boob that was easier to laugh at—and love.

FRASIER™

"The Good Son"

#61018-098

By David Angell
Peter Casey
& David Lee

ACT ONE

Scene A

A BLACK SCREEN. IN WHITE LETTERS APEARS, "THE JOB." FADE IN:
INT. RADIO STUDIO-DAY-DAY/1
(FRASIER, ROZ, RUSSELL (V.O.))

KACL - A TYPICAL RADIO STUDIO: TWO ROOMS SEPARATED BY A GLASS PARTITION AND A DOOR. ON ONE SIDE, FRASIER CRANE IS SEATED AT A DESK WITH A MULTI-LINE PHONE AND MICROPHONE. HE IS WEARING HEADPHONES. ON THE OTHER SIDE OF THE GLASS IS HIS CALL SCREENER, ROZ DOYLE. ANOTHER GLASS PARTITION IN THE STUDIO LOOKS OUT INTO THE HALLWAY. THE LIGHTS ARE LOW. FRASIER IS IN THE MIDDLE OF ANSWERING A CALLER.

Frasier: (FIRMLY, WITH CONCERN) Listen to yourself, Bob. You follow her to work. You eavesdrop on her calls. You open her mail. The minute you started doing these things, the relationship was over. Thank you for your call.

HE PUNCHES A BUTTON ON THE CONSOLE.

Frasier: Roz, I think we have time for one more.

ROZ SPEAKS INTO THE MICROPHONE IN THE BOOTH IN A SOOTHING RADIO VOICE.

Roz: Yes, Dr. Crane. On line four we have Russell from Kirkland.

FRASIER PUSHES A BUTTON ON THE PHONE.

Frasier: Hello, Russell, this is Doctor Frasier Crane. I'm listening.

Russell (V.O.): Well, I've been feeling, sort of, you know, depressed lately. My life's not going anywhere. It's not that bad. It's just the same old apartment, same old job. Sometimes I just . . .

ROZ SIGNALS FROM THE BOOTH THAT TIME IS RUNNING SHORT AND FRASIER HAS TO WRAP THIS UP.

Frasier: Uh, Russell, we're nearing the end of our hour. Let me see if I can cut to the chase by using myself as an example. Six months ago I was living in Boston. My wife had left me, which was very painful, then she came back to me, which was excruciating. On top of that, my practice had grown stagnant and my social life consisted of hanging around a bar night after night. You see I was clinging to a life that wasn't working anymore and I knew I had to do something, anything. So I ended the marriage once and for all, packed up my things and moved back here to my hometown of Seattle. Go Seahawks! I took action, Russell, and you can too. Move, change, do something. If it's a mistake, do something else. Will you do that, Russell? Will you? Russell? (TURNING TO ROZ) I think we lost him.

Roz: No, we cut to the news thirty seconds ago.

FRASIER TAKES OFF HIS HEADSET, GETS UP AND HEADS INTO ROZ'S CONTROL ROOM.

Frasier: Oh, for crying out loud. I finally bare my soul to all of Seattle and they're listening to ''Chopper Dave's Rush-Hour Roundup''? Well the rest of the show was pretty good. (THEN) It was a good show, wasn't it?

Roz: Here. (HANDS HIM A SLIP OF PAPER) Your brother called.

Frasier: Roz, in the trade, we call that avoidance. Don't change the subject. Tell me, what did you think?

SHE POINTS TO HER CONSOLE.

Roz: Did I ever tell you what this little button does?

Frasier: I'm not a piece of Lalique. I can handle criticism. How was I today?

Roz: Let's see. You dropped two commercials, you left a total of twenty-eight seconds of dead air, you scrambled the station's call letters, you spilled yogurt on the control board and you kept referring to Jerry with the identity crisis as ''Jeff.''

Frasier: (PAUSE) You say my brother called.

CUT TO:

Scene B

A BLACK SCREEN. IN WHITE LETTERS APPEARS ''THE BROTHER.''

Niles (V.O.): So I said to the gardner, ''Yoshi, I do not want a Zen garden in my backyard.

CUT TO:
INT. COFFEE HOUSE - LATER THAT DAY - DAY/1
(NILES, FRASIER, WAITRESS)

FRASIER AND HIS BROTHER, <u>DR. NILES CRANE</u>, STAND AT THE COUNTER.

FRASIER HAS HIS NOSE IN A MENU.

Niles: "If I want to rake gravel every ten minutes to maintain my inner harmony, I'll move to Yokohama." Well, this offends him so he starts pulling up Maris' prized camellias by the handful. Well, I couldn't stand for that, so I marched right into the morning room and locked the door until he cooled down. Tell me you would have handled it differently, Frasier.

AFTER A BEAT, FRASIER LOOKS UP.

Frasier: Oh, I'm sorry, Niles, I didn't realize you'd stopped talking.

Niles: You haven't heard a word I said.

Frasier: Niles, you're a psychiatrist. You know what it's like to listen to people prattling on endlessly about their mundane lives.

Niles: Touché. And on that subject, I heard your show today.

Frasier: And?

Niles: You know what I think about pop psychiatry.

Frasier: Yes, I know what you think about everything. When was the last time you had an unexpressed thought?

Niles: I'm having one now.

THEY BOTH CHUCKLE GOOD-NATUREDLY. A WAITRESS APPROACHES.

Waitress: You guys ready?

Frasier: (TO WAITRESS) Two cafe latte supremos.

NILES MOVES TO A CHAIR AND BEGINS TO DUST IT OFF WITH A HAND-KERCHIEF. HE OFFERS IT TO FRASIER.

Frasier (cont'd): No, thank you.

Niles: So, Frasier, how you doing on your own?

Frasier: I'm fine. I love my new life. I love the solitude. I miss Frederick like the dickens, of course. You know, he's quite a boy. He's playing goalie on the pee wee soccer team now. He's a chip off the old block.

Niles: You hated sports.

Frasier: So does he, the fresh air's good for him.

THEY BOTH LAUGH AT THIS.

Niles: Oh well, this has been fun, Frasier, but we have a problem and that's why I thought we should talk.

Frasier: Is it Dad?

Niles: I'm afraid so. One of his old buddies from the police force called this morning. He went over to see him and found him on the bathroom floor.

Frasier: Oh my God.

Niles: No, it's okay, he's fine.

Frasier: What? His hip again?

NILES NODS.

Niles: Frasier, I don't think he can live alone anymore.

Frasier: What can we do?

Niles: Well, I know this isn't going to be anyone's favorite solution, but I took the liberty of checking out a few convalescent homes for him.

HE REACHES INTO HIS BRIEFCASE AND TAKES OUT A PILE OF PAMPHLETS.

Frasier: Niles, a home? He's still a young man.

Niles: Well, you certainly can't take care of him. You're just getting your new life together.

Frasier: Absolutely. Well, besides, we've never been sympatico.

Niles: Of course, I can't take care of him.

Frasier: Oh, yes, yes, of course, of course. (BEAT) Why?

Niles: Because Dad doesn't get along with Maris.

Frasier: Who does?

Niles: I thought you liked my Maris.

Frasier: I do. I, I like her from a distance. You know, the way you like the sun. Maris is like the sun . . . except without the warmth.

Niles: Well then, we're agreed about what to do with Dad.

NILES PICKS UP A PAMPHLET FROM THE TABLE.

Niles (cont'd): (READING) ''Golden Acres. We care so you don't have to.''
Frasier: It says that?
Niles: Well, it might as well.
Frasier: (RESIGNED) Alright, I'll make up the spare bedroom.

Niles: Oh, you're a good son, Frasier.

Frasier: Oh God, I am, aren't I?

FRASIER BURIES HIS HEAD IN HIS HANDS AS NILES COMFORTS HIM. THE WAITRESS BRINGS THEM THEIR COFFEE.

Waitress: Two cafe supremos. Anything to eat?

Frasier: No. I've seemed to have lost my appitite.

Niles: I'll have a large piece of cheesecake.

CUT TO:

Scene C

A BLACK SCREEN. IN WHITE LETTERS APPEARS ''THE FATHER.''
FADE IN: <u>INT. FRASIER'S LIVING ROOM - DAY - DAY/2</u>
(FRASIER, NILES, MARTIN, DELIVERYMAN)

IT'S A SMART, CLEAN, METICULOUSLY DECORATED CONDO. THE FUR-
NISHINGS LEAN TOWARD THE CONTEMPORARY, WITH WELL CHOSEN
PIECES OF ART AND SCULPTURE. CENTER IS A VIEW OF THE SEATTLE
SKYLINE. THERE IS A <u>KNOCK</u> AT THE DOOR. FRASIER, AT THE PIANO,
GOES TO THE DOOR. HE STEELS HIMSELF AND OPENS THE DOOR. NILES
IS STANDING THERE WITH A FEW SUITCASES IN HIS HAND.

Frasier: Hi!

Niles: We finally made it.

NILES ENTERS FOLLOWED BY THEIR FATHER, MARTIN, USING A WALKER.

Frasier: Ah, Dad, Dad, welcome to your new home. You look great.

Martin: Don't B.S. me. I do not look great. I spent Monday on the bathroom floor. You can still see the tile marks on my face.

Niles: (SOTTO TO FRASIER) Gives you some idea about the ride over in
the car.

FRASIER CLAPS HIS HANDS AND RUBS THEM TOGETHER, TRYING TO
LIGHTEN THE MOMENT.

Frasier: Well, uh, here we are. Well, rest assured the refrigerator is stocked with your favorite beer, Ballantines, and we've got plenty of hot links and cole slaw. I just rented a Charles Bronson movie for later.

Martin: Let's cut the "Welcome to Camp Crane" speech. We all know why I'm here. Your old man can't be left alone for ten minutes without falling on his ass, and Frasier got stuck with me. Isn't that right?

FRASIER AND NILES LOOK AT EACH OTHER.

Frasier/Niles: No, no, no.

Frasier (cont'd): I want you here. It will give us a chance to get reacquainted.

Martin: That implies we were acquainted at one point.

NILES CHUCKLES. FRASIER SHOOTS HIM A LOOK.

Niles: Listen, why don't I take Dad's things into his new "bachelor quarters" so you two scoundrels can plan some hijinx?

NILES EXITS WITH THE BAGS DOWN THE HALLWAY TO THE BEDROOM.

Martin: I think that wife of his is driving him nutso.

Frasier: Yes, we Crane boys sure know how to marry. (THEN) Let me get you a beer, Dad.

FRASIER CROSSES TO THE KITCHEN. MARTIN LOOKS AROUND THE ROOM.

Frasier (cont'd): So, uh, what do you think of what I've done with the place? You know, Every item here was carefully selected. This lamp, by Corbu. The chair by Eames. And this couch is an exact replica of the one Coco Chanel had in her Paris atelier.

Martin: Nothing matches.

Frasier: Well, it's a style of decorating. It's called eclectic. (OFF HIS LOOK) Well, the theory behind it is, if you've got really fine pieces of furniture, it doesn't matter if they match. They will go together.

Martin: It's your money.

SFX: THE DOORBELL RINGS.

Frasier: Dad, what do you think of that view? (INDICATING) Well, hey, that's the Space Needle there.

Martin: Thanks for pointing that out. Being born and raised here, I never would have known.

AS NILES RE-ENTERS FROM THE OTHER ROOM, FRASIER CROSSES TO THE DOOR AND OPENS IT. IT'S A DELIVERYMAN.

Deliveryman: Delivery for Martin Crane.

Martin: Oh, in here.

Deliveryman: Coming through.

FRASIER STEPS BACK. THE <u>DELIVERYMAN</u> BRINGS IN A BARCALOUNGER.

Frasier: Excuse me, excuse me. Wait a minute.

Deliveryman: Where do you want it?

Martin: Where's the TV?

Niles: (INDICATING) It's in that credenza.

Martin: Point it at that thing.

Deliveryman: What about this chair?

Niles: The chair? Here. Let me get it out of the way.

NILES PICKS UP THE CHAIR AND MOVES IT. THE DELIVERYMAN REPLACES IT WITH MARTIN'S BACALOUNGER.

Frasier: Niles, Niles, be careful with that. That's a Wassily. (RE: LOUNGER) Uh, Dad, as dear as I'm sure that this piece is to you, I just don't think it goes with anything here.

Martin: I know. It's eclectic.

MARTIN PAYS THE DELIVERYMAN. HE EXITS.
Frasier: Niles, Niles, will you help me out here?

Martin: Well, you're going to have to run an extension cord over here so I can plug in the vibrating part.

Frasier: (BEATEN) Ah, yes, yes, that will be the crowning touch.

Niles: Well, now that you two are settled in, I've got to run. I'm late for my dysfunctional family seminar.

AS HE HEADS FOR THE DOOR:

Niles (cont'd): Dad, have you mentioned Eddie yet?

FRASIER TURNS TO MARTIN.

Frasier: (PANICKED) Eddie?

Niles: Ta ta.

NILES EXITS.

Frasier: Oh no, Dad, no, no, no. Not Eddie.

Martin: But he's my best friend. Get me my beer, will 'ya?

Frasier: But he's weird. He gives me the creeps. All he does is stare at me.

Martin: Oh, it's just your imagination.

Frasier: No, Dad, no, no. I'm sorry, but I'm putting my foot down. Eddie is <u>not</u> moving in here.

CUT TO:

Scene D:

A BLACK SCREEN. IN WHITE LETTERS APPEARS THE WORD, ''EDDIE.'' CROSS FADE TO:
INT. FRASIER'S LIVING ROOM - NIGHT - NIGHT/2
(MARTIN, FRASIER, EDDIE)

MARTIN IS SITTING IN HIS BARCALOUNGER WATCHING THE CHARLES BRONSON MOVIE. WE PAN OVER TO FRASIER ON HIS COCO COUCH. WE CONTINUE THE PAN. SITTING NEXT TO FRASIER IS <u>EDDIE</u>, A SMALL LONG-HAIRED JACK RUSSELL TERRIER. EDDIE STARES AT FRASIER. FADE OUT.

END OF ACT ONE

ACT TWO

Scene E

FADE IN:
<u>INT. COFFEE HOUSE - DAY - DAY/3</u>
(NILES, FRASIER)
NILES IS THERE, FRASIER RUSHES IN.

Frasier: Oh, Niles, there you are. Sorry I'm late. Just as I was leaving, Dad decided to fix lunch by the glow of a small kitchen fire. (BEAT) Oh, Niles, this last week with Dad, it's been a living hell. When I'm there, I feel like my territory is being violated and when I'm not, I worry about what he's up to. Look at me, I'm a nervous wreck. I've got to do something to calm down. (TO WAITRESS) Double espresso, please. (TO NILES) Niles, you don't still have the brochures from those rest homes, do you?

Niles: Of course I do. Don't forget Maris is five years older than I am. But do you really think that's necessary?

Frasier: I'm afraid I do. I don't have my life anymore. Tuesday night I gave up my tickets to the theater. Wednesday, it was the symphony.

Niles: That reminds me, weren't you going to the opera on Friday?

FRASIER TAKES TWO TICKETS OUT OF HIS POCKET.

Frasier: Yes. Here.

Niles: Thank you. (LOOKS AT TICKETS)

Frasier: Niles, you don't suppose there's a chance that you and Maris could . . . ?

Niles: Funny you should mention that. Maris and I were just discussing this. We feel we should do more to share the responsibility.

Frasier: You mean you'd take him?

Niles: Oh, dear God, no. But we would be willing to help you pay for a home care worker.

Frasier: A what?

Niles: You know, someone who cooks, and cleans, and can help Dad with his physical therapy.

Frasier: These angels exist?

Niles: I know of an agency. Let me arrange for them to send a few people over to meet with you.

Frasier: Niles, I can't ever thank you enough. I feel the overwhelming urge to hug you.

Niles: Remember what Mom always said: A handshake is as good as a hug.

Frasier: Wise woman.

THEY SHAKE HANDS.

cut to:

Scene H

A BLACK SCREEN. IN WHITE LETTERS APPEARS ''THE HOME CARE SPE-
CIALIST.''

FADE IN:

INT. HALLWAY OF FRASIER'S BUILDING - DAY - DAY/4
(Frasier)

ANOTHER APPLICANT. SHE APPEARS ROBUST, KIND, NEATLY DRESSED:
THE EPITOME OF COMPETENCE.

Frasier: I have never been more impressed with a human being in my life.

FRASIER CLOSES THE DOOR.
reset to:

INT. FRASIER'S LIVING ROOM - CONTINUOUS - DAY/4
(Frasier, Martin, Eddie, Daphne)

Frasier (cont'd): (BLOWING UP) Now what was wrong with that one?!!

Martin: She was casing the joint.

Frasier: Casing the joint? She spent two years with Mother Teresa.

Martin: Well, if I were Mother Teresa, I'd check my jewelry box.

SFX: THE DOORBELL RINGS.

Frasier: Now, this is the last one. Can you at least try to keep an open mind?

FRASIER OPENS THE DOOR TO REVEAL DAPHNE MOON, AN ENGLISH WORKING CLASS WOMAN IN HER MID TO LATE TWENTIES. AT THIS MOMENT, SHE IS REACHING INTO HER BLOUSE AND ADJUSTING HER BRA.

Daphne: Oh hello. Caught me with my hand in the biscuit tin. (EXTENDING HER HAND) I'm Daphne. Daphne Moon.

Frasier: (THEY SHAKE) Frasier Crane. Please come in.

Daphne: Thank you.

SHE ENTERS.

Frasier: This is my father, Martin Crane. Dad, this is Daphne Moon.

THEY EXCHANGE GREETINGS.

Daphne: Nice to meet you. (RE: EDDIE) And who might this be?

Frasier: That is Eddie.

Martin: I call him Eddie Spaghetti.

Daphne: Oh, he likes pasta?

Martin: No, he has worms.

Frasier: Uh, have a seat, Miss Moon.

Daphne: Daphne. Thank you. (RE: BARCALOUNGER) Oh, will you look at that. What a comfy chair. It's like I always say, start with a good piece and replace the rest (INDICATING FRASIER'S FURNITURE) when you can afford it.

SHE SMILES AT FRASIER. SO DOES MARTIN.

Frasier: Yes, well, um, perhaps you should start by telling us a little bit about yourself, Miss Moon.

Daphne: Well, I'm originally from Manchester, England.

Frasier: Oh really. Did you hear that, Dad?

Martin: I'm three feet away. There's nothing wrong with my hearing.

Daphne: I've only been in the U.S. for a few months but I have quite an extensive background in home care and physical therapy, as you can see from my resume. I . . .

SHE LOOKS AT MARTIN.

Daphne (cont'd): You were a policeman, weren't you?

Martin: Yeah. How did you know?

Daphne: I must confess, I'm a bit psychic. It's nothing big. Just little things I sense about people. I mean, it's not like I can pick the lottery. If I could, I wouldn't be talking to the likes of you two, now would I?

SHE LAUGHS. MARTIN FINDS THAT AMUSING.

Frasier: Yes, perhaps I should describe the duties around here. You would be responsible for . . .

Daphne: (TO FRASIER) Oh, wait a minute, I'm getting something on you. You're a florist.

Frasier: No, I'm a psychiatrist.

Daphne: Well, it comes and goes. Usually it's strongest during my time of the month. Oh, I guess I let out a little secret there, didn't I?

Frasier: It's safe with us. (CHECKING WATCH) Well, Miss Moon, I think we've learned just about all we need to know about you. And a dash extra.

Daphne: (TO EDDIE) You're a dog, aren't you?

Frasier: Well, we'll be calling you, Miss Moon.

Martin: Why wait? You got the job.

Daphne: Oh wonderful!

Frasier: But excuse me, excuse me. Aren't you just forgetting a little something here? Don't you think we should talk about this in private?

Daphne: Oh, of course you should. I completely understand. I'll just pop into the loo. You do have one, don't you?

Frasier: (INDICATING) Yes.

Daphne: Oh, I love America.

DAPHNE EXITS.

Frasier: Dad, what do you think you're doing?

Martin: You wanted me to pick one . . . I picked one.

Frasier: But she's a kook. I don't like her.

Martin: What difference does it make to you? She's only going to be here when you're not.

Frasier: Then . . . what's my problem? (CALLING) Daphne.

DAPHNE RE-ENTERS.

Frasier: (cont'd) You've been retained.

Daphne: Oh, wonderful. I had a premonition.

Frasier: Quelle surprise.

Daphne: I'll move my things in tomorrow.

Frasier: Move in? I'm sorry, there must be some misunderstanding. This isn't a live-in position.

Daphne: Oh dear. Well, the lady at the agency said . . .

Frasier: Well, the lady at the agency was wrong. This is just a part-time position. I'm afraid it just won't work out.

FRASIER STARTS TO USHER HER OUT.

Martin: Hold on there, Frasier. Let's talk about this.

Frasier: Dad, there's nothing to discuss.

Daphne: You two should talk about this. I'll pop back in here and enjoy some more of your African erotic art.

DAPHNE HEADS FOR THE BATHROOM.

Frasier: Daphne, Daphne, I think it would be best if you leave.

Daphne: Oh, well, all right then.

Frasier: Don't be alarmed. We'll contact you. If not by telephone, then through the toaster.

SHE EXITS.

Frasier: Dad, I'm not having another person living in this house.

Martin: Give me one good reason why.

Frasier: Well, for one thing there's no room for her.

Martin: What about that room right across the hall from mine?

Frasier: My study?! You expect me to give up my study? The place where I read, where I do my most profound thinking?

Martin: Ah, use the can like the rest of the world. (THEN) You'll adjust.

Frasier: I don't want to adjust. I've done enough adjusting. I'm in a new city, I've got a new job, I'm separated from my little boy, which in itself is enough to drive me nuts, and now my father and his dog are living with me. Well, that's enough on my plate, thank you. The whole idea of getting someone in here was to help ease my burden, not to add to it.

Martin: Oh, did you hear that, Eddie? We're a burden.

Frasier: Dad, Dad, you're twisting my words. I meant burden in its most positive sense.

Martin: As in "gee what a lovely burden"?

Frasier: Something like that, yes.

Martin: Well, you're not the only one who got screwed here you know. Two years ago I'm sailing toward retirement and some punk robbing a convenience store puts a bullet in my hip. Next thing you know, I'm trading in my golf clubs in for one of these. (HE HOLDS UP THE WALKER) Well, I had plans too, you know, and this may come as a shock to you, Sonny Boy, but one of them wasn't living with you.

Frasier: I'm just trying to do the right thing here, I'm trying to be the good son.

Martin: Oh, don't worry, Son, after I'm gone, you can live guilt-free knowing you've done right by your papa.

Frasier: You think that's what this is all about, guilt?

Martin: Isn't it?

Frasier: Of course it is! But the point is, I did it. I took you in. And I've got news for you. . . . I wanted to do it. Because you're my father. And how do you repay me? Ever since you moved in here, it's been a snide comment about this or a smart little put-down about that. Well, I've done my best to make a home here for you and once, just once, would it have killed you to say thank you? One lousy thank you?
there's a pause.

Martin: C'mon, Eddie. It's past your dinner time.

Frasier: I'm going out.

MARTIN AND EDDIE EXIT TO THE KITCHEN. FRASIER ANGRILY EXITS, SLAMMING THE DOOR BEHIND HIM.

CUT TO:

Scene J
A BLACK SCREEN. IN WHITE LETTERS APPEARS "LUPE VELEZ."
FADE IN:

INT. RADIO STUDIO - LATER THAT DAY - DAY/4
(FRASIER, ROZ, MARTIN (V.O.), CLAIRE (V.O.))

FRASIER COMES BLASTING IN TO HIS BOOTH.

Frasier: They have <u>got</u> to move the bathroom closer to the studio!

HE FLINGS HIMSELF INTO THE CHAIR AND PUTS ON HIS HEADPHONES. ROZ POINTS TO HIM. HE SPEAKS INTO THE MICROPHONE.

Frasier: We'll be right back after these messages.

HE PUNCHES A BUTTON ON THE CONSOLE.

Frasier: (TO ROZ, IRRITATED) Can't I put that on tape?

ROZ WALKS INTO FRASIER'S BOOTH.

Roz: What's eating you?

Frasier: Oh, I'm sorry, it's this thing with my father and this person he wants to hire. . . . I thought I started my life with a clean slate. I had a picture of what it was going to be like. And then, I don't know . . .

Roz: Ever heard of Lupe Velez?

Frasier: Who?

Roz: Lupe Velez. The movie star in the thirties. Well, her career hit the skids so she decided she'd make one final stab at immortality. She figured if she couldn't be remembered for her movies, she'd be remembered for the way she died. And all Lupe wanted was to be remembered. So she plans this lavish suicide. Flowers, candles, silk sheets, white satin gown, full hair and make-up, the works. She takes the overdose of pills, lays on the bed and imagines how beautiful she's going to look on the front page of tomorrow's newspaper. Unfortunately, the pills don't set well with the enchilada combo plate she sadly chose as her last meal. She stumbles toward the bathroom, trips and goes head first into the toilet. And that's how they found her.

Frasier: Is there a reason you're telling me this story?

Roz: Yes. Even though things may not happen like we planned, they can work out anyway.

Frasier: Remind me again how it worked for Lupe, last seen with her head in the toilet?

Roz: All she wanted was to be remembered. (BEAT) Will you <u>ever</u> forget that story?

ROZ GOES BACK INTO HER BOOTH, LOOKS AT THE CLOCK AND POINTS AT FRASIER.

Frasier: We're back. Roz, who's our next caller?

Roz: We have Martin on line one. He's having a problem with his son.

Frasier: Hello, Martin. This is Doctor Frasier Crane. I'm listening.

Martin (V.O.): I'm a first-time caller.

FRASIER STIFFENS.

Frasier: Welcome to the show. How can I help you?

Martin (V.O.): I just moved in with my son and, uh, it ain't working. There's a lot of tension between us.

Frasier: I can imagine. Why do you think that's so?

Martin (V.O.): I guess I didn't see he had a whole new life planned for himself and I kind of got in the way.

Frasier: Well these things are a two-way street. Perhaps your son wasn't sensitive enough to see how <u>your</u> life was changing.

Martin (V.O.): You got that right. I've been telling him that ever since I got there.

Frasier: I'm sure he appreciated your candor.

Martin (V.O.): Well maybe sometimes I've got to learn how to keep my trap shut.

Frasier: That's good advice for us all. Anything else?

Martin (V.O.): Yeah. I'm worried my son doesn't know that I really appreciate what he's done for me.

Frasier: Why don't you tell him?

Martin (V.O.): You know how it is with fathers and sons. They have trouble saying that stuff.

Frasier: Well, if it helps, I suspect your son already knows how you feel.

THERE IS A PAUSE.

Frasier (cont'd): Is that all?

Martin (V.O.): Yeah, I guess that's it. Thank you, Doctor Crane.

Frasier: My pleasure, Martin.

Martin (V.O.): You hear what I said? I said, thank you.

Frasier: Yes. I heard.

MARTIN HANGS UP. FRASIER JUST SITS THERE WITHOUT SAYING ANYTHING. ROZ INTERRUPTS.

Roz: Uh, Doctor Crane? We have Claire on line four. She's having a problem getting over a relationship.

Frasier: Hello, Claire. I'm listening.

Claire (V.O.): I'm, uh, well, I'm a mess. Eight months ago, my boyfriend and I broke up and I just can't get over it. The pain isn't going away. It's almost like I'm in mourning or something.

Frasier: Claire, you <u>are</u> in mourning. But you're not mourning the loss of your boyfriend. You're mourning what you thought your life was going to be. Let it go. Things don't always work out how you plan. That's not necessarily bad. Things have a way of working out anyway. Have you ever heard of Lupe Velez?

FADE OUT

END OF ACT TWO

Scene K

END CREDITS

<u>INT. FRASIER'S LIVING ROOM - LATER THAT NIGHT - NIGHT /4</u>
(FRASIER, MARTIN, EDDIE, DAPHNE)
WE PAN ACROSS THE APARTMENT TO SEE FRASIER AND HIS NEW ''FAMILY'' WATCHING TV. MARTIN IS SITTING IN HIS BARCALOUNGER. EDDIE, FRASIER AND DAPHNE ARE SITTING ON THE COUCH. AFTER A BEAT, EDDIE PUTS ONE PAW ON FRASIER'S LEG.

FADE OUT.

TEN

TRIVIA

Openings

The opening animation sequence of the Seattle skyline alternates in every episode of *Frasier*. They all start out drawing a Seattle skyline and the *Frasier* title, followed by some additional detail. For instance, there's:

- ◆ Flashing light on top of Space Needle.
- ◆ Elevator going up in Space Needle.
- ◆ Lights come on in buildings.
- ◆ Fireworks over the city.
- ◆ Helicopter flying over city.
- ◆ Storm cloud over city.
- ◆ Lightning strikes building.

As for the closing of the show, that changes every week as well. The first lines are always the same, but the last line often changes.

- ◆ A sampling:

"Hey baby, I hear the blues a-callin', tossed salads and scrambled eggs.

Oh, my.

And maybe I seem a bit confused; yeah maybe, but I got you pegged!

Ha, Ha, Ha, Ha!

But I don't know what to do with those tossed salads and scrambled eggs.

They're callin' again. Goodnight, Seattle, we love you!"

"Hey baby, I hear the blues a-callin', tossed salads and scrambled eggs.

Oh, my.

Mercy!

And maybe I seem a bit confused; yea maybe, but I got you pegged!

Ha, Ha, Ha, Ha.

But I don't know what to do with those tossed salads and scrambled eggs.

They're callin' again. Scrambled eggs all over my face;

What is a boy to do. Goodnight!"

"Hey baby, I hear the blues a-callin', tossed salads and scrambled eggs.

Oh, my.

Quite stylish!

And maybe I seem a bit confused; well maybe, but I got you pegged!

Ha, Ha, Ha, Ha.

But I don't know what to do with those tossed salads and scrambled eggs.

They're callin' again. Frasier has left the building!"

"Hey baby, I hear the blues a-callin', tossed salads and scrambled eggs.

Oh, my.

And maybe I seem a bit confused; well maybe, but I got you pegged!

Ha, Ha, Ha, Ha.

But I don't know what to do with those tossed salads and scrambled eggs.

They're callin' again. Thank you!''

"Hey baby, I hear the blues a-callin', tossed salads and scrambled eggs.

Oh, my.

Quite stylish!

And maybe I seem a bit confused; yea maybe, but I got you pegged!

Ha, Ha, Ha, Ha.

But I don't know what to do with those tossed salads and scrambled eggs.

They're callin' again. **Scrambled eggs all over my face;**
What is a boy to do. Goodnight, everybody!''

"Hey baby, I hear the blues a'callin', tossed salads and scrambled eggs.

Oh, my.

Quite stylish!

And maybe I seem a bit confused; well maybe, but I got you pegged!

Ha, ha, ha, ha.

But I don't know what to do with those tossed salads and scrambled eggs.

They're callin' again. See you next year, we love ya!''

As for what exactly "tossed salads and scrambled eggs" means, these words of wisdom from *Frasier* cocreator David Lee.

"It's been fun watching the different theories regarding the meaning of 'tossed salads and scrambled eggs' pop up over the years. I don't think *Hamlet* has been as closely scrutinized or more divergently interpreted. Here is what I (and the songwriters and the other two creators of the show) thought it meant when we decided on it.''

"Hey baby I hear the blues a'-callin'
(*Play on words. He's got the blues and referencing that he takes
    phone calls.*)
Tossed Salads and Scrambled Eggs
(*Mixed-up people who call in.*)

And maybe I seem a bit confused
Well, maybe, but I got you pegged.
(*The core of Frasier's character. He is a nutcase himself much of
    the time, but can analyze the problems of others.*)

But I don't know what to do with those
Tossed Salad and Scrambled Eggs
(*Except these damn callers.*)
They're callin' again. They're callin' again."

More trivia

True or false:
1. Since moving back to Seattle, Frasier has reunited for a
night with both Lilith and Diane?

2. The radio station's call letters are:
a. KCAL
b. KLAC
c. KACL

3. True or false: Since moving to Seattle, Frasier has won the
SeaBea award for broadcaster of the year?

4. Frasier told the gang at Cheers his parents were dead
because . . .

5. Name a typical coffee order for Niles.
a. Double cappuccino, half-caf, nonfat milk

b. Double espresso
c. Mocha java

6. True or false: With his coffee, Niles likes:
a. A sesame bagel.
b. Biscotti
c. A chocolate chip cookie.

7. Frasier dated a noted self-help author, who wrote a popular tome called *Don't Change, You're Perfect*. Her name was:
a. Honey
b. Sugar
c. Summer

8. Which of the following activities have Niles and Frasier not attempted together:
a. Opening their own gourmet restaurant.
b. Cowriting a book.
c. Cohosting a TV talk show.
d. Sharing offices at a psychiatric practice.

9. Which one of the following names hasn't Roz called Frasier?
a. Dirty Boy
b. Shower Boy
c. Radio Boy

10. Identify the duties of the various workers at the Dr. Niles Crane household:
a. Collette
b. Boris
c. Yoshi
d. Hightower

11. What does *Mein Kleine Leberknödel* mean, and who said it to Maris?

12. Which of the following doesn't Maris do at home?
a. Hang out in a sensory deprivation tank.
b. Hold meetings for her wine club.
c. Take dance classes.

13. Whom does Frasier call the "Princess of Darkness" and Roz refer to as "A nazi in nylons."

14. The local Seattle newspaper said it: "I Won't Fink, Says Kinky Shrink." What were they referring to?

15. Frasier's son Frederick's favorite TV show is:
a. *Pinky and the Brain*
b. *Crossfire*
c. *The Mighty Morphin Power Rangers*

16. Why was Martin once called "Boohoo Crane"?

17. Two significant women in Frasier's life have been to Frasier's favorite island retreat. Name the women and the island.

18. Frasier and Niles's mother was named:
a. Hester
b. Gertrude
c. Matilda
d. Ruth
e. Sophie

19. What did Frasier's mom do for a living?

Which of the following doesn't work at KACL?
a. Gil Chesterton
b. Bulldog
c. Chopper Dave
d. Henry "Scoop" Jackson

21. Frasier's first wife was named Nancy Gee, and appeared on one episode of *Cheers*. She was played by:
a. Meryl Streep
b. Susan Sarandon
c. Emma Thompson

22. Which of the following statements Frasier made on *Cheers* is false:
a. His father and mother were dead.
b. That he was an only child.
c. That he grew up in Manhattan.
d. That he went to Harvard.

23. Of the following actors, which ones haven't appeared on Frasier?
a. Griffin Dunne
b. Nathan Lane
c. Robin Williams
d. Mercedes Rhuel
e. Shannon Tweed
f. Anna Nicole Smith
g. JoBeth Williams
h. Dr. Joyce Brothers
i. Tea Leoni
j. Drew Carey
k. Tony Shalhoub
l. Ted Danson
m. Shelley Long
n. Woody Harrelson
o. Bebe Nuewirth

24. Eric Lutes made his first TV appearance as Frasier's gay boss on the episode entitled "The Matchmaker." Name the one other *Frasier* episode that Lutes also appeared on.

25. Funny thing about when Frasier and Niles visit the Café Nervosa. They always seem to be served by the same wait-

ress. Name the actress who plays the woman the writers call "Waitress."

26. What is Frasier's on-air catchphrase?
a. You're on the couch!
b. Let's talk about it.
c. I'm listening.
d. What is your problem?

27. How many times have we seen Maris?
a. Three
b. Two
c. Once
d. Never

28. What breed of dog is Eddie?
a. Cocker spaniel
b. Jack Russell terrier
c. Dachshund

29. Eddie's real name is:
a. Rover
b. Jim
c. Frasier
d. Moose

30. True or false: Daphne hails from Liverpool, England.

31. What is Martin's favorite beer?
a. Coors
b. Budweiser
c. Ballantine

32. Which of the following statements about Daphne is false?
a. She once starred in a British TV series.

b. She does a magic act for kids on the weekend.
c. She works nights as a standup comedian.
d. She's has psychic abilities.

33. Roz's mother is:
a. The president of the Wisconsin chapter of the Christian Coalition.
b. The attorney general for the state of Wisconsin.
c. The owner of Beth's Cheese House.

34. Name Frasier's apartment building.
a. Seattle Skyline View Apartments
b. Elliott Bay Towers
c. The Seattle

35. What is on Niles's license plate?
a. MARIS
b. SHRINK
c. BISCOTTI

36. Who has the highest-rated show at KACL?
a. Frasier
b. Bulldog
c. Gil Chesterton

37. True or false: Roz purchased Bulldog at the bachelor auction.

38. Which of the following statements about Maris isn't true?
a. She refuses to fly because she once flew coach and hated the experience.
b. She spends her days in a sensory deprivation unit.
c. Niles is her fourth husband and had to sign a pre-nuptial agreement before she would say "I do."

39. Niles and Maris met when . . .

a. She came to see him as a patient about her problems with society.

b. At Café Nervosa. He was infatuated with her beauty and walked over to introduce himself.

c. When she was locked out of her estate and banging on the electric gates with a tire iron.

40. How did Frasier keep his mind off the pain of his first tetanus shot?

Answers

1. False
2. C
3. False
4. Trick question. On *Frasier*, he told Sam that he had said Martin was dead because he called him a windbag and hung up on him on the phone at Cheers. But on the *Cheers* show, the subject came up when Frasier and Lilith were planning their wedding, and Frasier said he wouldn't be inviting his parents, because they were dead.)
(Answer: His father hung up on him and called him a windbag.)
5. A
6. B
7. A
8. C
9. C
10. A. cook, B. Handyman, C. gardener and D. secretary.
11. Gunnar, her fencing instructor, and it means "my little liver dumpling."
12. C

13. Kate Costas
14. The night Frasier and Kate did the wild thing on the air.
15. B
16. He cried while watching *Brian's Song*.
17. Bora Bora, Lilith and Madeline.
18. A
19. Psychiatrist
20. D
21. C
22. C
23. C, F, J and N
24. "Agents in America, Part 3," when Frasier's agent Bebe convinces her client to stage a walkout in order to renegotiate his contract.
25. Luck Hari
26. C
27. D
28. B
29. D
30. False
31. C
32. B&C
33. B
34. B
35. B
36. B
37. False. Daphne did.
38. C
39. C
40. By reciting the names of Puccini's operas.

Acknowledgments

The *Frasier* creators, David Angell, Peter Casey, and David Lee, have always gone out of their way to open their doors, so thanks guys, along with a very special nod to my cyberspace pal David Lee, who allowed me to be the first journalist to sit in on *Frasier* writers' sessions. He was also kind enough to read the manuscript in E-mail form and make Internet corrections.

Risa Kessler, Kim Conant, Trisha Drissi, Kristin Torgen, Susan Rosen, Cindy Collins, Bob Meyer, and the cast and the rest of the folks at the *Frasier* show were also of great help. A special nod goes to John Wentworth, who worked so hard to make this book happen.

Finally, how about some applause for the fine editor Pete Wolverton, the master agent Mel Berger, and the great people at *USA Today*, especially my friend and editor, Dennis Moore, as well as Mrs. G. and Sam, for putting up all these years with a husband/father who writes every morning, noon, and night.